POLITICS AT THE AIRPORT

POLITICS AT THE AIRPORT

Mark B. Salter, Editor

University of Minnesota Press

Minneapolis • London

Portions of chapter 2 were previously published in David Lyon, *Surveillance Studies: An Overview* (Cambridge: Polity, 2007); reprinted with permission of Polity Press.

Published by the University of Minnesota Press
111 Third Avenue South, Suite 290
Minneapolis, MN 55401-2520
http://www.upress.umn.edu

Library of Congress Cataloging-in-Publication Data

Politics at the airport / Mark B. Salter, editor.
    p. cm.
  Includes bibliographical references and index.
  ISBN 978-0-8166-5014-9 (hc : alk. paper)—ISBN 978-0-8166-5015-6
(pb : alk. paper)
    1. International airports—Security measures. 2. Terrorism—Prevention. I. Salter, Mark B.
HE9797.4.S4P65 2008
363.12'4—dc22   2008009095

Printed in the United States of America on acid-free paper

The University of Minnesota is an equal-opportunity educator and employer.

15 14 13 12 11 10 09 08   10 9 8 7 6 5 4 3 2 1

CONTENTS

ACKNOWLEDGMENTS

The workshop where these chapters were first presented, "Moving Targets: Politics of/at the Airport," was held with the support of the Globalization of Data Project, part of the Queen's University Surveillance Project. With funding from the Social Sciences and Humanities Research Council of Canada, David Lyon and I were able to bring together scholars from Europe, America, and Canada for serious conversation on the theme of the airport. We were fortunate to hold the conference concurrent with the first Canadian Aviation Security conference, with the support of the Canadian Air Transport Security Authority and the Canadian Advanced Technology Alliance. In particular, we would like to thank Tom Hodge, John Stroud, Norm Kirkpatrick, and Jacques Duscheneau for their constant encouragement and commitment. We also thank Debbie Lisle and Heather Cameron, who participated in the workshop but were unable to contribute to this volume. An individual research grant from SSHRC and support from the University of Ottawa have also been invaluable to my own work in this area.

David Lyon has been a keen supporter of this project, and I would like to acknowledge his open attitude, hard work, thoughtful advice, and frequent encouragement. The contributors to this volume have been extremely generous with their time and intellectual energy, which is greatly appreciated. The assistance of Joan Sharpe was key to the success of both the workshop and the subsequent book. Danielle Topic provided a keen editorial eye in the presentation, collation, and production of this manuscript. I also thank Pieter Martin and two reviewers at the University of Minnesota Press for their enthusiasm for this project.

Mark B. Salter
Ottawa, Canada

Introduction

AIRPORT ASSEMBLAGE

....

Mark B. Salter

Few sites are more iconographic of both the opportunities and the vulnera-
bilities of contemporary globalization than the international airport. The
popular imagination is filled with images of postmodern hubs that cater to
the contemporary road warriors and global nomads that philosopher Peter
Sloterdijk and architect Rem Koolhaus haved dubbed the "kinetic elite."[1]
Cities unto themselves—with all attendant institutions, social forces, politics, and anxieties—airports are both an exception to and paradigmatic of
present-day life. Using a Foucauldian frame, they can be understood as "het-
erotopias," social spaces that are "in relation with all other sites, but in such
a way to suspect, neutralize, or invert the set of relations that they happen
to designate, mirror, or reflect."[2] Airports are national spaces that connect
to international spaces, frontiers that are not at the territorial limit, and
grounded sites that embody mobility.[3]

In addition to being local sites of contestation, airports are representa-
tive of supermodern "nonplaces" in which social relations are based on
mobility rather than fixity.[4] As J. G. Ballard writes, "airports have become
a new kind of discontinuous city, whose vast populations, measured by
annual passenger throughputs, are entirely transient, purposeful, and for
the most part happy. Above all, airports are places of good news."[5] The
glamour and exoticism of the airport as a gateway to other places and the

ix

interstices of travel encourages flights of fancy.[6] Equally, airports have been represented as "a stress laboratory, a no man's land between the nation and the world, a surveillance machine for automated bodies, shepherded from control station to control state."[7] For cultural analysts, airports have long been a stock example of the *zeitgeist* that requires no serious or sustained analysis, fieldwork, or empirical evidence.

This collection addresses this naïve public optimism and the gap in current scholarly analysis. The authors respond to the emergent political, societal, economic, and ethical problems illuminated by this "metastable" institution—stable only in its instability:[8] How are flows of people, data, capital, symbols, meanings, and objects managed, controlled, restricted, and monitored? What kind of political, market, and social forces are in play? How are dominant modes of social sorting, coercion, normalization, and authorization reinforced, disrupted, or resisted? What can studying airports tell us about these processes? To what extent can airports be compared across time and space?

Though a growing community of scholars are concerned with the subject of airports, there is no institutionalization of "airport studies" in the social sciences or humanities—no research centers, journals, or professional associations. Aviation institutes and centers of aviation law treat airports as a set of management, business, technical, and design problems with little consideration of the wider analysis of social and political trends. Only cultural critics such as Alaistair Gordon, David Pascoe, and Mark Gottdiener provide interpretations of the meanings attributed to airports.[9]

As a sustained conversation about the airport, this volume remedies the absence of social science perspectives in this debate. We present a number of different perspectives on, methodologies about, and claims to the airport. It is clear that multidisciplinary studies are crucial for understanding the airport: social sorting and surveillance, design and culture, organization and management, public administration and multilevel governance, human geography, and political sociology are all crucial to the analysis of this microcosm. Theoretically, we want to "go beyond" the state and the market. As Debbie Lisle writes, "at the airport . . . power is increasingly characterized by its complexity, speed, and mobility. Airports are not only sites of extreme force, surveillance, and discipline. Rather, airports become politically interesting when they are also understood as sites of destabilitization, ambiguity, and constant movement. Just as people never stay put at airports, neither does power."[10] This introduction will use two key concepts to sort the multiple perspectives applied—governmentality and assemblage.

Governmentality

Airports have long been laboratories for new strategies of both technological and social control. As both legal and irregular international migration flows increase, and state attempts to control these flows become more energetic and more diffuse, airports have taken on an increased significance as ports of entry. They have become sites of intense surveillance, policing, and control. Public and private authorities have taken advantage of the liminal character of airports to conduct policing and border functions, which take place inside the state but at the margins of the law.[11] At the same time, more and more airports have accelerated lanes for the elite, transnational class and invisible corridors for the "deportation class."[12] But the attempts to control the space of the airport cannot be reduced to border guards, airline agents, and shopping mall attendants.

Governmentality is a useful addition to our theoretical and methodological toolbox because it includes not simply the institutional apparatus of government but also the instances, cases, and fields when "government" is practiced on all manner and spheres of conduct. In short, we are concerned with how particular problems come to be constructed as problems of government, rather than looking ex post facto at problem-solving theories.

Foucault argued in his Collège de France lectures *Security, Territory, Population* that he was concerned with the development of modern political rationality, which concerned "the notion of population and the mechanisms capable of ensuring its regulation."[13] He identified a shift from a pastoral to a managerial mode of sovereign control in the sixteenth and seventeenth centuries. The object of government comes to be constituted differently, not as a people but rather as a population: "a mass of living and coexisting beings who present particular biological and pathological traits and who thus come under specific knowledge and technologies."[14]

The focus of analysis consequently shifts toward "employing tactics rather than laws . . . to arrange things in such a way that, through a certain number of means, such and such ends may be achieved."[15] In particular, Foucault is concerned with how particular social issues come to be defined as problems, which are then to be solved by the government (such as insanity, sexual deviance, indolence, indigency, etc.). He uses the clinic, the prison, and the confessional as sites of these specific tactics of governmentality. We would argue that the airport becomes an extremely productive example of an "ensemble formed by the institutions, procedures, analyses, and reflections, the calculations and tactics that allow the exercise of this very specific albeit complex form of power, which has as its target population."[16] Though not a totalizing institution such as the prison or the clinic, the airport provides a fascinating example of how (inter)national mobility is first problematized and then managed.

Mobility becomes a governmental problem at the time of the consolidation of the sovereign-territorial state. If the modern mechanisms of population control use statistics and other indirect methods of observation and incarceration, how can the population be reckoned, understood, and managed when it is constantly mobile?[17] Stuart Elden's analysis of early French quarantine regulations and prison architecture demonstrates the importance of visibility and enclosure for Foucauldian analyses.[18] John Torpey, however, makes a different argument. He purports that the state comes to appropriate the "legitimate means of movement," in part, through the control of identity documents, just as it had appropriated the legitimate means of violence and the means of production.[19] In addition to fixed institutions, such as territorial borders, customs and border posts, traffic laws, infrastructure, and passports, the state also described "normal" routes of movement and acceptable modes of fixity.

Indigence suddenly becomes a governmental problem. The control of "security, population, and territory" is essentially a question of the management of mobility: the mobility of things and worth, symbols and ideas, and most importantly, the population. However, this control of mobility is not necessarily direct, through the use of identity papers and internal passes. The development of property rights, the enclosures of public land, the creation of cities as such—all speak to describing and controlling a dispersed system of national (im)mobility. A brilliant example of this kind of analysis is Jeremy Packer, who identifies how the regulation of mobility becomes central to modern governmentality, in his case through an analysis of automobile safety regulations.[20]

The airport lays bare some of these issues with regard to national identity, international mobility, and population control—and requires the analysis not simply of state institutions involved in the administration of the airport as a site but also the governmental construction by various actors, discourses, and practices of (un)acceptable, (ab)normal, and safe/dangerous mobility.[21] In short, in addition to the control of movement, there is a pedagogical function of airports. We follow Mika Aatola's argument that "airports are places where authority is recognized and instructions given for making 'proper' judgments and acknowledgements are given. . . . Airports teach people the central rituals of acknowledgement that are needed to navigate in the Byzantine structures of the modern hierarchical world order."[22] Passage through airports condition and normalize particular identities, certain authorities, and normalize ways of managing the mobility of a population. Thus, there are multiple governmentalities of the airport that describe and condition the possibility of mobility. This is not to say that airports are homogenous or monolithic. In fact, to present the airport as a controlled, centralized, panoptic, or orderly space is baldly ideological.

Assemblage

Airports are systems that are dense, fast, and contingent. We want to side-step the question of mobility qua mobility to focus on what the control of that mobility represents.[23] The concept of the "assemblage," from Gilles Deleuze and Félix Guattari, is particularly useful in analyzing the incomplete, fragmented, and dispersed nature of airport politics. The assemblage is a perspective that examines the "convergence of once discrete systems" of control over a particular space.[24] Building on notions of multiplicity and the rhizome,[25] for Deleuze and Guattari the assemblage represents an "increase in the dimensions of a multiplicity that necessarily changes in nature as it expands its connections. There are no points or positions in a rhizome, such as those found in a structure, tree, or root. There are only lines."[26] In examining multiplicities of institutions, practices, and processes embedded in a particular space or site, they develop a typology of modes of control that escapes the state/society dualism that has so dogged the social sciences.

Kevin D. Haggerty and Richard V. Ericson describe the *surveillant* assemblage: "discrete flows of an essentially limitless range of other phenomena such as people, signs, chemicals, knowledge and institutions. To dig beneath the surface stability of any entity is to encounter a host of different phenomena and processes working in concert."[27] Similarly, attempts to control mobility are precisely multiple, public, private, nascent, incomplete, overlapping, redundant, and untidy—yet the result of these attempts is not disorganized freedom but a kind of radical entanglement. The airport is a messy system of systems, embedded within numerous networks and social spheres; it does not simply create freedom or incarceration. Deleuze argues that the institutions of Foucauldian analysis of essentially a series of enclosures has been eclipsed by "a society of control," in which there is no finality but continual "progressive and dispersed installation of a new system of dominance."[28]

William Walters and Charlotte Epstein make similar arguments. The biopolitical organization of the modern state system is not simply exclusive or carceral but concerns the policing and monitoring of flows of bodies.[29] Airports are not total institutions but rather nodes in a network of networks that include social, economic, and political actors with differing preferences, goals, logics, intentions, and capabilities. Rather than seek the single key idea of the airport, critics should instead focus on the resultant system—essentially, systems of rule without systematizers, convergence without coordination. In contrast with the governmentality approach, which assumes a common impulse to govern and to render certain problems amenable to government, the assemblage theory simply takes the resultant field of human activity as the object of study.

For example, Haggerty and Ericson argue that although companies, governments, and individuals each engage in surveillance for different and often conflicting reasons, there is a resultant empirically proven escalation and intensification of surveillance that is not easily resisted or rejected. David Lyon argues that airports are designed "for maximal commerce and for national security . . . [and] although they are analytically separable into 'citizen' and 'consumer' domains, even these are increasingly blurred."[30] The advantage of using the airport assemblage is that these categories of official/unofficial, public/private, security/commercial, and incarceration/mobility become less analytically important than the resultant field of control, however messy, random, or antagonistic.

A Map of the Book

As the balance between global mobility and national security is renegotiated under the twin stars of globalization and the war on terror, this collection looks at politics at the airport—how movement, architectural spaces, discourses, and technologies are deployed to shape and structure the social sorting of safe and dangerous travelers. Oriented toward questions of mobility, space, and control, we examine how airports structure, and are structured by, contemporary political, social, and economic processes. The contributors pay particular attention to the ways that airports have become securitized and technologized. In placing scholars from geography, sociology, cultural theory, and political science in direct conversation with each other, this collection draws together distinct voices, methodologies, and ontologies—though not always in harmony. The collection combines empirically driven analysis by Mark B. Salter, David Lyon, Colin J. Bennett, Gallya Lahav, Francisco R. Klauser, Jean Ruegg, and Valérie November, whose chapters illustrate how to conduct positivist research into the flows of data and people through these spaces, with more theoretically inspired research by Benjamin J. Muller, Peter Adey, and Gillian Fuller, whose chapters use case studies to reflect on contemporary theories of mobility, subjectivity, and power.

Salter reviews the manifold pressures facing contemporary airports in terms of space, time, technology, governance, and security. In examining the ways that various national and international regulations and practices structure the management of the airport, he suggests that the convergences in the corporatization of global airports, neoliberal trends toward public–private partnerships, and the deregulation of the sector have led to the privatization of public security and the dispersion of airport security throughout urban space and among multiple actors and agencies.

Lyon is one of the key thinkers of surveillance studies, and his previous work describes the airport usefully as a "data filter" that is "structured and dominated by flows of capital and information."[31] Lyon uses the airport, along with passports, ID cards, and trends in global surveillance, to demonstrate a double analysis of mobile individuals and their "data-doubles." The securitization of identity is materialized at the airport as a key node in the global transportation network. While grounded in particular sites, Lyon's chapter extends the study of global surveillance to question how the mobility of individuals is conditioned by the "means of identification."

Bennett expands on his previous research to demonstrate that the exchange of data between specific "no-fly lists" is more limited than critics suggest. While not definitively reassuring, he certainly indicates the need for further empirical study of the international flows of data gathered in and used at the airport.[32] Bennett argues that a robust and responsible consideration of privacy must take into account the actual movement of "data-doubles." Following from the discussion of governmentality above, Bennett argues that just as states reclaim a public security function through the restriction of the freedom to fly, both American and Canadian governments will require "the willing cooperation of a variety of civil society actors, and especially airlines." Through a careful excavation of the legal and bureaucratic paths, along which personal data flows within these two programs, he argues that the networks of control that police the possibilities of mobility, though dispersed between private and public actors, are modest in scope.

Lahav has been published widely in the field of migration studies, and here she examines the privatization of border functions within the American aviation security system.[33] The question of security echoes the case of personal data. Through a careful cost-benefit analysis, Lahav believes that the "dispersal of responsibility among [public and private] actors whose interests do not necessarily coincide," nevertheless provides a relatively stable aviation security system. She demonstrates how the institutions, rules, and roles of different actors were negotiated to form a robust and flexible system for aviation and border security that is responsive to governmental, commercial, and public pressures.

Generating new and very compelling data, Klasuer, Ruegg, and November set out the micropractices of the CCTV (closed circuit television) surveillance program at Geneva International Airport. In this extension of previous research, Klauser et al. examine the effect of particular policing practices and policies that operate within a field of risk management.[34] In particular, they argue that surveillance focuses not on "the usual suspects," as commonly assumed, but rather on risky spaces. Approaching the overlapping desires by the public, public officials, commercial interests, and the police for security and consumption, they argue that the CCTV system has both "repressive" and "creative functionality" that simultaneously deterred and attracted users to the airport.

The ability of CCTV to police individuals, the mobile population, and the faith placed in the technology by the agents of control extends beyond the visual for Muller, whose previous work on biometrics demonstrates the need for close examination of the assumed isomorphism between identity and dossier.[35] Following the trajectory of trusted traveler programs, Muller examines how the application of biometric technologies produce particular kinds of disaggregated and deterritorialized borders that are instantiated at the interface between body and technology rather than the more familiar physical border. This kind of mediated subject, he argues, creates both new techniques of control as well as new possibilities for resistance.

Adey has already provided a number of important contributions to the study of airports.[36] In this volume, Adey continues his previous expansion of Lyon's work on social sorting to argue that "airports actually work to make these differences [in life chances] by sorting passengers into different modalities." While engaging the material and corporeal experiences of passengers within the terminal, he treats the airport as a "difference machine," producing flows and stoppages that create and reinforce other kinds of social, political, and economic separation. Adey connects these mechanisms of distinction and separation to registered traveler programs that engage frequent passengers to exchange privacy for speed of security screening.

Fuller inverts this obsession with confession and security to discuss the design and architecture of airports as seemingly transparent spaces. She argues that though "the airport offers a seemingly unmediated spectacle of movement," one can distinguish, through the degree of ease within which individuals traverse the controlled spaces of the airport, socioeconomic and political subtexts in the design and operation of these airports.

This collection emerges as a result of the "Moving Targets: Politics of/at the Airport" workshop, which was held concurrently with the first Canadian Aviation Security Conference. The unique cross-pollination among policy makers, industry executives, government officials, and academics has informed our contributions, pushing us to engage with the ethical, political, economic, material, and practical concerns of the governance of the airport.

Consequently, we wish to take seriously the issues of methodology and policy relevance. These chapters are all informed by close empirical study of particular environments, attentive to the lived experiences and meanings of these social spaces given by the participants with no prejudice toward either elite or popular perceptions. Each of the authors discusses the contesting and overlapping structural pressures for profit and security, as well as the unique, particular solutions that individual agents and organizations have devised. In addition to the usual problems of access, studies of airports have become acutely sensitive in an age of generalized anxiety and increased attacks on civil-aviation facilities. Not only is the airport a crucial site of politics, but it is also an important site of study of contemporary global life.

Notes

1. Stephen Graham, "Flowcity: Networked Mobilities and the Contemporary Metropolis," *Journal of Urban Technology* 9, no. 1 (2002): 7.
2. Michel Foucault, "Of Other Spaces," *Diacritics* 16, no. 1 (1986): 24.
3. Mark B. Salter, "Governmentalities of an Airport: Heterotopia and Confession," *International Political Sociology* 1, no. 1 (2007): 49–67.
4. Marc Augé, *Non-places: Introduction to an Anthropology of Supermodernity*, trans. John Howe (New York: Verso, 1995).
5. J. G. Ballard, "Airports," *The Observer*, September 14, 1997, http://www .jgballard.com/airports.htm (accessed August 29, 2006).
6. Pico Iyer, *The Global Soul: Jet Lag, Shopping Malls, and the Search for Home* (New York: Vintage, 2001); Alain de Botton, *The Art of Travel* (New York: Pantheon, 2002).
7. Orvar Löfgren, "Crossing Borders: The Nationalization of Anxiety," *Ethnologia Scandinavica* 29 (1999): 17.
8. Gillian Fuller and Ross Harley, *Aviopolis: A Book about Airports* (London: Black Dog Publishing, 2005), 104.
9. Alaistair Gordon, *Naked Airport: A Cultural History of the World's Most Revolutionary Structure* (New York: Metropolitan Books, 2004); Mark Gottdiener, *Life in the Air: Surviving the Culture of Air Travel* (London: Rowman and Littlefield, 2001); David Pascoe, *Airspaces* (London: Reaktion Books, 2001).
10. Debbie Lisle, "Site Specific: Medi(t)ations at the Airport," in *Rituals of Mediation: International Politics and Social Meaning*, ed. François Debrix and Cynthia Weber (Minneapolis: University of Minnesota Press, 2003), 4.
11. Didier Bigo, "Detention of Foreigners, States of Exception, and the Social Practices of Control of the Banopticon," in *Borderscapes: Hidden Geographies and Politics at Territory's Edge*, ed. Prem Kumar Rajaram and Carl Grundy-Warr (Minneapolis: University of Minnesota Press, 2007), 25–26.

12. William Walters, "Deportation, Expulsion, and the International Police of Aliens," *Citizenship Studies* 6, no. 3 (2002): 265.

13. Foucault, "Security, Territory, Population," in *Michel Foucault Ethics: Subjectivity and Truth*, ed. Paul Rabinow (New York: New Press, 1997), 67.

14. Ibid., 71.

15. Foucault, "Governmentality," in *The Foucault Effect: Studies in Governmentality*, ed. Graham Burchell, Colin Gordon, and Peter Miller (Chicago: Chicago University Press, 1991), 95.

16. Ibid., 102.

17. Barry Hindess, "Citizenship in the International Management of Populations," *American Behavioral Scientist* 43, no. 9 (2000): 1486–97.

18. Stuart Elden, "Plague, Panopticon, Police," *Surveillance and Society* 1, no. 3 (2003): 243.

19. John Torpey, *The Invention of the Passport: Surveillance, Citizenship and the State* (Cambridge: Cambridge University Press, 2000), 4. See also David Lyon's chapter in this volume.

20. Jeremy Packer, "Disciplining Mobility: Governing and Safety," in *Foucault, Cultural Studies, and Governmentality*, ed. Jack Z. Bratich, Jeremy Packer, and Cameron McCarthy (Albany: SUNY Press, 2003), 145.

21. Salter, "Governmentalities of an Airport."

22. Mika Aaltola, "The International Airport: The Hub-and-Spoke Pedagogy of the American Empire," *Global Networks* 5, no. 3 (2005): 261.

23. Michael Crang, "Between Places: Producing Hubs, Flows, and Networks," *Environment and Planning A* 34, no. 4 (2002): 569–74; Tim Cresswell, "The Production of Mobilities," *New Formations* 43, no. 1 (2001): 11–25; John Urry, *Sociology beyond Societies: Mobilities for the Twenty-first Century* (London: Routledge, 2000).

24. Sean P. Hier, "Probing the Surveillant Assemblage: On the Dialectics of Surveillance Practices as Processes of Social Control," *Surveillance and Society* 1, no. 3 (2003): 400.

25. Rhizomes, like the strawberry or "creeping Charlie" plant, do not have a consolidated root/branch structure but rather expand horizontally wherever possible—off-shoots become the hub of new growth.

26. Gilles Deleuze and Félix Guattari, *A Thousand Plateaus* (Minneapolis: University of Minnesota Press, 1987), 8.

27. Kevin D. Haggerty and Richard V. Ericson, "The Surveillant Assemblage," *British Journal of Sociology* 51, no. 4 (2000): 605–22.

28. Deleuze, "Postscript on the Societies of Control," *October* 59 (1992): 7.

29. Walters, "Deportation, Expulsion"; Charlotte Epstein, "Guilty Bodies, Productive Bodies, Destructive Bodies: Crossing Biometric Borders," *International Political Sociology* 1, no. 2 (2007): 149–64.

30. David Lyon, "Airports as Data Filters: Converging Surveillance Systems after September 11th," *Information, Communication, and Ethics in Society* 1 (2003): 13.

31. Ibid., 14.

32. Colin J. Bennett, "What Happens When You Book an Airline Ticket? The Collection and Processing of Passenger Data Post-9/11," in *Global*

Surveillance and Policing: Borders, Security, Identity, ed. Elia Zureik and Mark B. Salter (Cullumpton, UK: Willan, 2005), 113–38.

33. Gallya Lahav and Anthony Messina, eds., *The Migration Reader* (Boulder, Colo.: Lynne Rienner, 2006); Gallya Lahav, *Immigration and Politics in the New Europe: Reinventing Borders* (Cambridge: Cambridge University Press, 2004).

34. Jean Ruegg, Valérie November, and Francisco Klauser, "CCTV, Risk Management, and Regulatory Mechanisms in Publicly Used Places: A Discussion Based on Swiss Examples," *Surveillance and Society* 2, nos. 2/3 (2004): 415–29.

35. Benjamin J. Muller, "Borders, Bodies, Biometrics: Towards Identity Management," in *Global Surveillance and Policing: Borders, Security, Identity*, ed. Elia Zureik and Mark B. Salter (Cullompton, UK: Willan, 2005), 89–93; Muller, "(Dis)Qualified Bodies: Securitization, Citizenship, and 'Identity Management,'" *Citizenship Studies* 8, no. 3 (2004): 279–94.

36. Peter Adey, "Secured and Sorted Mobilities: Example from the Airport," *Surveillance and Society* 2, no. 3 (2004): 500–51; Adey, "Surveillance at the Airport: Surveilling Mobility / Mobilizing Surveillance," *Environment and Planning A* 36, no. 8 (2004): 1365–80; Adey, "Airports and Air-mindedness: Spacing, Timing, and Using the Liverpool Airport, 1929–1939," *Social and Cultural Geography* 7, no. 3 (2006): 343–63.

THE GLOBAL AIRPORT

Managing Space, Speed, and Security

....

Mark B. Salter

Airports are vital and vulnerable nodes in the global mobility regime. The coordinated exploitation of security gaps on 9/11 and direct attacks on Glasgow, Madrid, and other airports subsequently have demonstrated that the lure of adventure and exotic destinations has been overlaid with anxieties, frustration, and fear. Each of the major actors within the global airport face a different set of dilemmas and pressures. This chapter lays out the principal dilemmas in terms of space, speed, and security, based on the literature of airport management.

The increase of passenger and cargo flows, along with a simultaneous pressure for low-priced travel—represented by the growth in number of flights per day and by the enlarged size of aircraft—places two oppositional pressures on airports to both increase the efficiency of movement and extract the maximum levy possible from those passing through the airport by using forced waiting zones. Although technology has generally been viewed as a absolute gain for airport operators, business, and government officials alike, new technologies not only place additional stresses on scarce airport space and screening time but also create a public expectation for absolute security.

The standards and best practices for each of these areas are influenced by the complicated governance environment of international civil aviation, which is affected by global, national, and local pressures. The rubric of governmentality is useful as a framework for this chapter since we avoid pitting commercial and governmental pressures against one another as different species. Rather, the forces of efficiency and security cannot be parsed as simply commercial or statist—just as the motors of profit and risk drive public and private actors alike. As institutions, airports must become expert in the flow dynamics of people, objects, money, and authority as well as try to master space, speed, and security.

Arrivals

Worldwide, we see deregulation and privatization of the civil aviation sector and of airports in particular.[1] The increasing corporatization of airports represents a bid by governments to enjoy the economic benefits of airports while simultaneously "avoid[ing] the financial burdens associated with subsidizing airport capital investment."[2] Due to a global lack of capacity in airport facilities, this need for investment is particularly acute. As Michael Carney and Keith Mew argue, the expected growth in the number of passengers, aircraft movements, and air cargo has lead to widescale global "governance reform . . . aimed at attracting private capital."[3] Airports have been completely privatized in the United Kingdom, Austria, Denmark, and Australia; however, in each case, the monopoly is tightly regulated by the government.[4]

Though local governments publicly own American airports, there remains a great pressure to be profitable, as seen in the subcontracting of retail and operational concessions to international airport-management firms.[5] Canada has a mixed system in which private companies operate federally owned airports over the course of forty-year leases.[6] Asian airports are publicly owned but see increasing private participation in expansion plans.[7] Even the expectation of privatization is enough to reorient airport management toward profitability and customer service.[8] Large, global airport hubs (such as London, Frankfurt, Dubai, Singapore, Hong Kong, and so on.) are more market oriented.[9]

Globally, then, there is a trend of shifting the economic burden from local governments to private companies, or public–private partnerships, that has led to an increased emphasis on profit making, while deregulation has led to increased competition among airlines and airports themselves. Within this sector, "the apparent and only possible move to counteract market weaknesses and hypercompetition involves adopting a new form of marketing-driven approach by the airport authority as a whole."[10] Whether public, private, or some combination of the two, global airports operate within a complex web of international, national, and local authorities, typified by the common "airport management committee," whose stakeholders include the airport authority, airlines, land-side and air-side businesses, cargo agents and freight forwarders, catering and stores, police, immigration and other security officials, as well as regulators, inspectors, and government representatives. Airports are "high-reliability organizations" that must perform many complex functions while maintaining a low error rate in terms of accidents, crimes, acts of unlawful interference, compromised security, or lost bags.[11] We will discuss four major functions of the contemporary airport: (1) flight operations, (2) terminal operations, (3) cargo operations, and (4) the overarching task of aviation security.

Despite particular dips due to recessions—for example, during the severe acute respiratory syndrome (SARS) virus scare or following the 9/11 attacks—the volume of international passenger and cargo transported by civil aviation has been steadily increasing since the end of World War II, with projected exponential increases for the next twenty years. Airports Council International (ACI), the industry organization for global airports, reports that member airports served 4.2 billion passengers in 2005, and it predicts that this number will grow to 7 billion by 2020, by which time "airports estimate that capacity to accommodate demand w[ill] fall short by nearly one billion passengers."[12]

The International Civil Aviation Organization (ICAO) sets both safety and security standards for civil aviation. Since all global airports are connected, clear standards are required for communications, air-traffic control, signage, runway layout, security, and so on. The standardization of civil aviation regulations provides a fascinating case study for the evolution of international norms and regimes.[13] Flight operations comprise the movement of aircraft, including takeoff and landing, noncommercial flights, fueling, catering, deicing, and so on. Terminal operations include airline check-in, baggage sorting and reconciliation, retail, security screening, policing, fixed-base operations (such as charter aircraft, repair shops, and flying schools), and perimeter and access control. Cargo operations include warehouses, screening, and loading facilities. Finally, aviation security remains an underlying priority for all aspects of airport governance from architecture and design to standard operating procedures and emergency planning. Within this complex environment, authorities are continually pressured to make mobility and the commercial functions of the airport run as smoothly, efficiently, and securely as possible.

There are three general trends that structure the contemporary dilemmas of global airports: the increase in passenger volume, the steady persistence of criminal and terrorist attacks, and an international public and official demand for new security standards. Passenger and cargo volumes have increased steadily over the past twenty years. Following the drop in passenger growth in the aftermath of 9/11, there was a general worldwide trend toward greater-volume passenger travel. Air cargo is a vital sinew of globalization, and a large percentage of high-value, low-volume cargo is being shipped by air. Some experts have argued that the North American air carriers, which were severely affected by the terrorist attacks, stayed profitable through a combination of government subsidies and cargo shipments. The introduction and growth of low-cost budget airlines has seen a dramatic impact on all aspects of civil aviation, including ticket prices, average revenue per passenger kilometer, gate scheduling, landing fees, and airport expansion.[14] The latest generation of jet aircraft represented by the Airbus A380s and Boeing 787s will force airports to adapt runways, apron handling (management of airplanes between runways and gates), and passenger volumes in dramatic ways (similar to the introduction of wide-body jets in the 1970s).

Given the largely transitory population in airports, they are fertile grounds for criminal enterprises.[15] But surprisingly, there is also a general trend toward terrorist acts against airport facilities themselves, even though they are hardened targets.[16] Consequently, there has been demand for greater airport security in terms of passenger, baggage, and airport employees screening; perimeter and sterile area access; and terminal security. General trends in policing, such as the use of closed circuit TV (CCTV) technologies and community-policing models are also evident at global airports. As Peter Adey and David Lyon argue, there is also a coupling of surveillance and self-sorting of passengers according to socially constructed risk profiles. As indicated by this author, Gallya Lahav, David Lyon, and others, the role of many global airports as national ports of entry—in effect, sites of deterritorialized borders —makes these security requirements all the more intensive. The airport is correspondingly a site of concentrated anxiety and planning. The outlook for the next twenty years is one of continual expansion, amplification, and concentration of commercial and policing activity. Within this environment of accelerated change and increased public scrutiny, airports face five chief pressures: (1) space, (2) time, (3) technology, (4) governance, and (5) security.

Space

As Gillian Fuller and Ross Harley argue, airports are both sites of perpetual motion and are in perpetual motion themselves.[17] The pressures on urban space, terminal space, and facilities space lead to an impasse: bodies, equipment, and access routes compete for finite space, leading to a kind of horizontal airport sprawl across the urban landscape and a vertical intensification of the core. Airport facilities extend underground, up into the surrounding airspace, and throughout the local neighborhood. Within terminal buildings, baggage, departures, transfer passengers, arrivals, and commercial and administrative areas are often stratified vertically (e.g., baggage in the basement, arrivals on the ground floor, departures and retail above, and administration and air-traffic control in the upper levels). Expansion and renovations mean that "airports [are] never finished. They [are] in a constant state of flux, flirting with obsolesce, reshaping themselves, and adapting to new technologies."[18]

New facilities and runways in Hong Kong, Sydney, and Tokyo are all built on reclaimed land. Airport expansion plans in other communities are often the focus of intense public debate and resistance, such as the campaign against Terminal Five at Heathrow, Runway Three at Sea-Tac, or recurring protests at the airports in Frankfurt, Sydney, and Toronto.[19] Tension leads to contentious development between urban planners and local officials who wish to accommodate the airport's clear economic benefits with the desire to avoid environmental and noise pollution.

The crowding of terminal space is matched by the congestion of airspace. American and European governments recognize the coming problems with the current organization of civil airspace. In the United States, one of the largest ever multidepartmental agencies in government history has been convened to develop a Next Generation Air Transportation System (NGATS). The Joint Planning and Development Office (JPDO) coordinates the work of the Federal Aviation Administration (FAA); the National Aeronautics and Space Administration (NASA); and five federal divisions, the Departments of Transportation, Commerce, Defense, and Homeland Security as well as the White House Office of Science and Technology Policy. The JPDO is developing of a set of new standards, processes, and technologies to decrease the congestion in American airspace. The JPDO predicts that American "demand for air transportation is expected to triple by 2025; in Europe, it's expected to double soon after 2020."[20]

NGATS is a public–private enterprise that is developing new technologies, standards, and regulations for anticipated implementation in 2025, which will encompass environmental, security, and safety changes.[21] Eurocontrol, the European Organization for the Safety of Air Navigation, is taking a private-sector approach exclusively for air-traffic control, which aims to create a seamless regional system. Currently, there are thirty-four separate air-traffic control operators within Europe.[22] There are no similar plans or agencies for the Asia-Pacific, although the organization Asia-Pacific Economic Cooperation (APEC) has a transportation working-group, which has aviation security, aviation safety, and air services as well as the Secure Trade in the APEC Region (STAR) series of conferences.

Contemporary airspace is overcrowded, with major overhauls required in North America and Europe to avoid delays or safety and security issues. This has lead primary hub airports to float expansion plans and secondary airports to court the business of low-cost air carriers and cargo companies. Legacy carriers, such as national or flag airlines (British Airways, KLM, Air France, and so on), are awarded landing slots based on grandfathered rights (i.e., a proportion of the landing slots available at the airport, despite expansion or competition).[23] Sean D. Barrett argues that in the regulated European air market "hub airports abdicated control over their vital runway capacity to airline scheduling committees chaired by the national airlines."[24] This has led low-cost airlines to choose secondary airports, which offer lower landing fees.[25]

Airport architecture has moved away from the original layout of a railway terminus toward the style of a contemporary shopping mall. Inside the terminal space a similar overcrowding exists. With a continual expansion of passenger and baggage volumes, and the increase in cargo facilities and fixed-base operators (FBOs), airport managers are continually trying to balance the architects and retailers' desires for wide-open shopping arcades with the police or security screeners' desires for closed, easily containable spaces. Alistair Gordon writes, "antiterrorist measures turned the airport into an electronically controlled environment rivaled only by the maximum security prison. It was more than mere coincidence that the architects responsible for some of these fortified terminals had also designed penitentiaries."[26]

Twentieth-century airports tended to architecturally gesture toward flight itself, whereas contemporary terminals attempt to act as signposts, impelling motion in their very design.[27] As the drive toward more retail space and more marketing campaigns that feature the airport as a destination in itself progressed, the gray concrete cells were transformed into large, windowed corridors, such as the new Chek Lap Kok airport in Hong Kong. Deyan Sudjic writes,

> it is not its sheer size that makes Chek Lap Kok so impressive. It is the sense of order and calm that [Norman] Foster has brought to the interior that makes it so memorable. He has eliminated as much of the visual noise as possible, restricting the structure and the range of finishes to the minimum. At the same time he has brought sunlight right into the heart of the building. The structure is planned to make it as clear as possible in which direction passengers should be heading at every stage of their journey.[28]

As Fuller and Harley suggest, the question of path finding has become more pressing as terminals grow in size and complexity.[29] Current space requirements are determined by dividing total concourse space by the number of transiting passengers and are measured by the ease of traversing the terminal.[30] Some have even suggested that new airport construction aims for a strategic balance of space, speed, and customer satisfaction.

The profits derived from retail space are increasingly important to private or public–private airports. In one example, the private British Airport Authorities "has raised the amount of revenue derived from unregulated commercial sources from 49.5 [percent] in 1984/85 to 71.5 [percent] in 1998/99."[31] Airports are thus pressured to increase the amount of retail space available.[32] Because competition between airports for long-distance, transfer, and budget passengers drive down other prices, airports are pressured to generate profit from nonaviation sectors. Budget airlines in particular often seek reduced or bulk landing fees, leaving the airport to generate revenue from facilities exclusively.[33] Airport management companies also attempt to include destination attractions: "Frankfurt airport in Germany opened a disco inside the Terminal building, while Amsterdam Schiphol launched a casino in the transit area. . . . Malpensa airport, more sporadically has been organizing music concerts inside Terminal [One]'s walls."[34]

The efficiency or capacity of airport space is also under new pressure from passenger volumes and security screening regulations. Most global airports engage in "'smart' scheduling and preferential gate assignments" so that large aircraft and transfer passengers have the least distance to move and the most time to make connections.[35] In particular, the Airbus A380s and Boeing 787s will average five hundred passengers per flight, depending on the configuration, in contrast to current A380s or 747s, which average three hundred passengers per plane. Global hubs, such as Heathrow, Schiphol, and Frankfurt, are actively courting the A380 market with demonstrations of capacity for increased passenger volume and other facilities. An example of the retrofitting needed for a similar generational shift in aircraft can be seen in the necessary changes to aircraft terminals in the 1970s, with the broad adoption of wide-body and stretch jets, which increased average passenger volume from two hundred to three hundred passengers per plane. As Mark Gottdeiner argues, "their introduction [twenty] years ago necessitated the alteration of nearly every airport in the country."[36]

In addition to spatial tension between fixed terminals and the increased space required for security screening and security equipment, there are three key technological dilemmas that face global airports. Technology is widely seen as a "force-multiplier" for both security and facilitation by increasing efficiency and effectiveness, but it also faces a rush to obsolescence. Since there is pressure on global airports to be profit generators, managers, regulators, and operators are faced with difficult decisions about which technologies to make mandatory, balancing unclear security benefits and clear cost.[37] As will be discussed later in the chapter, security is a diffuse good that is hard to quantify in business terms as a return on investment (ROI).

Adherence to government regulations or international ICAO Standards and Recommended Practices (SARPs) is by contrast much clearer; but, by necessity, those standards are much slower than innovations in the market or the security-threat environment. Some airports are experimenting with the use of radio frequency identification devices (RFIDs) on luggage, for greater precision of tracking, which aids both facilitation and security. Other airports are using integrated CCTV systems for the surveillance of all areas of the airport. General Electric Security, for example, has a program called "Facility Commander v2," which it claims will integrate emergency management, crowd and flow control, and passenger security. However, Kelly Leone and Rongfang Lui suggest that the majority of screening technology operates under capacity because of the relative slowness of human operators needed to clear alarms.[38] Thus, although an in-line checked baggage screening X-ray might possibly clear 360 bags per hour, its actual flow rate is half that. The human is the weakest, and the most adaptive, element of secure flow-management.[39]

The pressure for scarce space has led several groups to suggest the delocalization of the airport, which goes beyond online check-in or self-serve kiosks within the passenger terminal. Airport managers are pushing passenger, baggage, cargo, and security operations away from the physical site of the airport. For example, there is remote check-in at Paddington rail station for flights from Heathrow. Also, American passengers deplane at Vancouver International Airport and are transported to their Alaskan-bound cruise ships without officially "entering" Canada for customs or border control purposes. New programs will be tested in Vancouver for the 2010 Olympics. For example, air passengers will be able to check themselves and their baggage at a number of remote sites, and will then be securely transported to the airport.

The Simplifying Passenger Travel (SPT) Interest Group, affiliated with the industry organization International Air Transport Association (IATA) and many other commercial and government stakeholders, suggests a refinement of security and facilitation procedures through remote airline check-in, home or hotel baggage pick-up, automated check-in at the airport, integrated security screening and travel document assessment, and flexible airport design.[40] One of the keys to the smooth operation of SPT's "Ideal Passenger Flow" is the incorporation of biometric information into identity documents. To guard against worries about data protection, privacy, and identity theft,[41] the SPT Interest Group has developed a novel and very interesting notion of "disposable biometrics," which would be collected and verified at the "one-stop" check-in and used at each subsequent security check, including passenger screening, cabin baggage examination, and boarding. The data would then be erased at departure.[42] The SPT group represents aviation sector leaders' best attempt to think through the provision of security and facilitation simultaneously, rather than seeing them in competition with one another. By aiming for a security/facilitation process that exceeds current governmental regulations, the sign of the plan's success will be the ability of governments to manage the industry. One of the hurdles of the SPT interest group has been the development of standards that are acceptable to multiple jurisdictions.

The delocalization of international borders forces air carriers and foreign airports to be the front line of border control. Consequently, passengers are given "board" or "no board" status from foreign governments before departing: pushing the virtual border into the airport. Such a no-fly system is currently in play with flights to Australia, and plans are in the works for one with American-bound European flights and with the Passenger Protect program in Canada. Thus, spatially, one enters the border zone of the destination airport before leaving the departing airport. Similarly, for layover passengers, Changi Airport and Schiphol Airport offer tours of Singapore and Amsterdam, respectively, without officially "entering" the country—the tour bus becomes a mobile instantiation of the airport's transit zone. In these ways, the airport space is being dispersed throughout the city.

The space of the airport thus extends rhizomatically into the atmosphere —integrated into transport and critical infrastructure, throughout government regulations and business relations, into the surrounding city and country, and across territorial frontiers. Rhizomes such as the strawberry plant or "creeping Charlie" are apt metaphors for the current systems of control at play in the airport, since they expand horizontally in the space provided. In this context, airports represent an assemblage of multiple actors operating according to different and often conflicting logics that lacks a single root-branch architecture, but nevertheless expand across the urban and global landscape. The pressures of security, scarcity, profitability, accountability, and governance create a dense, overdetermined, chaotic, networked topology where the dominant impetus is the management of speed.

Speed

As Paul Virilio writes, "the loss of material space leads to the government of nothing but time."[43] The accommodation of current passenger and baggage flows is a continual balance of efficiency and convenience—essentially a government of time and mobility. As with all modes of transport, global airports go through traffic-volume peaks and troughs. Early morning and early evening flights are in high demand, with off-peak flights such as red-eyes and middays occurring much less frequently. Given the structuring of the common workday into eight- or twelve-hour shifts, airports are chronically under- or overstaffed, and correspondingly under- or overcapacity. This creates problems throughout the airport system: air-traffic control, apron movement and gate assignment, passenger and baggage control, facilities (catering, refueling, cleaning crews, etc.) and stores, and security screening. To some extent, cargo operations are able to make use of this "downtime" in airport schedules, but they also run up against noise restrictions for early morning or late-night flights.

Of course, these schedules are arrayed around hubs in Europe and America. This location has colonial overtones insofar as flights from the Middle East, Asia, and Africa are often timed to arrive at the beginning of the European/American business day. The structuring of aircraft movements around the "typical" business day, and the natural clash with shift scheduling at the airport itself, leads to chronic inefficiency at security screening, passenger and baggage handling, and facilities and retail. The overcrowding of air space has led to ATC delays for global airports.

Budget airlines operate on a point-to-point rather than a hub-and-spoke architecture (as legacy carriers do), and often demand less of the airport in terms of facilities or network connections.[44] Budget airlines—such as EasyJet and RyanAir in Europe; WestJet and Porter Air in Canada; Virgin Blue in Australia; Air Asia in Malaysia; or Ted, Blue, and Southwest in the United States—base their profit margins on reducing the turnaround time of aircraft at the gate, and choosing secondary airports whose landing fees are smaller.[45] These companies aim to keep their planes airborne for as much time as possible, limiting the downtime to twenty to twenty-five minutes for disembarking, cleaning, refueling, restocking, and embarking. (For example, cabin crew act as cleaners in between flights to quicken the process.) These stakeholders put pressure on airport authorities to guarantee that security screening facilities, retail, and catering are available to passengers within very short periods of time.

Legacy carriers operate large hubs—such as United at O'Hare, Delta at Hartsfield-Jackson in Atlanta, British Airways at Heathrow, or KLM at Schiphol—and consequently require much greater baggage, passenger, and facility infrastructure.[46] New airport screening requirements, including in some airports the required rescreening of incoming passengers or baggage (since U.S. and EU requirements for baggage screening are not compatible), have led to a dramatic slowdown in airport flow.[47] In Canada, increased security precautions and a corresponding air-security service charge may be responsible for the dramatic drop in demand for regional air routes, whose convenience can be topped by rail or bus links. There is some evidence, however, that customer satisfaction is not based solely on wait times.[48] Passengers must be convinced that screening procedures are effective and efficient in order to endure much more stringent security than other modes of transport.[49]

Legacy and budget airlines both pressure airport managers in terms of cost and efficiency, measured by average and maximum wait times for security screening, facilities, and passenger/baggage check-in. But as airports themselves are increasingly under pressure to become profit-making centers, there is a movement toward the creation of "malls for the mobile."[50] In evaluating the tension between the "dwell-time" necessary for the commercial viability of the airport terminal itself and the necessity for the quick flow of aircraft turnaround, Peter Adey is exemplary.[51] He argues persuasively, along with Lloyd, that the airport creates and depends on "dwell-time," or enforced waiting periods to create retail opportunities.[52]

Unsurprisingly, the more dwell-time, the greater the passengers' expenditure—although both business and leisure passengers seem to stabilize their purchases after about two hours.[53] As Fraport AG, the operator of Frankfort Airport City, puts it, "the *homo aeroportis globalis* is a new but by no means rare species . . . all of these people are consumers, whose behavior patterns are changing and are increasingly difficult to predict; marketing experts talk about hybrid, adaptable consumers who switch between luxuries and basics."[54] Thus, airport managers find themselves needing to present both the image of efficiency and ease of facilitation as well as the image of retail opportunities for the "kinetic elite." This entails not the creation or elimination of delays but rather the management of speed as a resource—the study of which Paul Virilio calls "dromology."[55]

Just as there is competition between regional airports for local business, there is competition between global airports for international business. Network analysis indicates that the airports that were most connected within the global aviation network were not the most centrally located.[56] The hub-and-spoke structure of international civil aviation leads to intense competition for global transit points, such as London and Amsterdam, Dubai and Abu Dhabi, Singapore and Hong Kong, and so on. Airports are selling themselves to international passengers as destinations in their own right. Competition both for global leisure-time and for expedited use of facilities is evident in the expansion campaigns in the Persian Gulf: "Airports in the UAE [United Arab Emirates] are investing over AED [UAE dirham] 46 billion [12.5 billion USD] in airport expansion projects which will increase their capacity from 33 million passengers annually at present to 120 million passengers by 2008."[57] These hub airports are investing in infrastructure such as shops, cinemas, spas, hotels, gardens, churches, and medical facilities, so that the time spent on the ground at airports is not seen as "dead-time" but rather can be quickly soaked up by the institutions of social and commercial life. In this way, airports can be seen as microcosms of society—although critical analysis on this point needs to be taken further.

Security

New security requirements have also fundamentally altered the social and political dynamics of contemporary airports.[58] Despite the incredible investment in aviation security since the 9/11 attacks, the protection of global airports requires a wholesale revamping of domestic security and foreign policy.[59] There are three major dilemmas within contemporary airport security: space, speed, and sharing. First, security competes with static commerce and flow dynamics for limited space within the terminal buildings. Second, there is continuous pressure to increase the flow of passengers through security checkpoints, while providing secure dwell-time within commercial areas and securing layover passengers (regardless of the security of their embarking point). Finally, airports are vulnerable nodes and high-value targets in an incredibly complex framework of national and international security. Consequently, the question of responsibility and management of security tasks is often contested.[60] Facilities, stores, catering, and cargo already engage in off-site security, for which they enjoy fewer checks at the airport perimeter. Israeli airport security, which is often lauded as exemplary, does security checks on the buses, trains, and cars destined for the airport some ten to fifteen kilometers away.

The integration of international civil-aviation routes means that the security at core global-hub airports is only as good as the peripheral feeder airports providing the passengers. Since passengers arriving at a global airport may have boarded anywhere, the global aviation security system is hostage to the least secure airport. Developing countries do not have the same resources to spend on aviation security, although a great deal of the work conducted by ICAO falls into the category of assistance.[61] The Pacific Islands Safety Office, for example, aims to equip all airports in member countries with similar metal detection wands and archways to ensure a degree of consistency, although this level of passenger screening would not be up to standards elsewhere. ICAO aims to provide some certainty to the system by its newly inaugurated security audits.

In terms of secured space, airports are divided into public and restricted areas. Sterile areas are those public spaces that have been security screened. Restricted areas cover all nonpublic spaces for which authorization by the National Civil Aviation Authority is required. Landside operations refer to those within the terminal; airside refers to spaces with airplanes such as runways, taxiways, and aprons. However, airport security regulations have changed dramatically in response to terror attacks.

Airport security has always been reactive.[62] The model of terminal and aircraft security in the 1960s and early 1970s focused on the threat of hijacking and screened individuals immediately before they boarded the plane, allowing the majority of terminal space to be public. Since terrorists were assumed to want publicity rather than a high body count, pilots were advised to hand the plane over to terrorists with no struggle. After the attacks in Rome and Athens in 1973, the American Federal Aviation Authority (FAA) imposed new rules: "narrow points of control were established at the 'throat' of each concourse."[63] However, as terrorist attacks on airports increased, notably in Europe, security screening moved farther and farther away from the gate toward centralized screening points, as seen today in the majority of North American and European airports. This allows airport officials to concentrate expensive, large, labor-intensive technology in one site and maximizes the amount of sterile space for retail outlets of passengers who have time to shop.[64]

Technological solutions are seen as the primary way to overcome the challenges of speed and security. The technologies of handheld metal detection wands and walk-through archways are thirty years old, with little improvement over that time. But the space required for security screening has undergone a rapid and profound shift since 9/11, with the inclusion of a wide range of new machines, processes, and technologies. Distinct from the holding-cells or interrogation rooms, which might grace the airport police station, there are increasing requirements for airport security. In addition to the screening of cabin luggage with explosive trace detection involving new machines, techniques, and space, the majority of global airports are mandated by government regulations to provide space for secondary searches of individuals.

The next-generation of scanning technology requires much more space within the screening area than current walk-through metal detectors. Millimeter-wave scanners, back-scatter X-rays, or personal Explosive Detection Systems (EDS) equipment are all currently on trial in a number of U.S. airports. These new machines require two to three times the floor space for the actual machine than current walkthrough archways. This is equally true for checked-baggage screening, which has undergone dramatic changes since the Air India, Lockerbie, and 9/11 incidents. The need for passenger–baggage reconciliation requires tracking systems and EDS equipment that is integrated into the checked-baggage system.

The chief managerial dynamic in the adoption of technologies for airports is the pace of change, dictated in terms of both capacity and the perceived threat. Expansion and overhaul efforts in all regions of the world demonstrate that passenger and cargo volumes are predicted to rise dramatically over the next twenty years. As the milestones before it—the arrival of the jet, the wide-body, the next-generation passenger jet, next-day courier and cargo delivery, and global supply chains—the emergence of global terror threats to civil aviation, including the use of planes as weapons themselves, has dramatically altered the shape and processes at the airport. Since positive and negative clients (passengers and terrorists) are adaptive, airports are constantly under pressure to adapt to the latest technology—for example, dedicated lanes for self-selected frequent flyers and extra equipment to detect liquid explosives.

The model approach for aviation security is the layering of security systems, but there is no global consensus on the methodology for this layering. Because of ICAO's consensus-based governance model, which will be discussed later, Chicago Treaty Annex 17 aviation-security standards are expressed in ways that are goal oriented rather than prescriptive. Since ICAO required, in Amendment 10 of Annex 17, that all international hold baggage be subject to security screening by January 1, 2006, airports have had to modify their processes according to the different national regulatory interpretations of this requirement.

Thus, with the implementation of new standards for the screening of all checked luggage (not hold baggage, which is a wider category that includes postal shipments and courier packages), we see a technological difference between European and American systems. All checked baggage must be screened, but there is no international consensus on the best way to implement effective screening. European systems have a five-level security screening system, in which bags that are suspect are given more and more intense security until a final check by CT scanner and personal inspection. The American norm is the opposite, seeing the CT scan as the primary and first step toward baggage clearance. The Europeans thus boast of the small number of bags sent to the final level-five CT scan; Americans boast that all bags go through a CT scan but few are opened. Canada, caught between these two great hubs, opted for the European-style system of baggage screening, which has led to all baggage going through the United States to be rescreened at the first American airport it enters, leading to delays and disruption. Other jurisdictions have also reacted differently to recent threats regarding the use of liquid explosives, with Australia opting out of new screening procedures in place in Europe and North America. This lack of technical consensus is not a deficiency in itself, but it places a strain on the consistency of the global aviation security system and the facilitation activities of global airports.

One of the most pressing governmental issues for aviation security is privatization of security. Market-driven security providers are assumed to be more efficient, whereas government-provided solutions are more stable and more secure.[65] Before the creation of the Transportation Security Authority (TSA), airlines were responsible for passenger and baggage screening, and local authorities were responsible for nonpassenger screening (employees, staff, mechanics, etc.). Since 2001, the TSA has taken over all of these key functions.

In Canada, the Canadian Air Transport Security Authority (CATSA) is responsible to Transport Canada for passenger, baggage, and nonpassenger screening but subcontracts the task to service providers. For example, Transport Canada is responsible for the Security Screening Order, which the CATSA carries out through private service providers, who are in turn inspected by Transport Canada. In the United States, the FAA, under the authority of the Department of Transport, provides the regulations for airport operators, but the Transport Security Agency, under the authority of the Department of Homeland Security, is responsible for airport security screening, regulations, and equipment. In Europe, the majority of countries use federal or local police.

There is a tension between the desire for both efficiency and security.[66] But security is an indirect benefit: passengers, airlines, and terminal retailers are chiefly interested in the processing time rather than security outcomes (except in the event of a disaster). In the American case, about the chronic "underinvestment" in security, Paul Seidenstat observes, "achieving a greater level of security inevitably requires that a higher level of costs be incurred. From the vantage point of airport and airline managers operating in a competitive environment, the benefits flowing to their organizations from tightened security did not justify the added cost."[67] To meet international and national standards, airports have to invest great resources into security with little direct return.

Governance

The governance environment for any particular global airport is a combination of international treaties, national regulations and legislation, local bylaws, and management practices.[68] In North America and Europe, we see a similar structure (although other regions vary). ICAO sets Standards and Recommended Practices, which are endorsed and enacted by the National Civil Aviation Authority. Global best practices are defined by ICAO and the industry groups: IATA and ACI. The National Civil Aviation Authority sets security and safety regulations. Airport authorities are responsible for the operation and expansion of the facilities, and increasingly airport management companies are becoming globalized. Subcontractors, such as catering, facilities, fuel, and so on, are also responsible for safety and security standards, usually monitored, inspected, and licensed by the national authority. Air-traffic control is provided by a not-for-profit corporation in both England and Canada, and by the FAA in the United States, but apron-traffic management is performed by the airport authorities.

While many global airports maintain their own private security forces, local police, customs and excise, and border agents are almost always present as well. Following the trend toward privatization, security screening is performed by public authorities, such as the Transportation Security Administration in the United States; private authorities, such as the British Airports Authority in the United Kingdom; and public–private corporations, such as the Canadian Air Transport Security Authority. Thus, although always under national and international regulation and law, a passenger might pass through the jurisdiction of the local police, private airport security, security screeners, customs and excise, immigration, the national police, and the airline that is responsible for the passenger once they board the plane. This complex environment means that airport authorities must familiarize themselves with ICAO's SARPs, IATA- and ACI-recommended best practices, national regulation, and local bylaws and ordinances.

ICAO is a specialized agency of the United Nations and was formed under the Treaty of Chicago (1944) in order to formalize shared standards of national civil-aviation standards in pursuit of safety, security, and efficiency. The annexes to the treaty deal with all manner of standardization, including rules of the air, aeronautical charts, facilitation, communications, security, and aerodromes.[69] Given its nature as an international organization of sovereign states, as one would expect, once a SARP is communicated to member states, governments are offered the opportunity to file a "notification of difference," by which the government acknowledges how its national aviation regulations or practices differ from the global norm. This "notification of difference" will be amended to the relevant annex and thus become part of public law. Started in 1998, the Voluntary Safety Oversight program encompasses both government licensing of aviation workers, operation of aircraft, and airworthiness; it was recently made universal and mandatory on January 1, 1999 (Resolution AC 32-11). Rather than "black-listing" of airlines or airports, the ICAO Universal Safety Oversight Audit program aims to identify weaknesses and remedial action plans.

Annex 14, Volume I, of the Chicago Treaty, which has been subject to thirty-nine amendments since 1947, comprises many different aspects of aerodrome design, planning, management, and practices. [70] At the heart of the annex are the design parameters for the landing, taxiway, and apron areas of the airport. Following the prioritization for safety and security, it also includes SARPs regarding fire fighting and rescue equipment and procedures, visual aids for navigation, communications equipment and lighting standards, and the prevention of bird strikes (collisions between birds and aircraft, which can result in crashes). While airport design has evolved from a single railway-like terminus to the large, windowed hallways of contemporary airports, Annex 14 ensures that light colors, apron markings, and runway lengths are standard throughout the signatory countries. Annex 9 contains SARPs regarding the facilitation of passengers and baggage.

Regarding airport security, Annex 17 of the Chicago Treaty, Safeguarding International Civil Aviation against Acts of Unlawful Interference, was adopted in 1974, incorporating language and directives from the Tokyo (1963), Hague (1970), and Montreal (1971) Conventions.

> [It] requires each member state to establish a government institution for regulating security and establishing a national civil aviation security program [that must] prevent the presence of weapons, explosives or other dangerous devices aboard aircraft; require the checking and screening of aircraft, passengers, baggage, cargo, and mail; and to require that security personnel be subjected to background checks, qualification requirements, and adequate training.[71]

Annex 17 has been revised twelve times since 1944 to adapt to new risks and challenges, shifting focus since the 1970s from hijacking to attacks on facilities, to sabotage, including the use of aircraft as weapons of mass destruction.

After 9/11, the ICAO adopted Amendment 10, by which domestic aviation is held to the same standards as international aviation security set by the ICAO in a dramatic extension of its powers.[72] Although this extension has subsequently been undone in Annex 11 (published July 1, 2006), there was a reaffirmation of the importance of domestic security for international aviation security. In 2002, the ICAO Council swiftly approved the "Aviation Security Plan of Action," which requires regular security audits of member states. At present, the Universal Security Audit Program requires all signatory states to undertake an audit by ICAO inspectors on their adherence to

Annex 17 standards, including evaluation of the National Aviation Security Plan and national airports. Audit results are secret and not made public.

Roughly 30 percent of all global airports are in North America, and more than 50 percent of global civil aviation flights occur within American airspace, with Europe contributing a large percentage of the remainder.[73] Consequently, the FAA and the European Civil Aviation Conference (ECAC) play dominant roles in the definition of global standards and norms. The ECAC is a regional civil aviation organization whose membership comprises nearly all members of the European Union. Closely associated with ICAO and European Organisation for the Safety of Air Navigation (EUROCONTROL), ECAC seeks to "harmonise civil aviation policies and practices amongst its Member States." Together with the European Joint Aviation Associations, the representatives work to establish common safety, air-traffic management, and security standards across the European Union. Both Joint Aviation Authorities (JAA) and ECAC work with the United States for the harmonization of standards. As suggested above, the difference in baggage-screening protocols falls within this realm of disagreement, although standards regarding the screening of liquids have been recently agreed upon.

National civil aviation authorities, such as the FAA in the United States, Transport Canada in Canada, and the Civil Aviation Authority in the United Kingdom, are responsible for the regulation and legislation of the aviation industry. Though historically airports (and airlines) were seen as national assets, trends toward privatization within the past twenty years have seen the majority of European countries, Canada, and the United States all move to privatize airports. National civil aviation authorities thus are left to regulate rather than operate. Traditionally, national regulations have been prescriptive, describing exactly the equipment, procedures, and policies that must be in place. But as the aviation sector adopts a risk-management approach more generally, national regulators are moving slowly toward a results-based regulatory frame.

The Civil Aviation Authority (CAA) of New Zealand commissioned the Swedavia-McGregor Report in 1988, which urged the shift toward results-based regulation. The CAA of New Zealand now conducts "sampling" of safety practices, rather than the usual "inspections," with a much greater flexibility allowed in the operational details of the security and safety policies.[74] JAA has expressed a desire to move in this direction, as has Transport Canada, although the time horizons vary dramatically across jurisdictions.[75] Flight routes are authorized by the National Civil Aviation Authority, which often involves a security audit of the target airport. For example, for the authorization of a route between Beirut and Toronto, regardless of the carrier, Canada's government officials would assess the security at the Lebanese airport before approval. The norm within the industry is bilateral rather than multilateral agreements on air routes.

Airport management companies can be multinational companies with operations in multiple jurisdictions, British Airports Authority, for example, runs seven airports in the United Kingdom, has a ten-year contract to operate Indianapolis International Airport, holds a stake in Budapest and Napoli airports, and is responsible for retail management at Boston, Baltimore, and Pittsburgh airports.[76] The Vancouver International Airport Authority operates five other airports in Canada including Hamilton, Ontario, and Moncton, New Brunswick, and also international airports in Cyprus, the Dominican Republic, Jamaica, Barbados, and Chile.[77] Fraport AG out of Frankfort Airport also runs international airports in Cairo, Egypt, and Lima, Peru, as well as other German airports.[78]

The security, safety, and operations responsibilities at a global airport often fall to subcontractors as part of the neoliberal move toward corporatization and privatization.[79] In addition to private security firms, who often supplement national airport police, other companies at the airport play other important roles. Businesses that provide fuel, catering and retail, repair, or cargo facilitation—in short, any company that has access to sterile areas within the airport—assumes both safety and security responsibilities. Usually, these nonpassenger workers who transit between public and sterile areas are identified and verified through the National Civil Aviation Authority. But it is the responsibility of companies with access to airside or secure areas to ensure that there are safety and security protocols and procedures to guarantee that sterility is not compromised. In addition, some countries are moving toward the privatization of security screening at airports.[80]

Two dominant business practices of importance have been almost universally adopted by leaders in the industry and supported by industry associations and international organizations, such as ACI, IATA, ICAO, and ECAC: Security Management Systems and risk management.[81] Following the success of the safety revolution in the late 1980s and early 1990s, due to a number of accidents caused by a lack of safety protocols, the industry adopted the Safety Management System (SMS) approach. Within SMS, airports (airlines and other facilities) are required to demonstrate an ongoing and overarching system for ensuring consistent safety standards. The SMS approach entails a process for implementation and continual evaluation of the safety system, clearly laid out responsibilities and procedures such as a safety committee or safety officer, a clear risk-management system, and post-event assessment.

As the ICAO Accident Prevention Program describes, "An SMS is evidence-based, in that it requires the analysis of actual data to identify hazards. Using risk assessment techniques, priorities are set for reducing the potential consequences of the hazards. Strategies to reduce or eliminate the hazards are then developed and implemented with clearly established accountabilities. The situation is reassessed on a recurrent basis and additional measures are implemented as required."[82] The safety audits conducted by ICAO, ECAC, and IATA evaluate members for compliance as an enforcement measure, but the SMS approach aims to integrate safety into the business culture to go beyond simple regulatory compliance. Wanting to draw on the success of SMS for security, proponents of a Security Management System (SEMS) argue that a similar standard is required for civil-aviation security.

The political impetus for SEMS came from the 33rd ICAO Assembly meeting, which took place immediately after September 11, 2001.[83] Although IATA has advanced with the SEMS agenda faster than ICAO—as one would expect from an industry group compared to an intergovernmental organization—there is a broad consensus that SEMS is a vital component of the Universal Security Audit Program. SEMS also aims to incorporate risk analysis, policies, procedures, competencies, and continual assessment to push forward a "security culture" above and beyond prescriptive regulatory requirements.[84] The chief objects of SEMS are access control, including perimeter and airside security, preflight aircraft searches, and airport personnel identification; passenger and baggage security; checked-baggage security; cargo security; catering and stores security, risk, and threat assessment; security audits; and accountable document security.[85] SEMS programs are integrated into SMS and quality-management systems (QMS) to develop a sector-wide culture of safety, security, and quality. IATA audits for air transport carriers will include SEMS evaluation after 2007, but there is no deadline for the application of SEMS to airports.[86]

Risk management has become the governance touchstone of the post-9/11 world, arising in the academic fields of sociology and criminology, and the private fields of insurance and policing. It involves conceiving risk as a business asset just like any other. In other words, businesses, governments, and airport authorities must plan for failure and allocate resources, procedures, and policies according to the probability and impact of certain unavoidable risks. Risk assessment estimates the expected probability and severity of different potential events, and then ranks them in order of effect. Risk is then, mitigated, avoided, transferred, or accepted according to the abilities and environment of the authority. According to ICAO, risk management is "the identification, analysis and elimination (and/or control to an acceptable level) of those hazards, as well as the subsequent risks that threaten the viability of an organization."[87]

A full consideration of the impact of risk and risk management on the governance of public goods, such as aviation safety and security, is outside the scope of this chapter.[88] But there is good evidence from various quarters that because both the probability and impact of security breeches (and to a lesser extent accidents) are largely *incalculable*, the risk management approach is *inappropriate*. While the insurance industry and risk consultancies benefit from the wide-scale adoption of this scheme, it is unclear whether risk management benefits passengers, managers, or the general public. Risk management is an essential component for both SMS and SEMS. However, in SMS, the known threats are physical—the deterioration of component parts, weather, climate, and so on—and vary within a predictable scale. Security risks are both unpredictable and adaptive. Both criminal and terrorist groups are able to change tactics and strategies based on the preventative approaches taken by the airport.

Airport authorities are expected by governments and shareholders to manage their risk or exposure. For example, most of Canada experiences a cold and snowy winter, which creates problems of icing on the wings of aircraft bound to take off. Airports in Canada that experience such conditions consequently avoid or mitigate the risks of an accident by meteorological equipment and de-icing stations. The frequency of icing is high in the winter, and the impact depends on the size of the airport. Thus, the very busy Toronto International Airport has a capacity to allow twelve Boeing 737s to be concurrently de-iced at its central facility, while the smaller Ottawa airport has the capacity for two aircraft.[89] Furthermore, due to the risk of environmental damage by the de-icing fluid, the facilities have been designed to capture and re-use the majority of the glycol used to de-ice.

With environmental hazards, facility design, apron accidents, or aviation safety, there is a relatively robust scientific consensus on the probability and impact of events. However, there is no such database for criminal and terrorist activities that can act as a reliable predictor for the future. In short, the risk-management system attempts to quantify and rank dangers that are unquantifiable and cannot be ranked. Not only are terrorists and criminals adaptive in a way that the physical environment or aircraft part is not but also the political risk of terror attacks is openly and actively contested. Determining metal fatigue, the frequency of bird strikes, and the environmental impact of de-icing fluid is a science; determining the likelihood of a terrorist attack is not a science. Despite the global consensus on the integration of risk management into airport management, there is no compelling evidence that it will yield beneficial results.

Authority and corporate governance models seek to adapt quality- and safety-management systems to aviation security in order to create organizations that share a culture of quality, safety, and security that rises above the minimum standard of regulatory compliance. Leading this trend is a movement toward results-oriented regulation, as the New Zealand Civil Aviation Authority has enacted. Each jurisdiction depends on every other node in the global mobility network, but questions of development and capacity persist. If Europe and the United States cannot agree on a procedure or standard for checked-baggage screening, how might a consensus develop on security among nearly two hundred sovereign states of varying degrees of development, thousands of airports, and tens of thousands of aircraft?

Departures

New aviation security requirements and privatization have dramatically altered the management of global airports. Pushed to generate nonaviation profit centers and simultaneously to manage public safety and convenience, airports have reinvented the balance of sterile and public areas. Grand sky terminals and wing-shaped buildings have been replaced by glass-and-steel superstructures, which engender particular kinds of motion and immobility, under the watchful eyes of marketing gurus and surveillance experts. Airport managers struggle over the allocation of space, the apportioning of time, and the investment in technology. The Simplifying Passenger Travel Interest Group's "Ideal Process Flow" is indicative of the most advanced position in the industry, using technology to disperse the airport functions throughout the urban space and enhance facilitation by the capture and use of biometric information. Within this system of conflicting stresses, the regulatory environment is overdetermined by international, national, and local regulations. The modern airport is, in essence, a system of systems that functions as a single node in a complex global network.

As this chapter has demonstrated, the vast majority of the management literature views the airport as a series of technical, managerial, bureaucratic, and regulatory problems to be solved. The governmentality of the airport goes unquestioned: how is it that international mobility and civil aviation came to be a problem that needed this array of solutions? The power of the market, the state, and society are all for the most part ignored. There are three competing models for understanding the modern airport within social science: as a total institution, as a heterotopia ("other" space, which contains many contradictions), or as a rhizome.

Popular accounts often take the airport to be a self-contained institution, complete with health clinics, religious sites, entertainment, hospitality, and police power. Airports are thus read as a gauge of the power of the state and the relations between the state and society. The airport serves as a miniature example of other social processes of management and control: "a place where the underlying forces and anxieties of modern living are revealed."[90] They are seen as a microcosm that can illuminate the real dynamics of "models of our future."[91]

Critical voices often view the airport as a heterotopia by indicating how certain economic, political, and social processes operate at the limit of societies. Airports are not complete institutions, but liminal institutions that exist at the edges of the state.[92] In particular, the discussion of airports as "non-places" inverts the analysis from the institution or the framework to the social meaning given to the interactions of the individuals: the supermodern space "deals only with individuals (customers, passengers, users, listeners), but they are identified (name, occupation, place of birth, address) only on entering or leaving . . . the non-place is the opposite of utopia: it exists, and it does not contain any organic society."[93]

Both of these models, however, suggest an underlying rationale or logic—a sort of inner truth or final goal. A better assumption is that there is no teleology of the airport, but rather that the airport is better understood as a rhizome. While there is not a concerted "controller" of airports, each of the operating networks has an interest in an increase in the control of space and management of speed at the airport—both of which depend on a problematization of mobility. The airport is an exception to normal urban spaces and a laboratory for testing wider schemes of social control—simultaneously individualizing travelers and rendering individual mobility as a national security threat. The global airport is a barometer of the state of society and must be studied carefully by scholars—who measure not simply the economics or business cases but also the democratic and social implications of new modes of control and facilitation.

Notes

1. Anne Graham, *Managing Airports: An International Perspective*, 2nd ed. (Oxford: Elsevier, 2003), 8–36; Alexander T. Wells and Seth B. Young, *Airport Planning and Management*, 5th ed. (New York: McGraw-Hill, 2004), 32–34.
2. Paul Freathy and Frank O'Connell, "Market Segmentation in the European Airport Sector," *Marketing Intelligence and Planning* 18, no. 3 (2000): 102.
3. Michael Carney and Keith Mew, "Airport Governance Reform: A Strategic Management Perspective," *Journal of Air Transport Management* 9, no. 4 (2003): 223.
4. Sean D. Barrett, "Airport Competition in the Deregulated European Aviation Market," *Journal of Air Transport Management* 6, no. 1 (2000): 13–27; Paul

Hooper, Robert Cain, and Sandy White, "The Privatization of Australia's Airports," *Transportation Research Part E: Logistics and Transportation Review* 36, no. 3 (2000): 181–204.

5. Keith Mew, "The Privatization of Commercial Airports in the United States: What Is Wrong with the Federal Aviation Administration Privatization Program, and What Might Be More Successful?" *Public Works Management Policy* 5, no. 2 (2000): 99–105. British Airport Authorities, for example, has contracted to run the retail section of Pittsburgh International Airport.

6. Mary R. Brooks and Barry Prentice, "Airport Devolution: The Canadian Experience," paper presented at the World Conference on Transport Research, Seoul, Korea, 2001.

7. Paul Hooper, "Privatization of Airports in Asia," *Journal of Air Transportation* 8, no. 5 (2002): 289–300.

8. Asheesh Advani and Sandford Borins, "Managing Airports: A Test of the New Public Management," *International Public Management Journal* 4, no. 1 (2001): 97.

9. Ibid., 101.

10. David Jarach, "The Evolution of Airport Management Practices: Towards a Multi-point, Multi-service, Marketing-driven Firm," *Journal of Air Transport Management* 7, no. 2 (2001): 121.

11. George H. Frederickson and Todd R. LaPorte, "Airport Security, High Reliability, and the Problem of Rationality," *Public Administration Review* 62, Supp. 1 (2002): 33–43.

12. Airports Council International, *Understanding Airport Business* (Geneva, 2006), http://www.aci.aero/ (accessed September 5, 2006).

13. Christer Jonsson, *International Aviation and the Politics of Regime Change* (New York: St. Martin's, 1987); Mark Zacher and Brent Sutton, *Governing Global Networks: International Regimes for Transportation and Communications* (Cambridge: Cambridge University Press 1996).

14. Keith J. Mason, "Observations of Fundamental Changes in the Demand for Aviation Services," *Journal of Air Transport Management* 11, no. 1 (2005): 19–25.

15. See the chapter by Klauser, Ruegg, and November in this volume.

16. Federal Aviation Administration, *Criminal Acts against Civil Aviation* (Washington, D.C.: FAA, 2001).

17. Gillian Fuller and Ross Harley, *Aviopolis: A Book about Airports* (London: Black Dog, 2004), 104.

18. Alistair Gordon, *Naked Airport: A Cultural History of the World's Most Revolutionary Structure* (New York: Metropolitan Books, 2004), 167.

19. Hans-Jörg Trenz and Erik Jentges, *Beyond National Cleavages? The Case of Airport Protests in France and Germany*, paper presented at the European Consortium for Political Research, Budapest, 2005, http://www2.hu-berlin .de/struktur/forschung/projekte/civgov/trenz-jentges-airports.pdf (accessed October 16, 2006); Steven Griggs and David Howarth, "A Transformative Political Campaign? The New Rhetoric of Protest against Airport Expansion in the UK," *Journal of Political Ideologies* 9, no. 2 (2004): 181–201.

20. Joint Planning and Development Office, *SESAR and NGATS Connection* (2006), http://www.jpdo.aero/ (accessed October 15, 2006).

21. See Joint Planning and Development Office, *2005 Progress Report to the Next Generation Air Transportation Integrated Plan* (2006); Joint Planning and Development Office, *Next Generation Air Transportation System Integrated Plan* (2004), http://www.jpdo.aero/integrated_plan.html (accessed October 17, 2006).

22. Giovanni Bisignani, *Remarks to the German Aviation Press Club*, Frankfurt, September 28, 2006, http://www.iata.org/pressroom/speeches/2006–09–28–01.htm (accessed October 25, 2006).

23. For a full explanation of landing slots, see Graham, *Managing Airports*, 120–26.

24. Barrett, "How Do the Demands for Airport Services Differ between Full-service Carriers and Low-cost Carriers?" *Journal of Air Transport Management* 10, no.1 (2004): 34.

25. Barrett, "Airport Competition," 16.

26. Gordon, *Naked Airport*, 238.

27. Hugh Pearman, *Airports: A Century of Architecture* (New York: Abrams, 2004); Fuller, "The Arrow—Directional Semiotics: Wayfinding in Transit," *Social Semiotics* 12, no. 3 (2002): 131–44.

28. Deyan Sudjic, "Identity in the City," *The Third Megacity Lecture*, 1999, http://www.kas.de/upload/dokumente/megacities/TheThirdMegacitieslecture.doc (accessed September 14, 2006).

29. Fuller and Harley, *Aviopolis*, 127.

30. Peter Adey, "Surveillance at the Airport: Surveilling Mobility/Mobilising Surveillance," *Environment and Planning A* 36, no. 8 (2004): 1365—80; R. E. Caves and C. D. Pickard, "The Satisfaction of Human Needs in Airport Passenger Terminals," *Proceedings of the Institution of Civil Engineers: Transport* 147, no. 1 (2001): 9–15.

31. Graham Francis and Ian Humphreys, "Airport Regulation: Reflecting on the Lessons from BAA plc," *Public Money and Management* 21, no. 1 (2001): 49–52.

32. Freathy and O'Connnell, "Market Segmentation," 103.

33. Barrett, "How Do the Demands?" 35–38.

34. Jarach, "The Evolution," 124.

35. Michael Pitt, Fong Kok Wai, and Phua Chai Teck, "Technology Selection in Airport Passenger and Baggage Selection Systems," *Facilities* 20, no. 10 (2002): 317.

36. Mark Gottdiener, *Life in the Air: Surviving the New Culture of Air Travel* (New York: Rowan and Littlefield, 2001), 64–65.

37. Pitt et al., "Technology Selection," 314–26.

38. Kelly Leone and Rongfang (Rachel) Lui, "The Key Design Parameters of Checked Baggage Security Screening Systems in Airports," *Journal of Air Transport Management* 11, no. 2 (2005): 70.

39. Douglas H. Harris, "How to *Really* Improve Airport Security," *Ergonomics in Design* 10, no. 1 (2002): 17–22.

40. Simplifying Passenger Travel Interest Group, *SPT: Ideal Passenger Flow v. 1.0*, 2005, http://www.simplifying-travel.org/files/downloads/21/IPF_V1.0_Nov _2005.pdf (accessed November 3, 2006).
41. Alejandro Piera, "The Simplifying Passenger Travel Programme and Its Legal Implications," *Air & Space Law* 28, no. 33 (2003): 132–38.
42. Matthew Finn, "Ideal Process Flow," paper presented at AVSEC World 2006, Sydney, Australia, 2006.
43. Paul Virilio, "The State of Emergency," in *The Virilio Reader*, ed. Jame Der Derian (Malden, Mass.: Blackwell, 1998), 51.
44. Barrett, "How Do the Demands?" 36.
45. David Gillen and Ashish Lall, "Competitive Advantage of Low-cost Carriers: Some Implications for Airports," *Journal of Air Transport Management* 10, no. 1 (2004): 41–50.
46. Carney and Mew, "Airport Governance Reform," 223.
47. Leone and Lui. "The Key Design Parameters," 71.
48. Konstantina Gkritza, Debbie Neimeier, and Fred Mannering, "Airport Security Screening and Changing Passenger Satisfaction: An Exploratory Assessment," *Journal of Air Transport Management* 12, no. 5 (2006): 219.
49. Mark B. Salter, "SeMS and Sensibility: Security Management Systems and the Management of Risk in the Canadian Air Transport Security Authority," *Journal of Air Transport Management* 31, no. 6 (2007): 389–98; Salter, "Seeing Beyond the Horizon," paper presented at AVSEC World 2006, Sydney, Australia, 2006; Salter, "Thinking through Risk for Aviation Security," paper presented at the Canadian Aviation Security Conference, Ottawa, Canada, 2006.
50. David Lyon, "Airports as Data-Filters: Converging Surveillance Systems after September 11th," *Information, Communications, and Ethics in Society* 1, no. 1 (2003): 13.
51. Peter Adey, "Airports and Air-mindedness: Spacing, Timing, and Using the Liverpool Airport, 1929–1939," *Social and Cultural Geography* 7, no. 3 (2006): 343–63.
52. Justine Lloyd, "Dwelltime: Airport Technology, Travel, and Consumption," *Space and Culture* 6, no. 2 (2003): 94.
53. E. Torres, J. S. Domínguez, L. Valdés, and R. Aza, "Passenger Waiting Time in an Airport and Expenditure Carried Out in the Commercial Area," *Journal of Air Transport Management* 11, no. 6 (2005): 366.
54. Fraport AG, *2005 Annual Report* (2006), 26.
55. Paul Virilio, *Speed and Politics: An Essay on Speed*, trans. Mark Polizzotti (New York: Semiotext(e), 1986).
56. R. Guimèra, S. Mossa, A. Turtschi, and L. A. N. Amaral, "The Worldwide Air Transportation Network: Anomalous Centrality, Community Structure, and Cities' Global Roles," *Proceedings of the National Academy of Sciences* 102, no. 22 (2005): 7799.
57. Dubai International Airport, "Global Civil Aviation's Largest Gathering Concludes," September 19, 2006, http://www.dubaiairport.com/DIA/English/ Home/ (accessed October 20, 2006).

58. For example, the two dominant books in the field, Wilkinson and Jenkins (1999) talk very little about airport security, whereas Sweet (2004) deals extensively with airport screening and security. Kathleen M. Sweet, *Aviation and Airport Security: Terrorism and Safety Concerns* (Toronto: Pearson Prentice Hall, 2004); Paul Wilkinson and Brian M. Jenkins, eds., *Aviation Terrorism and Security* (London: Cass, 1999).

59. Joseph S. Szyliowicz, "Aviation Security: Promise or Reality," *Studies in Conflict and Terrorism* 27, no. 1 (2004): 47–63.

60. Paul Seidenstat, "Terrorism, Airport Security and the Private Sector," *Review of Policy Research* 21, no. 3 (2004): 275–91.

61. R. Abeyratne, "The Future of African Civil Aviation," *Journal of Air Transport Worldwide* 3, no. 2 (1998): 30–49.

62. Max H. Bazerman and Michael Watkins, "Airline Security, the Failure of 9/11, and Predictable Surprises," *International Public Management Journal* 8, no. 3 (2005): 365–77; Perry A. Russell and Frederick W. Preston, "Airline Security after the Event," *American Behavioral Scientist* 47, no. 11 (2004): 1419–27.

63. Gordon, *Naked Airport*, 233.

64. Adey, "If Mobility Is Everything then It Is Nothing: Towards a Relations Politics of (Im)mobilities," *Mobilities* 1, no. 1 (2006): 75–94.

65. Jens Hainmüller and Jan Martin Lemnitzer, "Why Do Europeans Fly Safer? The Politics of Airport in Europe and the U.S.," *Terrorism and Political Violence* 15, no. 4 (2003): 1–36.

66. Randy Lippert and Daniel O'Connor, "Security Assemblages: Airport Security, Flexible Work, and Liberal Governance," *Alternatives* 28, no. 1 (2003): 331–58.

67. Seidenstat, "Terrorism, Airport Security," 278.

68. See also Lahav's chapter in this volume.

69. International Civil Aviation Organization, *Annual Report of the Council*, 2005, doc. 9862, pp. 2–3. Annex 1, Personnel Licensing; Annex 2, Rules of the Air; Annex 3, Meteorological Service for International Air Navigation; Annex 4, Aeronautical Charts; Annex 5, Units of Measurement to be Used in Air and Ground Operations; Annex 6, Operation of Aircraft; Annex 7, Aircraft Nationality and Registration Marks; Annex 8, Airworthiness of Aircraft; Annex 9, Facilitation; Annex 10, Aeronautical Telecommunications; Annex 11, Air Traffic Services; Annex 12, Search and Rescue; Annex 13, Aircraft Accident and Incident Investigation; Annex 14, Aerodromes; Annex 15, Aeronautical Information Services; Annex 16, Environmental Protection; Annex 17, Security—Safeguarding International Civil Aviation against Acts of Unlawful Interference; Annex 18, The Safe Transport of Dangerous Goods by Air: International Civil Aviation Organization, *Annual Report of the Council*, 2005, doc. 9862.

70. International Civil Aviation Organization, *Annex 14 to the Convention on International Civil Aviation: Aerodromes (Volumes I and II)*, 4th ed. (2004).

71. Paul Stephen Dempsey, "Aviation Security: The Role of Law in the War against Terrorism," *Columbia Journal of Transnational Law* 41, no. 3 (2003): 659.

72. Ibid., 690.

73. Guimèra et al., "The Worldwide Air Transportation Network," 7795.

74. Chris Ford, "SEMS and Outcome-based Regulation," paper presented at AVSEC World 2006, Sydney, Australia, 2006.

75. See Salter, "SeMS and Sensibility."

76. British Airports Authority, *BAA Annual Report 2005/2006* (2006), 5.

77. Vancouver International Airport Authority, *YVR Annual Report 2005* (2005), 24–27.

78. Fraport AG, *2005 Annual Report* (2006), 141.

79. Advani and Borins, "Managing Airports," 98; L. J. Truitt and M. Esler, "Airport Privatization: Full Divestiture and Its Alternative," *Policy Studies Journal* 24, no. 1 (1996): 100–110.

80. Hainmüller and Lemnitzer, "Why Do Europeans Fly Safer?" 1. The TSA ran pilot projects at five American airports, where the TSA described and inspected precise screening standards, but the duties themselves were left to private companies. This was done at the request of airport authorities, under an "opt-out" clause in the Aviation and Transportation Security Act.

81. Salter, "SeMS and Sensibility."

82. International Civil Aviation Organization, *ICAO Accident Prevention Program* (Montreal: Author, 2005), 4–7.

83. R. Abeyratne, *Aviation in Crisis* (Aldershot: Ashgate, 2004), 38.

84. International Air Transport Association, "Security Management Systems," 2006, http://www.iata.org/whatwedo/safety_security/security_issues/sems.htm (accessed October 16, 2006).

85. International Air Transport Association, "Security Management Systems (SEMS) for Air Transport Operators: Executive Summary," (2005), 3–4.

86. Colleen Blume, "Security Management Systems: Establishing a Security Culture," paper presented at AVSEC World 2006, Sydney, Australia, 2006; Mark Duncan, "Security Management System," paper presented at AVSEC World 2006, Sydney, Australia, 2006.

87. ICAO, *ICAO Accident Prevention Program*, Section 5:3.

88. Salter, "Imagining Numbers: Risk, Quantification, and Aviation Security," *Security Dialogue* 39, no. 2 (2008): 243-66.

89. Ed Salenieks and John Dejak "Central De-icing Facility at Toronto's Airport," *Environmental Science and Engineering* 12, no. 6 (2000).

90. Gordon, *Naked Airport*, 263.

91. Pico Iyer, *The Global Soul: Jet lag, Shopping Malls, and the Search for Home* (New York: Vintage, 2000), 43.

92. Salter, "At the Threshold of Security: A Theory of International Borders," in *Global Surveillance and Policing: Borders, Security, Identity*, ed. Elia Zureik and Mark B. Salter (Cullumpton, UK: Willan, 2005), 36–50; Leonard C. Feldman, "Terminal Exceptions: Law and Sovereignty at the Airport Threshold," *Law, Culture and the Humanities* 3, no. 2 (2007): 320–44.

93. Marc Augé, *Non-places: Introduction to an Anthropology of Supermodernity*, trans. John Howe (New York: Verso, 1995), 111–12.

2

FILTERING FLOWS, FRIENDS, AND FOES

Global Surveillance

....

David Lyon

The database is an instrument of selection, separation and exclusion. It keeps the globals in the sieve and washes out the locals.

—Zygmunt Bauman, *Globalization: The Human Consequences*

Apparently insignificant aspects of ordinary life—banking, traveling, using the phone—are routinely recorded, stored, processed, and retrieved. Those data, originating in or from our bodies, travel great distances not only within organizations or countries but also across borders. Global mobility, much prized in the late-modern capitalist world system, generates large-scale surveillance as people physically cross borders through airports and other gateways, or as their data travel for trade, employment, law enforcement, or other reasons. New travel documents such as passports (for external movement) or

ID cards (for internal movement) carry even more data extracted from the body (biometrics) to permit global flows.

Data-doubles—that is, virtual identities located in networked databases —have far greater rates of mobility than their real-life counterparts; indeed, the travels of the one affect the travels of the other (especially if one is locally defined as an "other"). Some see in this the emergence of a global surveillance assemblage, and in some instances this is an appropriate—not to mention democratically dangerous—characterization. But significant differences also occur between different countries; surveillance experiences are far from uniform for a number of reasons. Different cultures, different social values—these are accentuated by globalization in local contexts and serve to shape surveillance and responses to it in various ways.

In the twenty-first century, surveillance is a global phenomenon. The capture, tracing, and processing of personal data occur today not only within local organizational settings but across national borders. Digital technologies permit the routine, real-time transfer of such data, relating to citizenship, employment, travel, and consumption, using far-flung networks that indirectly connect numerous agencies with the everyday lives of ordinary people. In particular, new biometric technologies make possible a growing array of systems for verifying identities, including upgraded passports and electronic national identity cards. This is the broad context in which specific security and surveillance initiatives are seen most prominently in airports, train stations, ports, and subways.

However, it is not the new technologies that create this state of affairs. They merely enable it to happen. Certainly, the long-term trend toward using electronic technologies for surveillance purposes has to be borne in mind, and along with it the pressure from high-technology companies to deploy such systems on an increasingly large scale. The political commitment to adopting those techniques cannot be discounted either. There is a deep vein of belief in the efficacy of new technologies to solve social and political problems, especially in North America. But the globalization of personal data and the surveillance capacities that this represents have to do with much more than mere technology.

The new links between bodies, borders, and biometrics are forged by other kinds of forces as well; the development of what might be called the "safety state," which also fosters increasingly accepted government processes of risk management; the routinizing of "states of emergency" and of "exceptional circumstances," a process that has been accentuated since the events and aftermath of 9/11; and the centrality of constant, accelerating mobility to global consumer-based capitalism. This last point may be made in relation to the now-extensive work on the relationship between information and communication technologies and globalization. As Manuel Castells shows, data-flows are essential to emerging modes of organization.[1] Coordination is achieved through electronic flows that permit global real-time economic and other activity. Indeed, such data-circulation is partly what constitutes globalization, as well as contributing to its growth. The main emphasis here is on personal data that may be used to impede or facilitate the actual movement of those persons to whom the data refer.

Thus, questions of immigration, international policing, and citizenship feature prominently as global surveillance issues. But they also do so in terms of what kinds of persons are acceptable, and what kinds are not, in a world of consumer capitalism. As Zygmunt Bauman suggests, one of the basic (unspoken) categories is that distinguishing "tourists" from "vagabonds."[2] Not everyone can be a tourist; indeed, their existence transforms others into vagabonds, who confront red rather than green lights in the form of immigration desks and nationality laws, "clean streets," and "zero tolerance."

Bodies, biometrics, and borders are vitally related to each other. They're implicated in the growth of these barriers. So in a world of global traffic in personal information, what happens to those data as they travel? What are the general implications of cross-border data-flows, of which the movement of data-and-bodies is a special case? If one considers call centers, or the "outsourcing" of data processing, some significant issues come into view. Unprotected by the data-privacy regimes of the originating country, personal information may be vulnerable to forms of fraud or other misuse among employees who handle the data. Equally, outsourcing may mean that data actually become subject to a data-handling regime with which customers may well disapprove, if they knew about it.

Thus, for example, in 2004 the British Columbia Privacy Commissioner publicly asked some important questions about the personal data of Canadian citizens as it migrates south into U.S. jurisdictions.[3] He observed that Canadian data in the hands of private corporations or U.S. government departments may not only be out of reach of Canadian legal protection, it could also be subject to the U.S. Patriot Act and therefore available to the Department of Homeland Security. To get a sense of the range of personal data that travel south of the Canadian border into the United States, consider the following: Canadian organizations may transfer data to other organizations, including employment records, for example. Canadian organizations may transfer data to foreign governments—for example, airline manifests. Canadian government agencies transfer data to foreign governments for policing, intelligence, immigration, and other purposes. Canadian government agencies may transfer data to foreign companies for outsourcing. And

Canadians may hand over personal data by presenting passports, visas, and drivers' licenses when asked.

In all of these ways, personal data travel across national borders routinely, and they may be intercepted, diverted, or in other ways used such that those to whom they refer may be affected, and possibly negatively so. The cases that are referred to in what follows, however, are ones in which the personal data in question are used to ease or to block the movement of persons across borders—that is, they relate to physical as well as virtual mobility. We examine first, the arguments surrounding the mobility of persons and data, in employment and law enforcement contexts; second, the "securitizing of identity" in the contexts of passports, ID cards, biometrics, and airlines; third, citizenship and identity management, with special reference to the "exploitation of identity" and the "ban"; and finally, the prospects and limiting factors for global surveillance.

Global Mobility

It is important to remember that the growth of global surveillance is not a conspiracy. The primary reason why surveillance is globalizing is that mobility is a fundamental feature of the flexible capitalism that now dominates the world of exchange, production, and consumption. The personal-information economy is an important aspect of this globalizing world, but mobile labor is as well, which means that employment records also migrate. Travelers of all kinds are emblematic of these multiple mobilities, and their data are embedded in passports, visas, and other identifying documents, are read by machines and officials, and are passed from place to place the world over. One's identity as a citizen is checked by these means and others, such as national or category-specific ID cards, which also bring the "border" to other locations than the "edges" or territory, thus further virtualizing it.[4]

At this point, it is worth commenting on one of these categories—labor—though I shall also return to it later. In a globalizing world, multiple mobilities include data (personal and other), goods, communications, wastes, and persons, such as tourists, businesspersons, and casual and manual workers. While some workers are engaged remotely as outsourced labor, in data-entry, editorial work, and customer service, for example, other labor from the global south is still required to move to fulfill tasks for which insufficient willing workers can be obtained in the global north. Because such foreign labor is often needed, but not necessarily wanted, in the global north, the issue has become a source of community tension—be it of Hispanic fruit workers in the United States or Canada, North Africans in

France, Southeast Asian workers in the United Kingdom, workers from Turkey in Germany or, for that matter, Indonesians in Malaysia or Chinese in Hong Kong.

The desire to control the movement of such workers is central to a number of significant surveillance efforts, generally overseen by immigration departments but also related to wider policy agreements. This also disproves an early piece of one-dimensional "globalization" nonsense, that borders would eventually be eliminated. Of course, borders do change, and new technologies are involved in this.[5] Certainly, for tourists, businesspersons, and trade relations, the world has never been as open as it is today. But simultaneously, borders are also becoming more tightly policed and patrolled, not least with regard to the category of "illegal aliens/immigrants." In fact, as Hélène Pellerin points out, borders have become "privileged places of regulation."[6] And in Europe and North America, the two most powerful regions of the world, what Naomi Klein calls "fortress continents" are under construction.[7] Europe and North America are being formed into sealed units to maintain a flow of trade and cheap foreign labor without risking attack or infiltration from outside their borders. The desire to create these zones had been present for some time, but the key opportunity was provided by 9/11.[8]

Global surveillance is also visible in policing and antiterrorist activity. Although terrorism became an increasingly significant phenomenon during the twentieth century—stimulating the growth of surveillance in Israel, for example, following the Munich Olympic attack in 1972 or in the United Kingdom during the British mainland campaign of the Irish Republican Army (IRA) since the 1970s—it was not until the attacks on New York and Washington, D.C., on September 11, 2001, that antiterrorist security and surveillance were seriously globalized. It must also be recalled, however, that previous "wars" before the "war on terror" included the "war on drugs," which also involved, and still involves, considerable cross-border surveillance.[9]

Global surveillance was intensified following 9/11, as the United States took the lead not only in declaring a "war on terror" but also in implementing measures that would inevitably affect countries other than itself. The locus of these measures was at airports, given that the attacks on the symbolic power centers of New York and Washington, D.C., were carried out using domestic airplanes and that these are the most obvious points of entry by potential enemies into any country.[10] And in the airports of the twenty-first century the dilemma of contemporary governments is magnified: as Canada discovered, horrifically, through the bombing of Air India flight 182 from Vancouver in 1985.[11] Global flows through the airport are a vital component of a commitment to economic growth and "free trade," and thus the airport must provide unimpeded conduits for those flows. But at the same time, the airport is seen as a very vulnerable site of attack or penetration by any unwanted persons of malign intent and thus must be guarded stringently in ways that would seem to contradict the first aim of free flows.

In his exploration of the development of the passport, John Torpey comments on the ways that state authorities have a monopoly of the "means of movement."[12] Border controls encapsulate this idea with their capacity to say who may enter and who may not. The analogy is, of course, with other monopolies, such as those over the means of production, but there is another possible monopoly emerging in this context that centers on the "means of identification." The ability to regulate the means of movement is clearly a strategic one, but it prominently includes the power to determine that people are who they say they are or, increasingly, to say who people are without hearing their own stories at all. The question of identification has become central and is now bolstered with the paraphernalia of biometrics and inclusion in searchable networked databases.

Airports are perhaps the most stringently surveilled sites in terms of the means of movement and of identification. They are also excellent places for social sorting, but the critical analytic literature on airports is still fairly thin. Although some treatments of airports romanticize them as points of departure for dream vacations and ultimate freedoms, or on the flip side as "nonplaces" of consumption, in reality, passage through the airport is highly uneven.[13] Indeed, this applies to both matters of privileging "preferred passengers" and of security checks and screening. Moreover these two may also be linked.

In both cases, the airport acts as a "data filter," sifting the travelers who pass through both as consuming opportunities and threat risks.[14] Major airlines pride themselves on their clear distinctions between different classes of passenger, which enable some to board straight from the lounge without waiting at the gate and others to remain patiently at the gate until their rows (i.e., ticket class—who would choose the nonview window over the wing or the cramped corner by the rear washrooms if he had a choice?) are called. And airports work with airlines and government authorities to ensure that some passengers with paid-for security clearance cards get through immigration and baggage checks rapidly, while others wait their turn and may even miss flights in endless Disney-esque lines. Those with "dubious" backgrounds take longer to be processed and those on watch-lists are not permitted to fly at all. Here again, the twin and apparently contradictory aims of the airport are made clear: to maximize but to regulate mobility.

Peter Adey's study of airports shows how from the early days of airport expansion (1960s) means were sought of "visualizing" the flows of passengers through airports using punched-card techniques.[15] This fairly abstract process was later augmented to enable the tracking of specific bodies through airport spaces, using scanning devices for fingers, hands, eyes, and faces. Passengers could thus be categorized, sometimes before they entered the airport space. This is where biometrics comes into the picture to provide, what are claimed to be, increasingly reliable means of verifying and identifying.[16] The bodies that pass through the system are reconfigured as information, which as such is readily sharable with other agencies in the quest for what in North America is called the "smart border."[17]

Not only does the "informatting" of bodies make the data sharable, it also facilitates sorting, categorizing and profiling. Adey observes that this is supposed to speed up the mobility of those within the terminal, but the process is achieved by treating different categories of passengers differently, based on their threat and opportunity profiles. True, Colin Bennett's inquiry into "what happens when you buy an airline ticket?" found that in his own case the answer was "not much that is negative," but one wonders how different things might have been were his name Bin Yamin or Basheer.[18] At any rate, Adey rightly argues that the airport is now a surveillance machine, an "assemblage where webs of technology and information combine."[19] For not only does profiling occur, simulations are also engaged—for example, dynamically to model the movement of passengers. Travelers are scanned like barcodes to be silently organized and processed through the airport, says Adey, a process that invites critical examination along with the underlying assumptions and concepts framing it.

Securitizing Identity

Questions of identity and identification have become increasingly central to citizenship and indeed to ordinary everyday life in today's society. Manuel Castells used the title *The Power of Identity* for the third volume of his magisterial work on "The Information Age," and today, as Richard Jenkins says, "identity, it seems, is bound up with everything from political asylum to credit card theft."[20] But as Jenkins hints in this quotation, and as the words I used earlier in this chapter indicate, it is "identity" and "identification" that are really important in this context. In the twenty-first century, identity questions cannot be answered without considering those of identification and vice versa. To quote Jenkins again, "the capacity of organizations to identify people—authoritatively or powerfully, as individuals or collectively—and to make those identifications 'stick' through the allocation of rewards and penalties, should not be underestimated."[21]

It is worth reviewing the background to this state of affairs. In a general sense, the means of communication, which had developed mainly during the twentieth century, were depopulated. That is to say, the interpersonal forms of communication predominant in earlier contexts were increasingly mediated by systems such as the telegraph, telephone, and then radio, television, and the internet. The bodies that were once involved directly in communication disappeared (even though images of bodies reappeared in photographs, television, and now in various kinds of digital camera technology). Rising geographical mobility plus the stretching of social relationships enabled by these new transport and communication technologies meant the general decline of face-to-face relationships. This does not necessarily mean that there are fewer such face-to-face relations today, rather that we simply communicate with many more people (and machines and systems) that we do not see.[22] The upshot is a demand for more and more "tokens of trust" to stand in for the forms of trust that were previously sustained (or challenged) by the face-to-face relation. Seals and signatures were supplemented with drivers' licenses, social insurance numbers, PINs and barcodes, and now, photo IDs and biometrics.

From a governmentality viewpoint, Nikolas Rose sees contemporary shifts in terms of the "securitization of identity."[23] As he says, in many contexts, the exercise of freedom requires proof of legitimate identity. And this has to be done in ways that link individuation and control. To gain privileges or entitlement, the ID holder must present a card that refers to a database record and each time a transaction is made, or access is gained, the "data-double" in the database is modified. This virtual identity may also be enhanced by cross-checking with other agencies—banks with insurance companies, for example—in a constantly spiraling search for further verification. Biometrics and DNA offer what many believe to be the most reliable ways of perfecting these tokens of trust. For Rose, the circuits of securitization are dispersed and disorganized and are best seen as "conditional access to circuits of consumption and civility," especially in relation to work and consumption.[24]

However, he also argues that citizenship is not now primarily realized in relation to the state or public sphere but rather in a variety of practices, in which work and shopping are paradigmatic. And though is it important to bear this in mind, for as we see elsewhere their impact on life-chances and choices is enormous, the state still has a very significant role to play, especially in relation to "national identification" and citizenship. In his own work, Rose comments on ways in which nation-states helped to develop a sense of "national identity"; in the British case, the "colonial experience and the codes of race" were particularly significant for forming "governable subjectivities."[25] And in the U.S. case, census data were also important in giving a picture to "foreigners" and "our own people" of "who we really are."[26] While census enumeration buttresses some freedoms of liberal democracy, it also helps to constitute and solidify social and racial divisions.[27] Today—especially after 9/11 but also in relation to other trends such as fears of crime, especially identity theft—national identification is very much bound up with citizenship. This may be explored through the prisms of passports, national ID cards, and biometrics, all of which are perhaps most evident in airports.

John Torpey invokes Karl Marx and Max Weber in order to indicate the extent of the transformation accompanying passports and identification documents in the modern world. While Marx analyzed the monopolization of the means of production by capitalists and Weber discussed the state's expropriation of the legitimate use of violence, avers Torpey, a third type of expropriation must be added: the "monopolization of the means of movement" by states and the international state system.[28] They regulate population movements and sort out who belongs where as well as helping to protect and police-state borders by these means. As Mark Salter adds, passports uniquely identify each individual who needs one, using a photo and number, and indicate the country of origin and the state to which the bearer may be deported.[29]

Increasingly, however, interest in national identification systems is becoming expressed in countries of the global north (several countries in the global south, and some in Europe, have had ID cards for some time). At the time of writing, the British *Identity Card Act* (2006) has been passed, but the procurement process for the actual roll-out has been slow; and the American *Real ID Act* program that standardizes state drivers' licenses and makes their attendant databases interoperable is similarly making hesitant strides toward reality (with some significant opposition). These go further than passports in the regulation of mobility, because they can be used internally to the nation-state, and in the securitization of identity, because unlike passports, they are likely to become compulsory for all citizens, and because they depend more and more on standardized coding for interoperability within regions.

While various rationales—from urgently felt needs for immigration control to the desire to demonstrate prowess in high technology[30]—have been forwarded for introducing electronic ID-card systems in other contexts, recent northern initiatives gained their imperative character from 9/11. Indeed, the proposal for a national ID-card system (from Larry Ellison of Oracle Corporation) was one of the first made following the attacks on the United States. Sometimes, of course, these rationales are combined.

While Chinese and Indian authorities may not see 9/11 as a vital spur to ID-card production, both are concerned with internal population movement, migrant groups, and developing electronics-based administration. Already existing systems in Hong Kong, Malaysia, or Japan also have mixed rationales, which similarly do not have a lot to do with 9/11. Conversely, it may turn out that even those countries using 9/11 as a reason for developing new ID-card systems have other, perhaps more long-term, concerns in mind, including the more general control of migration.

It is important to note that while various kinds of ID-card systems have been in place for many decades, or have been installed for specific exigencies such as national war efforts, today's proposals and projects are of a somewhat different character. For example, they depend on electronic information infrastructures that support a variety of functions through networked databases. Indeed, the route to successful implementation of "electronic government" (or "e-government") is through the establishment of a single code—the "Unique Personal Identifier." The general-purpose card scheme, such as those in Singapore and Malaysia, which may be used for access to several government departments and as a means of verifying the identity of citizens, is enabled by networked technologies.[31]

This also makes possible another new aspect of such ID cards; they can be used for commercial as well as governmental administrative purposes. This means that conventional national interests in personal identification may be connected more directly with those of consumers (with consequences that are as yet unclear). Also, the internal national purposes of ID cards may be linked with external ones through the passport. In the United Kingdom, the proposed ID card will be administered through both the driver's license and the passport office (although in the United States, the Real ID is a product of integrating state-based driver licensing). Thus conventional distinctions between government/commercial, domestic/international, territorial/nonterritorial, and inside/outside are all challenged by new ID-card schemes.

Crucially, ID-card schemes are intended to categorize populations, distinguishing especially between insiders and outsiders, or legitimate citizens and others. This is where the existence of the national registry database is so significant. The cards themselves raise questions about "internal borders" and about unwarranted apprehension by police officers, but it is the database that facilitates automated forms of social sorting. Within the "new penology," of which Malcolm Feely and Jonathan Simon wrote some time ago, "techniques for identifying, classifying and managing groups sorted by levels of dangerousness" were sought.[32] But this takes such governmentality to a more general level by connecting it with investigations of fraud (financial and identity) and to entitlement for benefits and services. It also assumes that the scheme in question is capable of reliably making such distinctions.

The reliability of new ID-card systems across a range of stated purposes is linked with the fast-growing technologies of biometrics. At its simplest, biometrics relates to body measurements or, in the language of a company promoting biometrics, to "automated methods of identifying or authenticating the identity of a living person based on a unique physiological or behavioral characteristic."[33] As Elia Zureik says, biometrics relies on pattern recognition, which converts images into a binary code by means of an algorithm.[34] To be authenticated (or "verified"), an individual must enroll by presenting some ID card, whose details are then linked with the biometric data from the eye, finger, hand, or face. Once the linked details are stored, the individual's stated identity can be confirmed when the card and linked data are presented again. Identification occurs when an ID card (in this case) is submitted to an airline agency, for example, to be checked against a no-fly list, or to a welfare department to be checked against a list of those who have already applied for the benefit in question.

The background to ID cards may be seen in various contexts in early modern times, not least in the "pass laws," which were introduced in Virginia in 1642 to target people such as poor, white Irish indentured servants trying to "flee their obligations."[35] By 1656 Native Americans entering the colony to trade had to carry "tickets." A few years later, as Christian Parenti has shown, slave owners required slaves to carry passes in Barbados, and by 1680 Virginia had a slave pass-law. A hundred years later, tin tags, stamped with the slave's occupation, date, and a number for recording annual slave taxes, were instituted in South Carolina. In time, analogous systems would also become the apparatus of criminal justice, and together with military passes and schemes for the control of immigrant labor, would provide part of the genealogy of contemporary ID and biometric devices.

By the nineteenth century, the colonial inheritance and the "codes of race," alluded to by Rose in respect of securitizing identity, come into their own again, especially in the case of biometrics. For biometrics brings into the present certain practices that have been evident since the earliest fingerprinting of colonial subjects during the nineteenth century in countries such as India and Argentina.[36] William Herschel first used fingerprinting techniques in India in 1858 and these were systematized by Edward Henry and Azizul Haque of the Bengal Police in 1893. As Shuddhabrata Sengupta says, "anthropometrical data, in the form of cranial radii, nasal indexes and finger length, were tested for their utility in developing the science of criminology, often aided by an ethnographic discourse that constructed an elaborate taxonomy of criminal tribes, deviant populations, and martial races."[37] In relation to this, the Indian colonial state kept detailed political intelligence on "subversive activities" that entered every domain of life. In the early twenty-first century, the "war on terror" appears to be following a similar but technologically upgraded path.

Zureik reminds us that the use of biometrics "has a direct bearing on racial and other types of profiling—welfare recipients for example—and indeed on governance as a whole."[38] And yet at the same time, his work, along with others, shows that biometrics also presents many difficulties in terms of accuracy. Unsubstantiated claims and persistent errors of matching tend not to be highlighted in the effort to promote these means of "fighting terror." Combined with the quest of governments, especially the United States, to find new means of amassing personal information, and technology companies urgently seeking new markets, the prospects are poor for carefully assessing the promise of biometrics to increase national security. As Benjamin Muller observes in his description of a Canadian Forum he attended on biometrics, the event itself was framed by the "common need for biometrics."[39] Such discourses make it hard to raise questions relating to privacy or civil liberties, despite the obvious problems associated with any reliable attempt to "secure" spaces for "legitimate" persons only, especially when the political climate is chilly for specific minority groups.

Airport Security and Screening

The processes of identity securitization are most intense in contemporary airports; although as Michael Sorkin notes, these sites may also be seen as vanguards for organizing cities into spaces of heavily surveilled, highly managed flows. As a "classification engine," he goes on, "airport design is a distilled version of the segregated efficiencies of transportation planning in general in which the grail is the separation of means and, thereby, of people and privileges."[40] Identity securitization is a crucial aspect of this. Arriving at the airport, however, this is not the first hoop through which would-be entrants must pass. As Salter shows, the airport as a "transient institution" has three spheres: the arrivals hall, where newly landed passengers sort themselves into citizens, foreigners, and refugees; the "confessional," where the border agent inquires about your provenance, destination, and—this becomes the third sphere—checks the passport. This last is the "hyperdocumentation" phase, where the "body-biometrics-file-profile" is central.[41]

If we look at the Anti-Terrorism Plan in Canada, developed in the wake of 9/11, it is clear that it was intended to keep the Canadian–U.S. border secure and open to legitimate trade, to increase front-end screening for refugee claimants, to improve both detention and deportation processes, to increase security staff hiring, and to upgrade technology, integration, and training practices. In fact, Canada had been pressing for a "smart border" agreement for some time, but 9/11 seemed to offer the vital opportunity. The border issues include both geographical and artificial border-control sites such as airports. Almost immediately after 9/11, armed undercover police officers and state-of-the-art explosives detection systems were introduced. In the expectation that passengers would have to pay some of the bill for this, a CDN$12 per flight charge was levied at first, which was reduced to CDN$7 in 2003. Other initiatives included technical improvements, such as replacing cockpit doors and locking them from take-off to landing (May 2003), and installing "dirty bomb" detectors in Ottawa Airport (November 2004).

One significant border initiative that accents the reliance on new technologies is the Advanced Passenger Information / Passenger Name Record Program (API/PNR). Under the Immigration and Refugee Protection Act of 2002, commercial carriers are required to provide the Citizenship and Immigration Canada (CIC) agency with passenger and crew information for analysis, so that any who appear to pose concerns may be identified and intercepted. Such data include five elements: the full legal name, gender, date of birth, nationality, and travel document number. In a novel move, airlines are now required to provide CIC with such passenger and crew data before they arrive in Canada. Under joint Canadian–U.S. agreements, various means such as CANPASS Air (or the Canadian–U.S. harmonized, iris-scan dependent NEXUS Air scheme) have been implemented (November 2004) to expedite the travel of "approved, low-risk travelers."

Another initiative that comprises both technical and personnel skills also followed the 9/11 attacks. The Canadian Air Transport Security Authority (CATSA) was created as a crown corporation in April 2002, initially with four training centers to teach effective preboard screening to three thousand new security personnel. By 2003 CATSA began building comprehensive, aggregated datasets of all travelers plus four thousand employees, from eighty-nine designated Canadian airports, in order to compile data reports. The idea was to improve seasonal travel warnings as well as to identify gaps in security training if a particular type of incident occurred more often in one airport than in others.

Despite these apparently stringent improvements, critical questions have been raised (in Canada as well as in the United States and elsewhere) about the adequacy of the new measures. In December 2004 the Canadian Senate Standing Committee on National Security and Defense reported on inadequate mail and cargo screening, unsatisfactory background checks on airport personnel, a lack of control over access to restricted areas, and insufficient training of part-time customs staff. And in March 2005 Canada's Auditor General, Sheila Fraser, reported on lax Passport Office practices, including inadequate watch lists, outdated technology, and poor record-checking to verify identification. She argued that computer links were not in place to flag applicants ineligible for passports because they are on parole or charged with serious crimes. She also expressed concerns about passenger and baggage screening. Also in 2005 a Canadian Senate report, entitled "Borderline Insecure," argued that security is inadequate and should be the priority on borders.[42] It seems, however, that airport security initiatives south of the Canadian border have not been much more successful. A U.S. Government Accountability Office (GAO) report on the Secure Flight program in 2005 complained that the Transport Security Authority (TSA) was not effectively managing the program, to the extent that it risked failure.[43]

Borders, Citizenship, and Exclusion

In a fast-paced, mobile world, the idea of borders as barriers to movement is an unacceptable irritation, but in a fearful and unsafe world such borders make a lot of sense. The post-9/11 world is also perceived as insecure and vulnerable, and thus borders have become the focus of political concern as well as academic attention. The dominant assumptions about the importance of mobility for economic growth in the global north hold sway even in so-called terrorist times, so the urgent quest is for means of improving the sorting capacity of borders to ensure that approved movement is as fluid as possible, while simultaneously ensuring that some fine-mesh devices prevent the passage of illegitimate entrants. Needless to say, those "illegitimate entrants" include a cluster of national groups that have become "suspect" since 9/11 (from Jordan, Saudi Arabia, Libya, Pakistan, etc.), along with those who have for a long time been lower priority for permission to enter.

This is why so much attention is currently paid to schemes for greater police cooperation and improved means of examining travelers, and to technical means of checking, verifying, and identifying persons who are in transit across physical and virtual borders, especially in airports.[44] From a surveillance perspective, personal information is under detailed scrutiny at borders as never before. And of course because the data are primarily digital, the "border" is not only virtual in the sense that airports are seldom at the physical edge of territory but also in the sense that the processing often takes place "upstream" of the actual location where documents may be checked. As well, it is worth recalling that not only personal data (or actual bodies) are under surveillance; airports provide a prime example of locations where things—especially baggage but also physical documents like passports, the airplanes, and other airport machines—are also surveilled.[45] Since 9/11, concern with "things," such as small knives, has been paramount, even to an obsessive degree. Although stopping terrorists traveling by air may be an impossible task, ensuring that when they do they have no access to such things may be the best one can hope for.

In so-called control societies, however, older means of determining who is "innocent/guilty," "approved/suspect," or "legal/illegal" seem to be at a lower premium. In an analogous way to that in which the "categorical suspicion" of today's policing renders everyone if not guilty at least dubious until proven innocent, so "identity management" seems to be encroaching on older definitions of citizenship.[46] The need for knowledge and visibility as management tools is clear here, which is why airports especially are dense surveillance sites. The key tool for identity management is biometrics and in this context the chief aim is to ensure that only eligible persons enter a country. Interestingly, the identity management model derives from online businesses' protocols and technologies for "facilitating and controlling users' access to critical online applications and resources—while protecting confidential personal and business information from unauthorized users."[47] These are "integrated solutions" that administer user authentication, access rights, passwords, and the like.

In the offline world of border controls, however, bodies become passwords[48] and the "access rights" have deeply consequential aspects. As Muller comments, the shift to identity management emphasizes the emerging distinctions between friend and foe (some of which were articulated by President George W. Bush after 9/11) and, like "categorical suspicion," plays down the role of citizen agency in border practices. There is something disturbing about this process, in which the protocols of online business-practice start to displace conventional citizenship discourses, but after 9/11 it was justified as being part of a package of emergency measures. The difficulties deepened several years later, however, as it became clear that what Giorgio Agamben calls the "state of exception" had actually become "business as usual."[49]

Agamben argues that the emergency situation following 9/11 has now solidified into routine practice, and this judgment seems even more warranted by the 2006 perpetuation of the U.S. Patriot Act, which began life with a built-in "sunset clause" that was to limit its life. In Agamben's work, surveillance studies come full circle, once again to focus on the activities of the state and on citizens or noncitizens. Starkly, Agamben sees the world from the point of view of concentration camps, where death was adjudicated and life directed. In *State of Exception*, Agamben argues a contemporary case that the declaration by President George W. Bush that he is "commander-in-chief" in a "war on terror" has a longer history, in which it had been the exception but had now become the rule. In the "state of emergency" after 9/11, the Bush administration authorized the indefinite detention of noncitizens suspected of terrorist activities and their subsequent trials by a military commission.

For Didier Bigo, Agamben's analysis of the "ban" that systematically excludes some groups[50] challenges Foucault's understanding of the Panopticon, prompting the neologism; the "ban-opticon."[51] Whereas Foucault's Panopticon excludes through the incarceration of the "deviant," Bigo argues that contemporary institutions incarcerate the "safe" or the "normal" while excluding the deviant. While the majority of mobile citizens of the global north are normalized travelers who accept the need for security passes for fast-tracking through the airport as they accept the need for frequent-flyer cards to get access to the club lounges, a focused surveillance is reserved for the *sans-papiers*, the potential terrorist, the refugee—those "trapped in the imperative of mobility." Police, military, and other professionals combine their efforts to become the new "in-security professionals." The "opticon" has a specific purpose—to "ban" some, to exclude. Mixing files from different sources leads to new classifications. This is how friends and foes are distinguished and treated differently.

Global Surveillance

To talk of global surveillance certainly sounds conspiratorial, but this is not the intention of this chapter. Surveillance has become globalized just because economic and political processes are themselves globalized, for better or worse.[52] Both flexible employment and transnational consumer corporations contribute to global surveillance, just as the quest for security and safety does. Indeed, they do so in a symbiotic fashion. While Bauman argues, "the database is an instrument of selection, separation and exclusion," he also says, "the database is a vehicle of mobility, not the fetters keeping people in place."[53] At one and the same time, databases of global corporations and international policing help to lubricate desirable planetary flows and also to slow or stop undesirable traffic.

In relation to the "war on terror," one of the most obvious signs of global surveillance is the agreement of the (UN-sponsored) International Civil Aviation Organization (ICAO) for its 188 contracted states to use standard machine-readable passports (MRPs) by April 2010. About 110 of these already use such MRPs and 40 of these are planning to upgrade to the biometrically enhanced version, or e-passport, by the end of 2006. Security, immigration, and customs checkpoints worldwide accept these MRPs, which are also accessed by embassies and consulates for visas. The aim is interoperability and global networking, although what is much less clear is how far Fair Information Principles govern the ways that personal data obtained from MRPs are handled in all the countries using MRPs and e-passports. For example, the 2001 Smart Border Agreement called for common biometric standards between Canada and the United States, a process that is still under way at the time of writing. From the start of 2007 Canadians crossing into the United States will be required to hold passports or other accepted documents (British Columbia and Washington state are both moving toward an enhanced driver's license), all of which will eventually carry biometrics.

The globalization of surveillance, just as with all other globalizations, is both a phenomenon in its own right and something that takes place in different ways in different countries, producing situations of complex interrelations. Surveillance in different countries is linked with many factors, including economic priorities, technological development levels, legal oversight, colonial pasts, and present relations with the United States. It is not uniform or homogeneous and may be constrained or enabled by any or all of these factors. And surveillance is also perceived differently in different countries, which also makes a difference to its actual operation.[54]

The globalization of surveillance may also call forth new responses such as Toshimaru Ogura's proposals for a new kind of identity politics based on opposition to what Ogura calls (biometric) "identity exploitation."[55] Arguing that the securitization of identity leads to both a biological reductionism in conceptions of human identity and to the minimizing of trusting and "hospitable" international relationships through the mounting "suspicions" of nationality and citizenship tests, Ogura argues for a proliferation of usable identifiers rather than a quest for increasingly unique single identifiers.

Conclusion

Among their other attributes, airports function as filters for flows of personal data. As we have seen here, however, those flows of personal data are filtered in ways that affect the flesh-and-blood people who originally generated those data by buying airline tickets and by showing up at the airport to check their bags and board their flights. As Bauman poignantly observes, databases work to select, separate, and exclude, but their effects are encountered by "globals," who can move freely across international borders, and "locals," who are confronted by persistent and sometimes insurmountable obstacles as they attempt to do so. This process is felt most acutely within the routines and discourses of presenting oneself at a ticket counter or a security check. Here the "securitizing of identity," with its historical baggage and its contemporary technological enhancement through biometrics, is both engaged and experienced.

Such processes are developing rapidly in ways that both give evidence of and simultaneously contribute to globalization. Surveillance is going global in many ways, but airport data-filters are one obvious manifestation of this. In a world that both prizes mobility and seeks the means of restricting it for some groups—that is, of distinguishing automatically and often remotely between "friends and foes"—much will be gained in efficiency and productivity but also in the perpetuation and extension of entrenched divisions that favor some groups at the expense of others. Such matters are far from "merely technical." They represent a dynamic combination of technological, economic, and political factors, historically produced in varying ways and with varying consequences.

Those consequences that are experienced in deeply negative ways by specific groups may be mitigated or even eliminated by an equally global process of awareness-raising and resistance by coalitions of concerned citizens who will use legal, technical, and sometimes direct means. The social sciences and investigative journalism offer opportunities for probing behind the facades of "national security" or "technical logics" in ways informed by ethical criteria to indicate how new airport protocols are actually experienced by ordinary people, particularly those from populations that are less-than-welcome in the countries of the global north. But while nation-states continue to adhere to current "states of exception" and while automated modes of screening passengers remain relatively opaque to those affected by them, attempting to alter the status quo will continue to be an uphill struggle.

Notes

1. Manuel Castells, *The Rise of the Network Society* (Malden, Mass.: Blackwell, 2000).
2. Zygmunt Bauman, *Globalization: The Human Consequences* (Cambridge: Polity, 1998), 77f.
3. British Columbia, Office of the Information and Privacy Commissioner, *Privacy and the USA Patriot Act: Implications for British Columbia Public Sector Outsourcing*, October 2004.
4. David Lyon, "The Border Is Everywhere: ID Cards, Surveillance, and the Other," in *Global Surveillance and Policing: Borders, Identity, Security*, ed. Elia Zureik and Mark B. Salter (Cullumpton, UK: Willan, 2005), 66–82.

5. Gary T. Marx, "The Declining Significance of Traditional Borders (and the Appearance of New Borders) in an Age of High Technology," in *Intelligent Environments*, ed. P. Droege (Oxford: Elsevier Science, 1997), 484–94.

6. Hélène Pellerin, "Borders, Migration and Economic Integration: Towards a New Political Economy of Borders," in *Global Surveillance and Policing: Borders, Identity, Security*, ed. Elia Zureik and Mark B. Salter (Cullumpton, UK: Willan, 2005), 51.

7. Naomi Klein, *Fences and Windows: Dispatches from the Front Lines of the Globalization Debate* (New York: Picador, 2002).

8. Lyon, *Surveillance after September 11* (Cambridge: Polity Press, 2003).

9. Peter Shields, "Beyond 'Loss of Control': Telecommunications, Surveillance, Drugs, and Terrorism," *Info: The Journal of Policy, Regulation and Strategy for Telecommunications and Media* 4, no. 2 (2002): 9–15.

10. Whether or not this made sense in terms of the imaginative strategies of potential terrorists or of other kinds of vulnerability is another question. Mine is merely an empirical observation.

11. This is discussed in Lyon, "Search for Surveillance Theories" in *Theorizing Surveillance: The Panopticon and Beyond* Lyon ed. (Cullompton, UK: Willan, 2006), 3–20, although the Air India disaster is mistakenly omitted from that chapter.

12. John Torpey, *The Invention of the Passport: Surveillance, Citizenship and the State* (Cambridge: Cambridge University Press, 2000).

13. Marc Augé, *Non-places: Introduction to an Anthropology of Supermodernity* (London: Verso, 1995).

14. Lyon, "Airports as Data-filters: Converging Surveillance Systems after September 11th," *Information, Communication, and Ethics in Society* 1, no. 1 (2003): 13–20.

15. Peter Adey, "Secured and Sorted Mobilities: Examples from the Airport," *Surveillance and Society* 1, no. 3 (2003): 1368.

16. Elia Zureik with Karen Hindle, "Surveillance, Governance and Security: The Case of Biometrics," *Studies in Political Economy* 73 (2004): 113–37.

17. Irma Van der Ploeg, "Biometrics and the Body as Information: Normative Issues of the Socio-technical Coding of the Body," in *Surveillance as Social Sorting: Privacy, Risk, and Digital Discrimination*, ed. David Lyon (New York: Routledge, 2003), 57–73; Mark B. Salter, "Passports, Security, Mobility: How Smart Can the Border Be?" *International Studies Perspectives* 5, no. 1 (2004): 69–89.

18. Colin J. Bennett, "What Happens When You Book an Airline Ticket? The Collection and Processing of Passenger Data Post-9/11," in *Global Surveillance and Policing: Border, Security, Identity*, ed. Elia Zureik and Mark B. Salter (Cullompton, UK: Willan, 2005): 113–38; see also Colin J. Bennett's chapter in this volume.

19. Adey, "Secured and Sorted Mobilities," 1375.

20. Richard Jenkins, *Social Identities* (New York: Routledge, 2004), 8.

21. Ibid., 174.

22. See the discussion of this in chapter 1 of Lyon, *Surveillance Society: Monitoring Everyday Life* (Philadelphia: Open University Press, 2001).

23. Nicholas Rose, *Powers of Freedom* (Cambridge: Cambridge University Press, 1999), 240f.
24. Ibid., 243.
25. Ibid., 47.
26. Ibid., 219.
27. Elia Zureik, "Constructing Palestine through Surveillance Practices," *British Journal of Middle Eastern Studies* 28, no. 2 (2001): 205–27.
28. Torpey, *Invention of the Passport*.
29. Mark B. Salter, *Rights of Passage: The Passport in International Relations* (Boulder, Colo.: Lynne Rienner, 2003).
30. Lyon, "The Border Is Everywhere."
31. Roger Clarke, "National Identity Schemes: The Elements," Australia National University, 2006, http://www.anu.edu.au/people/roger.clarke/dv/NatIDScheme Elms.html (accessed April 12, 2008).
32. Malcolm Freely and Jonathan Simon, *Actuarial Justice: The Emerging New Criminal Law in the Futures of Criminology* (London: Sage, 1994), 173.
33. Merkatum, "Biometrics," 2006, http://www.merkatum.com/biometrics.asp/ (accessed April 12, 2008).
34. Zureik, "Surveillance, Governance and Security," 117.
35. Christian Parenti, *The Soft Cage: Surveillance in America from Slavery to the War on Terror* (New York: Basic Books, 2003), 19.
36. Shuddhbrata Sengupta, "Signatures of Apocalypse" *MetaMute* 26 (2003): 1–14.
37. Ibid., 5.
38. Zureik, "Surveillance, Governance and Security," 129.
39. Benjamin J. Muller, "Borders, Bodies and Biometrics: Towards Identity Management," in *Global Surveillance and Policing: Borders, Identity, Security*, ed. Elia Zureik and Mark B. Salter (Cullumpton, UK: Willan, 2005), 91.
40. Michael Sorkin, "Urban Warfare: A Tour of the Battlefield," in *Cities, War and Terrorism: Toward an Urban Geopolitics*, ed. Stephen Graham (Oxford: Blackwell, 2003), 261–62.
41. Salter, "At the Threshold of Security: A Theory of International Borders," in *Global Surveillance and Policing: Borders, Identity, Security*, ed. Elia Zureik and Mark B. Salter (Cullumpton, UK: Willan, 2005), 47.
42. Senate Standing Committee on National Defence, *Borderline Insecure* (2005), http://www.parl.gc.ca/38/1/parlbus/commbus/senate/com-e/defe-2/rep-e/ repintmainjun05_e.htm (accessed April 12, 2008).
43. Government Accountability Office, *Aviation Security: Secure Flight Development and Testing Under Way, but Risks Should Be Managed as System Is Further Developed*, GAO-05-356 (Washington, D.C., 2005). See Gallya Lahav's chapter in this volume.
44. Mark B. Salter, "Governmentalities of an Airport: Heterotopia and Confession," *International Political Sociology* 1, no. 1 (2007): 49–67.
45. Adey, "Secured and Sorted Mobilities," 2004.
46. See Benjamin J. Muller's chapter in this volume.

47. Wikipedia, "Identity Management," http://en.wikipedia.org/wiki/Identity _management (accessed March 4, 2006).

48. Ann Davis, "The Body as Password," *Wired Magazine* (May 7, 1997), http://www.wired.com/archive/5.07/biometrics.html (accessed April 12, 2008).

49. Giorgio Agamben, *State of Exception* (Chicago: University of Chicago Press, 2005), 2.

50. Agamben, *Homo Sacer: Sovereign Power and Bare Life*, trans. Daniel Heller-Roazen (Stanford, Calif.: Stanford University Press, 1998).

51. Didier Bigo, "Globalization of In-security: The Field of the Professionals of Unease Management and the Ban-opticon," *Traces: A Multilingual Journal of Cultural Theory* 4 (2004): 109–57.

52. Lyon, "Globalizing Surveillance: Comparative and Sociological Perspectives," *International Sociology* 19, no. 2 (2004): 135–49.

53. Bauman, *Globalization*, 51.

54. An international survey of attitudes to surveillance and privacy has been undertaken by the Surveillance Project at Queen's University. See Elia Zureik et al., eds., *Privacy, Surveillance and the Globalization of Personal Information: International Comparisons* (Montreal: McGill-Queen's University Press, forthcoming).

55. Toshimaru Ogura, "Electronic Government and Surveillance Oriented Society," in *Theorizing Surveillance: The Panopticon and Beyond*, ed. David Lyon (Cullompton, UK: Willan, 2006), 270–317.

3

Unsafe at Any Altitude

The Comparative Politics of No-Fly Lists in the United States and Canada

······················

Colin J. Bennett

I know everybody's income and what
  everybody earns,

And I carefully compare it with the
  income-tax returns;

But to benefit humanity, however
  much I plan,

Yet everybody says I'm such a
  disagreeable man!

And I can't think why!

—King Gama in *Princess Ida*,
Gilbert and Sullivan

As some day it may happen that a
    victim must be found,

I've got a little list—I've got a little list

Of society offenders who might well
    be underground,

And who never would be missed—
    who never would be missed! . . .

The task of filling up the blanks I'd
    rather leave to you.

But it really doesn't matter whom
    you put upon the list,

For they'd none of 'em be missed—
    they'd none of 'em be missed!

—Koko in *The Mikado*,
Gilbert and Sullivan[1]

Gilbert and Sullivan would no doubt have found great satirical humor in the various attempts of governments to keep tabs on their citizens in the early twenty-first century. Each of these quotations implies an opposing theory about the motivations for surveillance. The chilling implications of the Lord High Executioner's "little list" is contrasted with the well-meaning attempts of King Gama to "benefit humanity" by correcting his "erring fellow creatures."[2] The arbitrariness of the former is contrasted with the meticulous and systematic approach of the latter. The motivations behind the "little lists" are justified to find scapegoats, whereas those of the King Gama are prompted by public purpose. One sees no need to justify his surveillance; whereas, the other, of course, does.

We supposedly now have more sophisticated models of surveillance that do not rely on assumptions about the arbitrary whims of tyrants or philanthropists. The little lists are now not so little, and they are generated by a variety of bureaucratic motives and technological imperatives. The comparison of data from different sources (such as earnings and income-tax returns) is now routinized, as we leave traces of personal information behind us when we engage in the normal transactions of modern society. Contemporary surveillance does not rely on the venal whims of a Lord High Executioner or the benign motives of the philanthropist, but even so, the collection and analysis of personal information is a structural condition of modernity.[3]

Even though the increasing securitization of airline travel is explained by trends and measures put in place well before the attacks of September 11, 2001, there is no question that those events have accelerated the development of a range of measures in different countries and different airports: new forms of biometric identification, secure cockpit doors, the increased sharing of advanced passenger-information data, trusted traveler programs, and so on. However, the success of many of these measures does, to a large extent, rely on the identification of a group of individuals (e.g., "terrorists") who pose a threat to airline safety and who should be the subject of extra precautionary measures before they are allowed to board an aircraft. The "lists" thus generated are the focus of this chapter.

It is commonly assumed that airlines have always held information on "problem travelers"—the person caught smoking in the toilet, the tedious alcoholic who harasses the flight attendant, the recalcitrant passenger who refuses to obey the seat belt signs, and so on. But practices have varied considerably, and the names were not necessarily centrally stored and disseminated as they are today. The generation of "no-fly lists" as a public-policy measure is a more recent development and needs to be understood in the context of larger systems for the prescreening of airline passengers, such as the Computer Assisted Passenger Profiling Systems (CAPPS), Secure Flight, and the Automated Targeting System (ATS) in the United States and Passenger Protect in Canada. This chapter begins with an overview and comparison of these programs and then analyzes what we do and do not know about how "no-fly lists" are generated and deployed in both countries, and how they have been resisted.

These lists should be regarded not only as tools of surveillance but as "policy instruments," as one, among many, "tools of government" that might be deployed to address a commonly perceived problem.[4] Prescreening airline passengers against a prior "list" is one of several instruments used to prosecute the "war on terror."[5] The extent, level, type, and distribution of surveillance practices are not only dependent on legal and regulatory measures, nor on high-level sociological theory about technology, bureaucracy, modernity, and so on, but rather on the "structural configurations of states," which structure policy outcomes in path-dependent ways.[6] This approach is rooted in political science rather than in law and sociology. It has been termed "neo-institutionalist" and can help us to understand different patterns of surveillance in similar jurisdictions.[7] This chapter concludes with an interrogation of no-fly lists as policy instruments, as well as with some critical commentary on surveillance studies.

Systems for Airline Passenger Prescreening

Ten years ago, little attention was paid to privacy issues in the airline industry or the airport environment, and it was difficult to find interested or expert officials within the airlines, or their regulatory agencies, who could provide accurate descriptions of the personal-data processing practices of the industry. Since September 11, 2001, the interrelated questions of who travels by air, who gets to see who travels by air, and who gets to prevent people from traveling by air have been brought sharply into focus. These questions have become some of the most important in contemporary studies of privacy and surveillance.

Computer Assisted Passenger Profiling System (CAPPS)

On September 11, 2001, the nineteen hijackers were screened prior to boarding their flights against a Computer Assisted Passenger Profiling System (CAPPS), which had been in place since the early 1990s. More than half of them were identified for further inspection, but only their bags were inspected. At that time, the program was implemented in a decentralized fashion by the airlines themselves. Security concerns constrained the U.S. government from listing all potential terrorist suspects or delivering that list to the airlines.[8] This colossal security failure explains a great deal about subsequent responses in both the United States and Canada.

In January 2003, the Transportation Security Administration (TSA) published a *Federal Register* notice announcing CAPPS II and a new Aviation Security Screening Records (ASSR) database.[9] The *Federal Register* notice described a system that would allow the government access to "financial and transactional data" as well as virtually unlimited amounts of data from other proprietary and public sources. The TSA also indicated that many private and public entities might gain access to the personal information used in the ASSR database. This second-generation system was to be centrally coordinated through the TSA and to apply to all flights to, from, and within the United States.

The proposal was met with almost uniform criticism from a range of groups.[10] In response, TSA officials clarified that the basic elements of CAPPS II would be confined to the routine information collected at the time of reservation and included in the Passenger Name Record (PNR): a passenger's full name, home address, home telephone number, and date of birth, as well as that passenger's itinerary.[11] In an effort to verify the traveler's identity, that information would then be checked against credit information and other data held by various private corporations that maintain files on the commercial activities of most American citizens. CAPPS II would then conduct a check against government databases (including intelligence and law-enforcement databases) to assign a risk assessment score to each passenger: green for minimal, yellow to spark heightened security procedures, and red for those "high risk" passengers judged to pose an acute danger and who should be referred to law enforcement. It was anticipated that the number of passengers so identified as high risk would be extremely small but critically significant in the context of homeland security.

The TSA would also delete all records of travel for U.S. citizens and lawful permanent-resident aliens no more than a certain number of days after the safe completion of their travel itineraries, though it gave no similar commitment about non-U.S. citizens. The assurances about more-limited data retention, as well as about procedures to challenge their own risk assessments, did little to quell the criticism of this program. As the Electronic Frontier Foundation (EFF) put it, "the good news is TSA does not plan to retain data on individuals. The bad news is that CAPPS II puts the riskiest element of the program—the determination of risk and the construction of rules for conducting background checks—into the realm of the more secretive intelligence and law enforcement programs and databases."[12]

This entire system relied, of course, on obtaining the PNR data from the airlines and the Global Distribution Systems (GDS), reservation systems such as Galileo and Sabre.[13] To this end, the TSA announced that it would conduct a pilot project with Delta Air Lines in three midsize airports in the spring of 2003. However, Delta Air Lines, after strong public opposition, decided not to provide its passengers' data. There was a more serious scandal over the revelation that JetBlue had provided five million passenger records to a defense contractor, in what was reported as an underhand transfer of data for the testing of the CAPPS II profiling system.[14] It was later revealed to the Senate Governmental Affairs Committee by Acting TSA administrator David Stone that Delta, Continental, America West, JetBlue, and Frontier Airlines, as well as the major GDSs, had all disclosed passenger records to the TSA's contractors in 2002 to test CAPPS II.[15]

Pressure also came from Congress. In September 2003, the conference committee responsible for reconciling the Department of Homeland Security (DHS) appropriations for the next fiscal year decided to put the program on hold until the U.S. Government Accountability Office (GAO) had an opportunity to report on the effectiveness and fairness of the system. Analysis by the GAO culminated in a report that indicated that the TSA had failed to address most of the originally identified issues of concern. It recommended a number of actions, including a "risk mitigation strategy."[16] The American Civil Liberties Union (ACLU) summed up seven reasons why the CAPPS II should be abandoned: (1) the secret nature of the risk analysis; (2) the absence of an increase in safety; (3) the possibility of mission creep; (4) the lack of notification, correction, or appeal; (5) the possibility of enabling the building of lifetime travel dossiers; (6) the unnecessary burden; and (7) the discriminatory impact.[17]

Under the weight of an enormous volume of criticism, Tom Ridge, the Secretary of Homeland Security, declared CAPPS II "dead" in July 2004, a statement that raised a series of further questions about what would happen to the millions of records already collected. At the same time, the Report of the 9/11 Commission strongly advocated a centrally coordinated screening system:

> Improved use of "no-fly" and "automatic selectee" lists should not be delayed while the argument about a successor to CAPPS continues. This screening function should be performed by the TSA, and it should utilize the larger set of watchlists maintained by the federal government. Air carriers should be required to supply the information needed to test and implement this new system.[18]

Shortly thereafter, Congress passed the Intelligence Reform and Terrorism Prevention Act, which directed the DHS to "commence testing of an advanced passenger pre-screening system that will allow the Department of Homeland Security to assume the performance of comparing passenger information . . . to the automatic selectee and no-fly lists."[19]

Secure Flight

In August 2004 the TSA announced that the successor would be named "Secure Flight" and published a federal register notice indicating that it was to set up a new system of records pursuant to the Privacy Act in order to create this program. It also issued an emergency notice ordering airlines to divulge by October 29, 2004, details of all passengers who had flown domestically during the month of June 2004. The airlines initially questioned the order because of concerns about privacy, but in the end all seventy-two airlines complied and the details of around forty-two thousand passengers were transferred. At a minimum, they were to divulge the passenger's name, reservation date, travel agent, itinerary information, form of payment, flight number, and seating information—in other words, the basic information on the PNR. At that time, it was unclear whether the GDSs were also expected to cooperate.

According to the TSA, Secure Flight was to meet the following goals: identifying, in advance of flight, passengers known or suspected of being engaged in terrorist activity; moving passengers through airport screening more quickly and reducing the number of individuals unnecessarily selected for secondary screening; and fully protecting passengers' privacy and civil liberties. This notice went on to explain that the PNR data was to be compared against the existing Terrorist Screening Database, maintained by the Terrorist Screening Center. Secure Flight was to automate the watch-list comparisons and allow for more "consistent response provisions."[20] The tests were designed to verify that Secure Flight was able to match and authenticate information on air travelers with records stored in government databases and with data purchased from unspecified commercial data aggregators.

It appeared at the time that the major difference between Secure Flight and its predecessors was the abandonment of any predictive computer algorithms designed to profile travel behavior that might be linked to suspicions of terrorism (e.g., buying a one-way ticket in cash). Also, the new system was only to look for known or suspected terrorists, not other law-enforcement violators. In addition, it was to include a redress mechanism, where people could resolve questions if they believed that they had been unfairly or incorrectly selected for additional screening. It was reported that the CAPPS system (at least in 2004) screened about one out of every six air passengers. Secure Flight was supposed to cut the number down drastically.

In the 2005 Appropriations process for the DHS, Congress mandated the GAO to audit the program and in particular to assess the effectiveness of using commercial data for prescreening efforts. The GAO produced a series of reports in February, March, and July of 2005 and recommended a number of measures to reduce the risk of error and to improve procedures by which individuals could mount challenges. They also found that the TSA was less than forthcoming about the purposes of collection in its original Privacy Act Notice.[21] Critical reports were also issued by the "Secure Flight Working Group," the Department of Justice Office of the Inspector General, and the House Select Committee on Homeland Security.

While conceding that Secure Flight was an improvement on CAPPS or the proposed CAPPS II, groups such as the ACLU, the Electronic Privacy Information Center (EPIC), and the EFF also maintained consistent pressure, submitting evidence, making Freedom of Information Act (FOIA) requests for DHS documents as well as assisting individuals who had been wrongfully selected for screening. There was also use of the Privacy Act to obtain records sent to the TSA by the airlines during the testing phase. An initial request by four Alaskan citizens for any PNR data held by the TSA set in motion a lengthy process of stonewalling, confused messages about the destruction of the data, as well as an amendment to the original Privacy Act notice.[22] In August 2005 the EFF put out "an action alert" urging members of the public to request the information collected about themselves by the TSA under the Privacy and Freedom of Information Acts. The EFF asked inquirers to request that all commercial data be preserved from deletion for closer examination.[23] The TSA was thus flooded with requests. The agency responded that they did not have the "capability to perform a simple computer based search to locate any responsive records."[24]

The Secure Flight program was originally planned to be implemented in September 2005. In February 2006 it was subjected to further criticisms from the GAO, which reported that the program fell short in protecting security and privacy, and that it was seriously in jeopardy of not meeting its stated goals.[25] At a subsequent set of hearings from the Senate Committee on Commerce, the head of the TSA, Kip Hawley, announced that the Secure Flight program would be suspended pending a comprehensive security audit: "We will move forward with the Secure Flight program as expeditiously as possible, but in view of our need to establish trust with all of our stakeholders on the security and privacy of our systems and data, my priority is to ensure that we do it right . . . not just that we do it quickly."[26] A year later it was reported that the implementation of Secure Flight would be delayed until 2010.[27]

The Automated Targeting System

By 2007, however, another system, the Automated Targeting System (ATS), arose to the attention of the media and civil-liberties advocates. The ATS is a system designed for the screening of cargo coming into the United States. Somewhere in the depths of the DHS, someone had the idea to use these existing screening programs and risk-assessment methodologies for passengers as well. We do not know when this screening started, or how many individuals have been affected. The only public acknowledgment of this system appeared in the routine Privacy Act Notice, published in November 2006, which stated the following:

> The risk assessment and links to information upon which the assessment is based, which are stored in the Automated Targeting System, are created from existing information in a number of sources including, but not limited to: the trade community through the Automated Commercial System or its successor; the Automated Commercial Environment system; the traveling public through information submitted by their carrier to the Advance Passenger Information System; persons crossing the United States land border by automobile or on foot; the Treasury Enforcement Communications System, or its successor; or law enforcement information maintained in other parts of the Treasury Enforcement Communications System that pertain to persons, goods, or conveyances. As part of the information it accesses for screening, Passenger Name Record (PNR) information, which is currently collected pursuant to an existing CBP regulation (19 CFR 122.49d) from both inbound and outbound travelers through the carrier upon which travel occurs, is stored in the Automated Targeting System.[28]

The notice went on to declare that "as noted above, this system of records notice does not identify or create any new collection of information, rather DHS is providing additional notice and transparency of the functionality of these systems."[29] Subsequently, the DHS published a Privacy Impact Assessment (PIA), which described the extent of the planned system and confirmed that "every traveler and all shipments are processed through ATS, and are subject to a real-time rule based evaluation. ATS provides equitable treatment for all individuals in developing any individual's risk assessment score."[30] These risk assessments are to be maintained for up to forty years.

These announcements raised suspicions that the ATS had been in existence for a number of years, without appropriate congressional approval, and that CAPPS and Secure Flight were perhaps distractions from the real surveillance that was going on. The response from civil liberties and privacy advocates was angry and swift. The EFF pointed out that the ATS

> will create and assign "risk assessments" to tens of millions of citizens as they enter and leave the country. Individuals will have no way to access information about their "risk assessment" scores or to correct any false information about them. But once the assessment is made, the government will retain the information for [forty] years—as well as make it available to untold numbers of federal, state, local, and foreign agencies in addition to contractors, grantees, consultants, and others.[31]

The EFF filed an FOIA suit against the DHS to extract more details on the program. The EPIC, writing on behalf of thirty organizations and sixteen experts, regarded the ATS as a secret government program in clear violation of the Privacy Act and another example of "mission creep."[32] The ACLU contended that the ATS "subverts the Fourth Amendment by allowing DHS to create a dossier on every American Traveler. In short, this program turns every American traveler into a criminal and terrorist suspect."[33] Security expert, Bruce Schneier, pronounced it a complete waste of money: "The idea of feeding a limited set of characteristics into a computer, which then somehow divines a person's terrorist leanings, is farcical. Uncovering terrorist plots requires intelligence and investigation, not large-scale processing of everyone."[34]

As of the summer of 2007 outsiders are hoping that the various congressional investigations, and mainly that of the Senate Judiciary Committee, will shed light on the operation of the ATS and determine its legality. The announcement also reignited a long-standing dispute with the European Union concerning the circumstances under which PNR data on European travelers could be stored in the United States and accessed by law-enforcement agencies. In the absence of adequate privacy-protection laws in the United States, and of an equivalent supervisory authority, European data-protection officials have insisted on some degree of oversight in the processing of PNR data in the United States.

Passenger Protect

Canadian policy on airline and passenger security has been inextricably linked to that of the United States because a very large proportion of flights to and from Canadian destinations intrude upon U.S. airspace. Furthermore, the U.S. government has required all airlines flying over American soil either to turn over the names of all passengers on board within fifteen minutes of take-off or to check those names against U.S. government watch-lists in an effort to prevent terrorists from entering U.S. airspace. Both options, handing over passenger rosters or checking those names against the U.S. lists, were considered unacceptable to the Canadian government. Checking the names against a more precise and "Canadian-made" list was regarded as a more palatable alternative. That decision set in motion a series of policy events, which, as in the United States, are still in flux and still very controversial.

The legislative history begins with the Public Safety Act, 2002, which received Royal Assent on May 6, 2004. This law made changes to the Aeronautics Act, under which the Canadian government has the authority to request and evaluate information about airline passengers. Section 4.76 authorizes the prime minister to respond to immediate threats to aviation security. Section 4.81 authorizes the prime minister to require the submission of passenger information from air carriers for security purposes. Together these sections have been read as giving Transport Canada, Canada's federal transportation ministry, the authority to create a list of persons who may pose an "immediate threat to aviation security."[35] Section 4.82 of the Aeronautics Act authorizes Royal Canadian Mounted Police (RCMP) and Canadian Security Intelligence Service (CSIS) officials to access air-passenger information and match it against information under their control in order to identify threats to transportation and national security.

Thus, Section 4.81 is seen as an initial step in passenger assessment that will establish a list of persons who pose an immediate threat to aviation security, against which airlines can check their passengers. Section 4.82 is intended to build on section 4.81 by allowing for a more-advanced technological approach to passenger assessment. Since the summer of 2005, the government has proceeded on a two-track approach to implement sections 4.81 and 4.82. The 2005 budget allocated $16 million over 5 years for the assessment and development of systems to collect information about passengers to enhance transportation security.

The first official acknowledgment that a Canadian no-fly list was being developed came in August 2005:

> Beginning in August 2005, Transport Canada will consult with the Privacy Commissioner, airlines and other stakeholders on the implementation of a passenger assessment program, known as Passenger Protect. Under the program, the Government of Canada will create a list of individuals who pose an immediate threat to aviation security and who will be prevented from boarding aircraft. The program, targeted for implementation in 2006, will lay the foundation for future passenger assessment initiatives and allow airlines to provide information on individuals on this list to the federal government.[36]

Under section 4.82, Public Safety and Emergency Preparedness Canada (PSEPC) was also supposed to commission an independent feasibility study on the implementation of the "automated passenger assessment system."

In July 2006 Jennifer Stoddart, the Privacy Commissioner of Canada, sent a list of twenty-four questions to Transport Canada about the operation of this program.[37] In a press release two days after the announcement, she stated that the no-fly list "represents a serious incursion into the rights of travelers in Canada, rights of privacy and rights of freedom of movement." She complained that she had not received any in-depth briefing on the project nor any assurance that a Privacy Impact Assessment (PIA), addressing her questions, would be forthcoming.[38] The British Columbia Civil Liberties Association (BCCLA) also weighed in with complaints about the lack of consultation and a reminder of the many problems encountered with similar programs in the United States.[39]

Based on a leaked internal focus-group study, an article by Jim Bronskill reported that Canadians were much divided on the value of such lists, and that many reported difficulty in understanding how the prescreening process would work and how the list would be constructed according to what criteria. The study reported that the government was thinking very seriously about an appropriate redress mechanism for those mistakenly included on the list.[40] The same journalist also reported that Canadian Airlines had been using the larger and more cumbersome U.S. version, even though there was no requirement under Canadian law to do so. The result has been complaints from forty to fifty Canadians who were denied boarding on the basis of a match against the U.S. list.[41] A further development was the suspicion that the sharing of these lists with the U.S. government led to the wrongful apprehension of Maher Arar in New York and his subsequent deportation to Syria.[42] Therefore, when the government eventually announced the no-fly list in late 2006, a good deal of skepticism was already in the air.

Nonflyers, Selectees, Specified Persons, and "Derogs"

So what are "no-fly" lists and how are these instruments being implemented in the United States and Canada? The first watch-lists in the United States go back at least as far as 1990. This mandate was provided under the Aviation Security Improvement Act of 1990 (P.L. 101-604), which required "the agencies of the intelligence community [to] . . . ensure that intelligence reports concerning international terrorism are made available . . . to . . . the Department of Transportation and the Federal Aviation Administration [FAA]." The agencies responsible for producing most of the intelligence on terrorism are the Central Intelligence Agency (CIA), the Department of State (DOS), the Federal Bureau of Investigation (FBI), the National Security Agency (NSA), and the Defense Intelligence Agency (DIA). Between 1990 and 2001, the FAA issued several security directives and companion emergency amendments that identified persons whom carriers could not transport because they posed a threat to civil aviation. On September 11, 2001, only three of these directives were in effect.[43]

After 9/11 there have been several initiatives to try to coordinate the development, updating, and dissemination of these lists.[44] The broadest, and least exclusive, database of terrorist identities is called the Terrorist Identities Datamart Environment (TIDE). The TIDE database includes "all information the U.S. government possesses related to the identities of individuals known or appropriately suspected to be or have been involved in activities constituting, in preparation for, in aid of, or related to terrorism, with the exception of purely domestic terrorism information."[45] Entries in the TIDE database might stem from a variety of sources within the federal government but are primarily the result of derogatory nominations ("derogs") submitted by the FBI, CIA, and the newly created Office of the Director of National Intelligence (ODNI).

These entries are then reviewed by the Terrorist Screening Center (TSC) at the FBI to determine whether they meet the criteria to be included within the Terrorist Screening Database (TSDB) described as follows:

> Under Homeland Security Presidential Directive (HSPD) 6, the TSC now provides "one-stop shopping" so that every government screener is using the same terrorist watchlist—whether it is an airport screener, an embassy official issuing visas overseas, or a state or local law enforcement officer on

the street. The TSC allows government agencies to run name checks against the same comprehensive list with the most accurate, up-to-date information about known and suspected terrorists.[46]

The aforementioned presidential directive of September 16, 2003, stated,

The heads of executive departments and agencies shall, to the extent permitted by law, provide to the Terrorist Threat Integration Center (TTIC) on an ongoing basis all appropriate Terrorist Information in their possession, custody, or control. The Attorney General, in coordination with the Secretary of State, the Secretary of Homeland Security, and the Director of Central Intelligence shall implement appropriate procedures and safeguards with respect to all such information about United States persons. The TTIC will provide the organization referenced in paragraph (1) with access to all appropriate information or intelligence in the TTIC's custody, possession, or control that the organization requires to perform its functions.[47]

Although, the name obviously changed from the TTIC to the TSDB, the inclusion of names is still driven by the secret "terrorist criteria" outlined pursuant to HSPD-6. We know that "only individuals who are known or appropriately suspected to be or have been engaged in conduct constituting, in preparation for, in aid of, or related to terrorism are included in the TSDB." We are also assured that "the purpose of the TSDB is not to hold information on individuals who have been convicted of a crime; however, an individual appropriately included in the TSDB may also have a criminal history. None of the information pertaining to the criminal history is contained or referenced in the TSDB."[48] The TSDB then supplies certain government users with more precise subsets of individuals who might be of interest to government agencies, including the selectee and no-fly lists, which would be made available to the DHS and its TSA.[49]

The no-fly lists are the most stringent lists kept, and the staff at the TSC regularly rejects nominations.[50] The criteria for inclusion in these subsets, however, are not published. A memo from the Acting Associate Under-Secretary in Transportation Security Intelligence, dated October 16, 2002, was obtained by the EPIC under the FOIA; it concedes that there are two primary principles that guide the placement on the lists, but these principles have been withheld.[51] What is also unclear is how the opaque ATS system interacts with the creation of these lists. The TSC does not, we are told, engage in profiling or providing risk-assessment scores,[52] but one must assume that nominations from this larger prescreening reach the TSC at some point.

Two lists are shared with the airlines and the TSA. A "no-fly" match requires the agent to call a law-enforcement officer to detain and question the passenger. Someone on the "selectee," or "S," list has a special mark printed on their boarding pass, and the person then receives additional screening at security but presumably without any further intervention from law-enforcement officials. The FBI will neither confirm nor deny whether an individual is on these lists. How many names are on this list? The center's director, Donna A. Bucella, told Congress in March 2004 that the list was 120,000 names long. Other reports suggest that upward of 300,000 names would be a more accurate estimate. Since January 2005, the TSC has undergone a systematic scrub of all the information in the database. CBS News allegedly saw a list of 44,000 names in August 2006, not including a further 75,000 on the automatic selectee list.[53] By the time of this writing, in 2007, the numbers have probably become somewhat lower.

Increasing concerns about these lists, and about the lack of transparency and due process, has motivated a good deal of litigation. The most important suit was lodged by the ACLU. In April 2004, the National ACLU and the ACLU of Washington brought the first national lawsuit to challenge any aspect of the no-fly-list system. *Green et al. v. TSA* was brought on behalf of "false positive" passengers who had no method of resolving recurrent problems with being targeted by security even after they had been cleared for flight. The lawsuit and the related publicity led Congress in December 2004 to direct the TSA to maintain its lists in a manner that "will not produce a large number of false positives" and to create an appeal system for persons wrongly placed on the lists.

The overall public scrutiny forced government officials to admit there indeed were problems with these procedures and caused Congress to require the TSA to improve its processes for removing innocent people from the lists.[54] For those with names similar to those on the watch-lists, there is now a "TSA Passenger Identity Verification Form," through which individuals provide a range of personal information to allow the TSA to determine whether their check-in can be expedited. There is also an ombudsman in the TSA who is supposed to provide neutral and confidential services for employees and the public concerning TSA policies.[55] At the same time, there has been a more radical challenge to the very policy that airlines should require identification from airline travelers at all.[56]

Details of the Canadian government's implementation of the Passenger Protect program finally surfaced in the spring of 2007, when it published regulations on how the screening of people on the new "Specified Persons List" (SPL) would work. The lead agency is Transport Canada, which compiles the SPL based upon information received from the various Canadian security and intelligence agencies. It is assisted by a Passenger Protect Advisory Group, comprising senior officers from CSIS, RCMP, the Department of

Justice, and others to assess information on a case-by-case basis and make recommendations to the prime minister concerning the threat to aviation security. Under Transport Canada guidelines, a person will be added to the SPL if there is a determination the he poses an immediate threat to aviation security, including

> An individual who is or has been involved in a terrorist group, and who, it can reasonably be suspected, will endanger the security of any aircraft or aerodrome or the safety of the public, passengers or crew members; An individual who has been convicted of one or more serious and life-threatening crimes against aviation security; An individual who has been convicted or one or more serious and life-threatening offences and who may attack or harm an air carrier, passengers or crew members.[57]

It is clear that these criteria are not exclusive. In one sense they are narrower than those in the United States, because the list is meant to be confined to those who pose an "immediate threat" to aviation security. In another respect, the criteria are broader, because the list might also include many who have no connection to terrorism.

The SPL contains the name, date of birth, and gender of each person. The information for each specified person listed is reviewed at least once every thirty days. Under the Identity Screening Regulations,[58] airlines are required to compare each person's name as it appears on her government-issued ID against the specified-persons list before issuing a boarding pass, for any person who appears to be twelve years of age or older. The regulations take into account the various ways in which the boarding pass may be obtained, whether at a kiosk, off the Internet, or at an airport check-in counter. When the airline verifies that an individual matches in name, date of birth, and gender with someone on the list, the airline is required to inform Transport Canada to verify the person's identity. Once a match between a person wishing to board an aircraft and someone on the SPL is discovered by an air carrier, and subsequently confirmed by Transport Canada, that person will be denied boarding.[59]

Transport Canada has certainly taken steps to minimize the risk of false matches of persons with the same or similar name as someone on the list. Further an Office of Reconsideration provides an independent review mechanism for anyone with complaints or inquiries. Under the new procedures, this office will reevaluate cases, and if false positives are found, will "update the SPL with additional information to ensure the same individual will not be confused with a specified person in future."[60] It is not clear whether the individual's name will actually be removed. The SPL is expected to be more defined, limited, and hopefully effective than previous programs. Press reports suggest no more than two thousand names.

Although it is quite apparent that the government had tried to draw lessons from the mistakes made by the United States and is desperately trying to avoid the same embarrassments, this "made-in-Canada" program has not satisfied critics. Within two weeks of the program's beginning, there appeared a string of critical editorials and reports about false-positive cases.[61] Moreover, federal and provincial privacy commissioners passed a resolution in June 2007 calling for the referral of the program to parliament for review and scrutiny, the enactment of legislative criteria governing the use of no-fly lists (given that the Aeronautics Act clearly does not supply those criteria), the establishment of an independent oversight body to review the SPL, and the suspension of the program until the review had been completed. The commissioners were especially concerned that Transport Canada could not give assurances that the SPL would not be shared with foreign governments.[62] It is still not clear whether this smaller list would satisfy U.S. law-enforcement agencies, and if not, whether the airlines would continue to use the longer U.S. versions.

What Is Wrong with No-Fly Lists?

So what is wrong with trying to prevent those who pose threats to aviation security from boarding aircraft? The arguments against no-fly lists tend to group into four categories: effectiveness, due process, discrimination, and security. There are first a range of *effectiveness* questions. If the program cannot be demonstrably proven as effective, then why should civil liberties be put in the balance? With respect to Secure Flight, U.S. security expert Bruce Schneier states the issue as follows:

> Imagine for a minute that . . . we can ensure that no one can fly under a false identity, that the watch lists have perfect identity information, and that Secure Flight can perfectly determine if a passenger is on the watch list: no false positives and no false negatives. Even if we could do all that, Secure Flight wouldn't be worth it. Secure Flight is a passive system. It waits for the bad guys to buy an airplane ticket and try to board. If the bad guys don't fly, it's a waste of money. If the bad guys try to blow up shopping malls instead of airplanes, it's a waste of money.[63]

This leads him and others to conclude that the money spent on these passenger prescreening systems would be better spent on more proactive investigative measures or emergency-response systems. A more essential question asks whether one should really care whether somebody on an airplane has connections with terrorism, so long as he/she is not going to harm that particular flight. Behavior-based, rather than identity-based, screening is more appropriate.

Of course, any prescreening system embodies a range of *due process* concerns. The lists are secret. The criteria for appearing on lists are vague. There will always be false positives and false negatives. Therefore, many nondangerous passengers have either been mistakenly put on the lists or detained for having the same or similar name as someone on the list. Some have been subjected to stigma and detention with no meaningful opportunity to remedy these errors or appeal their status. Most notably, U.S. Senator Ted Kennedy told a Senate Judiciary Committee hearing on border security that he had been prevented from boarding flights because his name appeared on a watch-list; the problem was only corrected after a call from Senator Kennedy to Secretary Tom Ridge. Other journalists offered reports of babies, lawyers, academics, and famous pop-singers appearing on no-fly lists. A CBS *60 Minutes* in October 2006 reported that the list still contained fourteen of the nineteen dead 9/11 hijackers, François Genoud (was a Nazi sympathizer and has been dead for ten years) and Evo Morales, the president of Bolivia.[64] Further, anyone with the common name David Nelson risked intrusive screening and interrogation, prompting an ACLU supported lawsuit on behalf of someone with that name.[65]

A third and related problem of *discrimination* is also raised. Critics have noted the obvious issue of how socially constructed understandings of the kinds of people likely to engage in terrorism will inform the construction of watch-lists and the interpretation of behavior. We simply do not know the extent to which these prescreening programs rely on religious or racial profiling, or on the targeting of those with unsympathetic political beliefs. For example, plaintiffs in the 2004 American Civil Liberties Association constitutional challenge to no-fly lists included staff members of the ACLU and of the Nobel Peace Prize–winning pacifist organization the American Friends Service Committee.[66]

Finally, no comprehensive passenger prescreening program can be free of *security* problems. Individuals can purchase tickets and attempt to board with false identifications. Individuals may try to fly on someone else's ticket. There is also error that will naturally occur in the front-end verification match of thousands of airline transactions daily. The system of ID verification is always subject to human and computer error. And yet the risk to the individual is direct, immediate, and easily grasped.

No-Fly Lists and Theories of Surveillance

So what are no-fly lists and how can we better understand their development? It is readily apparent that the image of one discrete and bounded list in the hands of one authority is misguided. No-fly lists are dynamic, as they are constantly being updated, expanded, and refined. Donna Bucella, the head of the TSC, has likened the process to painting a bridge; as soon as you finish one end, you have to start again at the other.[67] One FBI agent has described the initial screening process as a "massive data dump" of anybody with a connection to terrorism, which the TSC has been trying to clean up ever since.[68]

From the outside, the apparent costs of these systems far outweigh any benefits. For many surveillance practices, the countervailing interests are normally quite evident. The case for passenger prescreening programs against no-fly lists, however, has clearly not been convincingly made, either in the United States or Canada. So what, then, explains the persistence of this idea? What theories of surveillance can help us come to grips with the dogged manner in which passenger prescreening programs have been developed in the United States, and then later emulated in Canada in the face of constant criticism, and the obvious and embarrassing fact that these systems still cannot adequately distinguish between terrorists and famous politicians or babies. The deep contradictions within this concept have been best expressed by Schneier: "Remember what the no-fly list is. It's a list of people who are so dangerous that they can't be allowed to board an airplane under any circumstances, yet so innocent that they can't be arrested—even under the provisions of the Patriot Act."[69]

It is now commonplace to try to understand surveillance practices in terms of the structural conditions of postmodern society.[70] The "conditions of possibility" for no-fly lists are obviously complex organizations employing the latest technologies. Airports are sites of discipline, where passengers become passive subjects and bearers of the power relations that force compliance. The "war on terror" is a further extension of the normalizing gaze of the panopticon. No-fly lists are the manifestation of authorities' attempts to marginalize—to separate the suspicious and abnormal from the innocent and normal. Surveillance is also supposed to have changed in character and degree. New patterns of information-capture inform the procedures by which individual behaviors might be discovered and interrogated. One persistent theme is that surveillance is now "routine" or "everyday"; it is the by-product of routine engagement with modern institutions.[71]

Contemporary surveillance is not, therefore, characterized by centralized "Big Brother" or "panoptic" control. It is, rather, decentralized and disaggregated in the form of different computer networks within government, outside government, and most notably within the gray areas in between collecting information about identity and behavior. In this environment, we talk less of "databases." The dispersed and networked information environment has created a more diffuse and elusive "surveillant assemblage."[72] In this model, surveillance operates by abstracting human bodies from their contexts and separating them into a series of discrete flows. These flows are then reassembled by different institutions in different locations to produce a series of "data-doubles" for each individual. Like a rhizome, our digital personae operate beneath the surface and then emerge in different forms for different institutional purposes and agendas. Thus, the surveillant assemblage transforms the hierarchies of surveillance and the nature of personal privacy.

The contemporary sociological literature on surveillance embodies many powerful insights into the ways modern institutions keep tabs on unsuspecting subjects. It does not, however, help us explain the patterns documented in this article. Indeed, it is interesting to reflect on how little this literature tends to talk about "lists." Watch-lists are as old as government, and no-fly lists are perhaps a throwback form of surveillance. They are definitely not routine and they are highly centralized. They also are not necessarily dependent upon sophisticated methods of information extraction and monitoring. "Lists" seem too discrete and too simple. They are also deeply and inescapably political. They evoke images of the most intrusive and discriminatory forms of government surveillance. No person would ever wish to be on a no-fly list. On the other hand, we have inherent interests in having our names on the electoral rolls, the banking systems, the credit-reporting agencies, and a host of other government systems. The problem with many contemporary information systems is how the information is used and disclosed *once collected*. If one's name is on a no-fly list, one has a problem, regardless of how it will be used and disseminated.

Paradoxically, these lists might also be easier to regulate, from the point of view of existing privacy regimes. The American and Canadian Privacy Acts date from 1974 and 1982 respectively. It is commonly agreed that both pieces of legislation are unequal to the depths and complexities of contemporary privacy challenges. Both, for example, rest on the outmoded concept of a "system of records," a bounded "list" of personal information, which could be more easily identified and regulated before the emergence of current models of computing architecture, based on dispersed networks. It is, however, instructive that the EPIC and the ACLU were able to get a handle on the CAPPS, Secure Flight, and ATS systems by invoking the statutory obligations within the Privacy Act to produce a notice in the *Federal Register* whenever a new "system of records" was being constructed. The TSA was even caught at one point violating Privacy Act requirements. These notices are, to be sure, vague and insufficient; however, they do provide a starting point for further litigation, for FOIA requests and for outside scrutiny. And in Canada, there has never been a more united, and forceful, opposition to any surveillance measure than that expressed against Passenger Protect.

Privacy is often faulted in the critical surveillance literature for its central reliance on the risks associated with individualized subjects rather than with the larger societal consequences. To be sure, the language and policy instruments of privacy are not the only antidote to curbing the effects of excessive surveillance.[73] They do, however, have an emotive appeal against the relatively crude construction of "lists." This conclusion also suggests that privacy legislation constitutes a necessary, if not sufficient, strategy to fight excessive surveillance.

If one is seeking an explanation for the development of no-fly lists, then perhaps the neo-institutionalist literature on policy instruments, referred to earlier, can assist. When faced with a common problem, governments possess a finite inventory of policy instruments, and they draw lessons from their counterparts. The "tools of government" have been a matter of academic inquiry and practical policy-analysis for about twenty years.[74] This approach eschews the old-fashioned and descriptive "institutionalism." It leads naturally to a range of fascinating comparative questions: Which tools appear in the "toolbox" of different societies? Why are some preferred over others? Is the correct tool being used? The metaphor should not be overdone. As we point out in *The Governance of Privacy*,

> In a toolbox, each instrument is suited to a different purpose and has a specific use. But most of the tools are used separately, not in conjunction with each other, and there is no overall single purpose for their use. Throw away the screwdriver, the drill and the saw, yet the hammer remains, still capable of doing its job and driving the nail home. But it cannot do what the other tools can do, and its efficacy as a nail-driver may depend, in part, on factors to do with the person who wields it. Among these is the ability to recognize what is a nail, and what is not.[75]

Christopher Hood makes a basic distinction between "effecting" tools (the means by which government can impact on the outside world) and "detecting" tools (the instruments that government uses for taking in information).[76] Government then uses its "nodality, treasure, authority, and organization to perform these roles" the distinctions are not clear-cut, but we are unmistakably analyzing "tools of detection" here: "government needs a set of tools for examination, inspection, monitoring, watching and detecting, tools which must be applicable to a wide range of objects."[77]

He further distinguishes between nodal receivers (information that government obtains simply by maintaining a passive presence at the center of the social network); rewards (where resources are used to obtain information); requisitions (where information is provided under threat of sanction for noncompliance); and ergonomic detectors (where government puts the emphasis on physical or mechanical devices for obtaining information involuntarily or without the cooperation of an informant).[78] Here then is a useful taxonomy of how government collects personal information. It may get it for free (when, for example, individuals call "hotlines"); it may pay for it (though rewards, information exchanges, or active propositions); it may demand it and impose a sanction if it is not provided (through obligations to notify, tax returns, interrogations, or inspections); it may set up fixed or mobile systems to observe all who pass (turnstiles, or mobile and hidden scanners).

How are nodality, treasure, authority, and organization deployed by governments to address the problem of airline security? In both Canada and the United States all of these tools have been used to develop passenger prescreening programs. Both use their "nodality" to assert a central coordinating role in the "war on terror," in response to the obvious failure of a more dispersed and fragmented system of prescreening. Both the DHS and Transport Canada use their organizational powers to coordinate and consult with relevant stakeholders. But economic power is perhaps used more in the United States, where it provides incentives to database companies to share proprietary data for identity verification; U.S. federal privacy laws do not generally prevent intelligence agencies from purchasing personal information from commercial data-aggregators.

In an era when policy making in advanced industrial-states is characterized by new governance arrangements, by innovative ways to use institutions in civil society to coregulate society, and by a conventional wisdom that many tools are necessary for the delivery of public goods, no-fly lists do stand out as a classic, authority-based model of government, based on command and sanction. In both countries, statutory authorizations are necessary conditions for the construction of lists (from other agencies) and the provision of mandates to airlines to prescreen against flight manifests and PNRs.

No-fly lists are one reflection of the resurgence of the state's attempt to reassert its sovereignty and perhaps a reversal of the transnational, complex, and multilevel aspects of policy making that characterized the political science and international relations of the 1990s.[79] At the same time, both the Canadian and U.S. governments cannot implement this policy without the willing cooperation of a variety of civil-society actors, especially airlines. The tendency to download costs and responsibilities to nongovernmental actors is definitely a feature of the contemporary form of governance, characterized by coregulatory activity rather than "do-it-alone" government.[80] These patterns are also consistent with theories of governmentality, in which devolution of governmental responsibility is enacted through a number of policy instruments or technologies to manage risk.[81]

However, if one is seeking a robust explanation for these policy developments in both countries, then one needs to look no further than September 11 and the obvious failure to apprehend any of the perpetrators before they boarded the planes, even though it is reported that half of them were already flagged on the watch-lists of the day. That experience creates a powerful legacy for newly created bureaucratic agencies with a need to justify their existence and budgets. The particular dynamics of policy development produce bureaucratic and technological legacies. No-fly lists are, therefore, path dependent. They are explained neither by the arbitrary whims of the sovereign with his "little list" nor by the protective motivations of the benign philanthropist. Rather, the pattern is better explained by an overwhelming motivation to "be on the safe side" within contemporary risk societies and by the fact that the range of policy instruments available to contemporary policy makers is inherently limited.[82]

Notes

1. Both quotations are from the Gilbert and Sullivan archive, http://math .boisestate.edu/GaS/index.html.
2. "If you give me your attention, I will tell you what I am:
   I'm a genuine philanthropist—all other kinds are sham.
   Each little fault of temper and each social defect
   In my erring fellow-creatures, I endeavour to correct"
   (King Gama in *Princess Ida*, Gilbert and Sullivan).
3. Anthony Giddens, *The Consequences of Modernity* (Cambridge: Polity Press, 1990); David Lyon, *Surveillance Society: Monitoring Everyday Life* (Buckingham: Open University Press, 2001).
4. Christopher Hood, *The Tools of Government: Public Policy and Politics* (Chatham, N.J.: Chatham House, 1983); Michael Howlett and M. Ramesh, *Studying Public Policy: Policy Cycles and Policy* (Oxford: Oxford University Press, 2003).
5. Philip B. Heyman, *Terrorism, Freedom and Security: Winning without War* (Cambridge, Mass.: MIT Press, 2003).
6. Theda Skocpol, "Bringing the State Back In: Strategies of Analysis in Current Research," in *Bringing the State Back In*, ed. Peter Evans, Dietrich Rueschemeyer, and Theda Skocpol (Cambridge: Cambridge University Press, 1985), 3–42.
7. James G. March and Johan P. Olsen, "The New Institutionalism: Organizational Factors in Political Life," *American Political Science Review* 78, no. 3 (1984): 734–49; Colin J. Bennett, "The Public Surveillance of Personal Data: A Cross-national Analysis," in *Computers, Surveillance, and Privacy*, ed. David Lyon and Elia Zureik (Minneapolis: University of Minnesota Press, 1996), 237–59.
8. The 9/11 Commission, *Final Report of the National Commission on Terrorist Attacks upon the United States* (New York: Norton, 2004), 392.

9. *Federal Register* 68, no. 10 (January 15, 2003): 2101–3.

10. See, for example, the comments of the Electronic Privacy Information Center, *Air Travel Privacy*, http://www.epic.org/privacy/airtravel/ (accessed April 11, 2008).

11. *Federal Register* 68, no. 148 (July 31, 2003): 45265–69.

12. http://www.eff.org/Privacy/TIA/20030324_capps_letter.php (accessed April 11, 2008).

13. The travel industry is served by four main "reservation-system" service providers—"Global Distribution Systems." Two companies have emerged as giants of the industry: Sabre, the larger of the two companies and pioneer of the service, and Galileo. Both offer computerized reservation systems to airlines, travel agencies, rental companies, and hotel chains. The others are Worldspan and Amadeus.

14. Ryan Singel, "JetBlue Shared Passenger Data," *Wired Magazine*, September 18, 2003, http://www.wired.com/news/politics/privacy/0,60489-0.html (accessed April 11, 2008). See also Gallya Lahav's chapter in this volume.

15. http://www.epic.org/privacy/airtravel/stone_answers.pdf (accessed April 11, 2008).

16. Government Accountability Office, "Computer Assisted Passenger PreScreening System Faces Significant Implementation Challenges," GAO Report No. 04-385 (February 2004), http://www.gao.gov/htext/d04385.html (accessed April 11, 2008).

17. American Civil Liberties Union, "The Seven Problems with CAPPS II," April 6, 2004, http://www.aclu.org/privacy/spying/15258res20040406.html (accessed April 11, 2008.

18. The 9/11 Commission, *Final Report*, 393.

19. Intelligence Reform and Terrorism Prevention Act Public Law, 108-458 (2004).

20. Federal Register, "TSA, Reports, Forms and Record Keeping Requirements: Agency Information Collection Activity under OMB Review, Docket No. TSA: 2004-19160," *Federal Register* 29 (September 24, 2004): 65619–27.

21. These General Accounting Office (GAO) reports are all linked from the EPIC Secure flight page, http://www.epic.org/privacy/airtravel/secureflight.html (accessed April 11, 2008).

22. See http://www.alaskafreedom.com (accessed April 11, 2008).

23. https://secure.eff.org/site/SPageServer?pagename=ADV_secureflight&JServ SessionIdr006=sevnmibej1.app6a (accessed April 11, 2008).

24. http://www.tsa.gov/research/privacy/faqs.shtm (accessed April 11, 2008).

25. General Accounting Office, "Aviation Security: Significant Management Challenges May Adversely Affect Implementation of the Transportation Security Administration's Secure Flight Program," GAO-06-374T (February 9, 2006), http://www.gao.gov/new.items/d06374t.pdf (accessed April 11, 2008).

26. Hawley, Kip, "Testimony by Kip Hawley," February 9, 2006, http://www.tsa.gov/press/speeches/speech_1002.shtm (accessed April 11, 2008).

27. http://www.epic.org/privacy/airtravel/secureflight.html (accessed April 11, 2008).

28. *Federal Register* 71, no. 212 (November 2, 2006): 64543–46, http://edocket .access.gpo.gov/2006/06-9026.htm (accessed April 11, 2008).

29. Ibid.

30. Department of Homeland Security, "Automated Targeting System Privacy Impact Assessment," November 22, 2006, p. 2, http://www.dhs.gov/xlibrary/ assets/privacy/privacy_pia_cbp_ats.pdf (accessed April 11, 2008).

31. Electronic Frontier Foundation, "American Travelers to Get Secret 'Risk Assessment' Scores," November 30, 2006, http://www.eff.org/news/archives/ 2006_11.php (accessed April 11, 2008).

32. http://www.epic.org/privacy/pdf/ats_comments.pdf (accessed April 11, 2008).

33. American Civil Liberties Union, "ACLU Backgrounder on ATS," January 10, 2007, http://www.aclu.org/privacy/gen/27928pub20070110.html (accessed April 11, 2008).

34. Bruce Schneier, "Automated Targeting System," December 22, 2006, http:// www.schneier.com/blog/archives/2006/12/automated_targe.html (accessed April 11, 2008).

35. Section 4.81 states:

   The Minister, or any officer of the Department of Transport authorized by the Minister for the purposes of this section, may, for the purposes of transportation security, require any air carrier or operator of an aviation reservation system to provide the Minister or officer, as the case may be, within the time and in the manner specified by the Minister or officer, with information set out in the schedule

   a) that is in the air carrier's or operator's control concerning the persons on board or expected to be on board an aircraft for any flight specified by the Minister or officer if the Minister or officer is of the opinion that there is an immediate threat to that flight; or

   b) that is in the air carrier's or operator's control, or that comes into their control within 30 days after the requirement is imposed on them, concerning any particular person specified by the Minister or officer.

36. Transport Canada, "Government of Canada Moving Forward on Air Passenger Assessment," August 5, 2005, http://www.tc.gc.ca/mediaroom/ releases/nat/2005/05-gc009e.htm (accessed April 11, 2008).

37. Office of the Privacy Commissioner of Canada, "Questions Submitted to Transport Canada, Regarding Plans for a 'No-fly List,'" August, 9, 2005, http://www.privcom.gc.ca/media/nr-c/2005/ques_050809_e.asp (accessed April 11, 2008).

38. The author made an access-to-information request for this Privacy Impact Assessment (PIA). A version, conducted by Deloittes and dated December 16, 2005 was released with several significant redactions in September 2007.

39. British Columbia Civil Liberties Union, "Letter to Ms. McLellan and Mr. Lapierre, Re: Opposition to Proposed 'No-fly' List," June 10, 2005, http:// www.bccla.org/othercontent/05nofly.html (accessed April 11, 2008).

40. Jim Bronskill, "No-Fly List May Not Fly, Federal Study Warns," *Globe and Mail*, March 17, 2006.

41. Jim Bronskill, "U.S. No-Fly List Mistakenly Snagging Dozens of Canadians," *Edmonton Journal*, July 18, 2006.

42. See http://www.ararcommission.ca (April 11, 2008).

43. TSA Watchlists Memo, http://www.epic.org/privacy/airtravel/foia/watchlist _foia_analysis.html (accessed April 11, 2008).

44. I am very grateful for the insights provided by Lyn Rahily, Privacy Officer of the Terrorist Screening Center, and Tim Edgar, Deputy Civil Liberties Director at the Office of the Director of National Intelligence on the panel on "No-fly Lists in Canada and the United States" at the Computer, Freedom, Privacy (CFP) Conference, Montreal, May 3, 2007.

45. The National Counterterrorism Center, "Terrorist Identities Datamart Environment" (TIDE), http://www.nctc.gov/docs/Tide_Fact_Sheet.pdf (accessed April 11, 2008).

46. http://www.fbi.gov/terrorinfo/counterrorism/faqs.htm (accessed April 11, 2008).

47. Office of the Press Secretary, White House, "Homeland Security Presidential Directive/Hspd-6," September 16, 2003, http://www.whitehouse.gov/news/ releases/2003/09/20030916-5.html (accessed April 11, 2008).

48. Ibid.

49. See FAQs, http://www.tsa.gov/research/privacy/faqs.shtm#0 (accessed April 11, 2008).

50. Comments by Lyn Rahily, Privacy Officer at the Terrorist Screening Center, Computer Freedom Privacy (CFP) conference, May 3, 2007.

51. TSA Watchlists Memo, http://www.epic.org/privacy/airtravel/foia/watchlist _foia_analysis.html (accessed April 11, 2008).

52. Lyn Rahily, CFP conference, May 3, 2007.

53. CBS News, "Unlikely Terrorists on No-Fly List," *Sixty Minutes*, October 8, 2006.

54. American Civil Liberties Union, "Grounding the No-fly List," August 12, 2005, http://www.aclu-wa.org/inthecourts/detail.cfm?id=252 (accessed April 11, 2008).

55. http://www.tsa.gov/join/benefits/careers_benefits_ombudsman.shtm (accessed April 11, 2008).

56. In *Gilmore v. Gonzales*, the court found that there was no inherent constitutional right to travel anonymously. They did uphold the airline's policy that one either presents identification or opts to be treated as a "selectee" and undergo more intensive screening. The entire story is told at http://www .papersplease.org/gilmore/index.html (accessed April 11, 2008).

57. Transport Canada, "Passenger Protect Program," June 8, 2007, http://www .tc.gc.ca/vigilance/sep/passenger_protect/menu.htm (accessed April 11, 2008).

58. Aeronautics Act, Identity Screening Regulations P.C. 2007-602, April 26, 2007, http://canadagazette.gc.ca/partII/2007/20070516/html/sor82-e.html (accessed April 11, 2008).

59. Transport Canada, "Specified Persons List," June 6, 2007, http://www.passenger protect.gc.ca/specified.html (accessed April 11, 2008).

60. Transport Canada, "Office of Reconsideration," June 7, 2007, http://www.tc .gc.ca/reconsideration/menu.htm (accessed April 11, 2008).

61. For example, "Boy on No-Fly List Advised to Change Name," *The Ottawa Citizen*, June 29, 2007.

62. Office of the Privacy Commissioner of Canada, "Resolution of Canada's Privacy Commissioners and Privacy Enforcement Officials. Passenger Protect Program—Canada's Aviation No-Fly List," June 28, 2007, http://www.privcom.gc.ca/nfl/res_20070628_e.asp (accessed April 11, 2008).

63. Bruce Schneier, "TSA's Secure Flight," January 31, 2005, http://www.schneier.com/blog/archives/2005/01/tsas_secure_fli.html (accessed April 11, 2008).

64. CBS News, "Unlikely Terrorists on No-Fly List."

65. American Civil Liberties Union, "Statement of David C. Nelson," April 6, 2004, http://www.aclu.org/safefree/resources/17468res20040406.html (accessed April 11, 2008).

66. British Columbia Civil Liberties Union, "Letter to Ms. McLellan."

67. Quoted in CBS News, "Unlikely Terrorists on No-Fly List."

68. Jack Cloonan, quoted in ibid.

69. Bruce Schneier, "Schneier on Security: Definition of No-Fly," September 26, 2005, http://www.schneier.com/blog/archives/2005/09/secure_flight_n_1.html (accessed April 11, 2008).

70. See chapters by David Lyon, Benjamin J. Muller, and Peter Adey in this volume.

71. Lyon, *Surveillance Society*.

72. Kevin D. Haggerty and Richard V. Ericson, "The Surveillant Assemblage," *British Journal of Sociology* 51, no. 4 (2000): 605–20; see Mark B. Salter's chapter in this volume.

73. Lyon, *Surveillance Society*, 119; Felix Stalder, "Privacy Is Not the Antidote to Surveillance," *Surveillance and Society* 1, no. 1 (2002): 120–24.

74. Howlett and Ramesh, *Studying Public Policy*.

75. Colin J. Bennett and Charles Raab, *The Governance of Privacy: Policy Instruments in the Twenty-First Century* (Toronto: University of Toronto Press, 2003), 164.

76. Hood, *The Tools of Government*, 3.

77. Ibid., 91.

78. Ibid., 91–105.

79. Edgar Grande and L. Pauly, *Complex Sovereignty: Reconstituting Political Authority in the Twenty-First Century* (Toronto: University of Toronto Press, 2005).

80. Jan Kooiman, *Governing as Governance* (London: Sage, 2003).

81. Nicholas Rose, "Governing 'Advanced' Liberal Democracies," in *Foucault and Political Reason: Liberalism, Neo-liberalism and Rationalities of Government*, ed. Andrew Barry, Thomas Osborne, and Nicholas Rose (Chicago: University of Chicago Press, 1996), 37–64.

82. Ulrich Beck, *World Risk Society* (Cambridge: Polity Press, 1999).

4

MOBILITY AND BORDER SECURITY

The U.S. Aviation System, the State, and
the Rise of Public–Private Partnerships

· · · · · · · · · · · · · · · · · · ·

Gallya Lahav

Immediately following the terrorist attacks of September 11, 2001, the United States shut down its air-traffic system for several days, and rerouted an estimated forty-five thousand passengers to Canada. The creation of Operation Yellow Ribbon by Canada's Department of Transport marked the first time in history that Canada shut down its own airspace.[1] Beyond lending testament to spectacular international cooperation, these dramatic events revealed the expansive and interdependent nature of contemporary border control, now including foreign states, and other nonstate and private actors such as airlines. Moreover, the implications of the presence of foreigners in the terrorist attacks reflected the dramatic realization of new global threats emanating from private, nonstate actors, in groups as diverse as terrorists, drug traffickers, human smugglers, migrants, and foreign students. They visibly exposed the changing nature of threat, while masking some of the dramatic qualitative changes that have occurred since September 11.

The subsequent surge of policy instruments and public–private partnerships brought to light the link between security and mobility in a global world of people on the move. The linkage between security and mobility concerns has coincided with the proliferation and incorporation of nonstate actors, who have the economic, political, and technological resources to facilitate or curtail travel, migration, and return.[2] Actors such as airlines and transport companies, travel agencies, employer groups, and foreign states have been co-opted in an extended regulatory framework of migration and border control. In the literature, they have invariably been understood as "deputy sheriffs,"[3] "agents,"[4] or "tools of government"[5] involved in processes of "remote control,"[6] delegation,[7] externalization,[8] outsourcing, neocorporatism, or privatization.[9]

Regardless of the type of arrangement, the emergence of public–private partnerships, as illuminated by the U.S. aviation "system" explored here, is suggestive of new modes of cooperation and control. In all cases, the development of the relationship between states and nonstate actors in meeting security and mobility goals captures a global era marked by both a political desire to control movement, and agents willing and able to play on the link between mobility and security. The question is to what extent do these actors open up new channels and opportunities for state regulation over borders, or represent a transformation and abdication of state sovereignty and diminished democratic governance? To a large degree, the answers depend on the nature of the relationships that keep these dynamics in motion, and the degree of collaboration, co-optation, or level of autonomy of each actor.

By providing a disaggregated view of the U.S. aviation "system," this chapter examines the nature of an extended regulatory field, which includes both central state and nonstate actors in border security and regulation. A cost-benefit analysis of the interests of multiple stakeholders engaged in aviation security offers some empirical insight into the stakes involved and the logic behind border control. With special focus on private actors, I review four issues in aviation security: (1) passenger screening and Passenger Name Record (PNR) data; (2) virtual border and airport infrastructure; (3) government outsourcing; and (4) carrier sanctions. In each case, I highlight the relationship between private and public actors in managing border control. Finally, I consider the implications for effective border management and broader issues of state sovereignty and democratic governance.

Theoretical Framework: Security and Mobility

The uncovering of terror plots against airlines and the involvement of foreigners (and foreign networks), in addition to stoking the national security debate, has critically extended to the politics of mobility. On the heels of the horrific events of September 11, 2001, the United States formally institution-alized the link between domestic security and foreign travelers by creating the Department of Homeland Security (DHS), which merged twenty-two branches of the U.S. government, including immigration processing and enforcement bureaucracies. The creation of the DHS was the first significant addition to the U.S. government since 1947, when President Harry Truman amalgamated the various branches of the U.S. Armed Forces into the Department of Defense to better coordinate the nation's defense against mil-itary threats. The new DHS created the U.S. Visitor and Immigrant Status Indicator Technology (US-VISIT) program (an automated entry–exit system that collects biographic and biometric information at ports of entry). Originally designed to determine whether visiting foreigners overstayed their visas, the system became a tool to combat terrorism, and according to the DHS, has both immigration law-enforcement and antiterrorism missions.[10]

A surge of initiatives were launched to these dual ends. As well as the formation of the new DHS to coordinate activities with a reorganized Immigration and Naturalization Service (INS), the 2001 U.S. Patriot Act paved the way for all types of new modalities of regulation. These include electronic innovations, visa screening, racial and ethnic profiling, accelera-tion of procedures, unprecedented security checks, the modernization of immigration controls to include the latest technology through the use of biometrics, and the Student and Exchange Visitor Information System (SEVIS) database for foreign students. By 2007, the United States was esti-mated to have increased Border Patrol manpower by 30 percent since President Bush took office—from 9,500 to 12,500 agents—an intensifica-tion met with comparable results.[11]

These dramatic national policies represent the most obvious state responses to regulate borders. However, they overlook the more far-reaching changes on the ground, such as administration decisions and, most impor-tantly, the network of diverse nonstate actors involved in policy implemen-tation. These public–private partnerships offer a more accurate picture of the nature of border and migration control, and especially the venues where such policies are truly realized. In the multitude of policy initiatives lays the under-lying character of implementation—a policy of pushing border inspection and security agenda out to nonstate actors (including other nations and pri-vate, international, and local players) and co-opting new gatekeepers. Though many of these mechanisms have theoretically existed prior to 9/11, they have become more central to contemporary border control.

Indeed, considering the changes since 9/11, there is ample reason to argue that the politics of border control and migration may prevail at the implementation level,[12] where these policies are shaped, elaborated, and implemented.[13] In the United States, for example, these policy initiatives and information technology existed well before September 11, 2001, but their implementation was finally prompted by Congress's demands after the attacks on that day.[14] A number of ideas based on extending the U.S. borders, sealing the supply chain, designating a lead agency for port security, and using public–private partnerships to improve port security (apart from homeland security) were proposed before 9/11.[15] Before the catastrophic events, these security efforts lacked urgency and serious implementation strategies.

Notwithstanding structural and cultural variations, the role and liabilities of nonstate actors in sharing the burden of regulation has developed almost uniformly in Europe and North America, and are manifest in public–private partnerships.[16] These shifts in liabilities represent an incorporation of nonstate, mostly private actors in state regulatory functions; they also constitute more general trends occurring in other policy areas, namely to shift the externalities of policy making outside of the central government. Privatization, loosely defined as the shift of a function from the public sector to the private sector, involves a dependence on market forces for the pursuit of social goods, and may turn local actors or contractors into regulators.[17] Both the incorporation of private actors through sanctions and the privatization of migration regulation through "contracting out" of implementation functions have substantial implications for state control, sovereignty, and democratic governance.[18]

Yet, this new and complex regulatory field has not been adequately addressed in the political science literature for several reasons. First, the role of nonstate actors, particularly private actors, has been difficult to conceptualize in an international order dominated by the Westphalian notion of a state system. Second, although "globalization" has gained common currency, with some exceptions,[19] approaches to security have remained largely rooted in traditional assumptions about independent nation-states and conflicts. Responses to security threats tend to focus on increased border controls, intelligence, and steps to stem unwanted flows. Controlling migration through tighter border controls however may not be the most effective response in a transnational world, where threats originate both from within our own borders and without. Finally, the creation of transnational spaces, such as airports, airspace, seas, and cyberspace, challenge traditional border control and national sovereignty. They also represent areas where rights may be circumvented. According to some human rights groups, these types of spaces have been known to "create a corporate equivalent of Guantanamo Bay"—a virtual rules-free zone in which perpetrators are not likely to be held accountable for breaking the laws.[20] Combating nonstate actors with non(central)state actors has resulted in an array of new regulators in what have been traditionally state regulatory functions.

In a global era of new security threats, Western democracies are increasingly caught between their global market and rights-based norms, and political and security pressures to protect their borders—what I describe as "the migration-security-rights trilemma."[21] On the one hand, the realist's pursuit of state sovereignty to protect national territory has envisioned more protectionist approaches to terrorism and international mobility. On the other hand, global economic imperatives of open markets, trade, and tourism coupled with societal interests in civil liberties, social cohesion, democratic values, and constitutional guarantees has promoted liberal norms and practices.[22] In this article, I argue that liberal states have reconciled these cross-pressures by developing and institutionalizing public–private partnerships designed to shift the liability, overcome normative constraints, and simultaneously increase the capacity for more cost-effective border regulation.

Airlines and airport space epitomize this dynamic. Like shipping and other travel services, airlines may provide unique resources of personnel, services, and access to migrants, but states, by virtue of owning airspace (according to the Paris Conference of 1919), make private actors (airlines) dependent on them for market operations. These private actors may be enlisted in an enlarged control system, providing the state with the technological and resourceful means to effectively sort through travelers. At the same time, states are able to circumvent constraints, which may be present at the national or international level, by judicial and civil rights groups, since transnational spaces such as international airports constitute "no-man's land" zones where lawyers and humanitarian groups are notably absent.[23]

The "politics at the airport" as this volume is aptly called, encapsulates the growing intersection between different actors (federal, local, private, and international), interests, strategies, and tools employed in the management of border control. In order to assess the dynamic of this relationship (i.e., level of cooperation, collusion, compulsion, constraints), it is necessary to disaggregate the various stakeholders and stakes involved in these regulatory modalities. An institutionalist analysis of the aviation "system" allows us to go beyond state-level instruments and identify not only the various actors involved in border control but also the implications for states.

A Cost–Benefit Analysis of Border Security at the Airport: The Stakes and Stakeholders

In the aftermath of 9/11, the federal government's chief fiscal and program watchdog, the U.S. Government Accountability Office (GAO), recommended that the country allocate its security resources on the basis of a risk-management approach (i.e., based on assessments of threat, vulnerability, and criticality).[24] Although this strategy has been supported by most experts, its implementation is difficult because risks are difficult to measure and quantify, and also because there are enormous transaction costs (both direct and indirect) imposed on nonstate parties, who are typically being protected.[25] A cost–benefit analysis of each actor in the U.S. aviation security system lends some insight into the extent that the various interests converge (or do not) and into the types of outcomes that are possible.

The Stakes

There are myriad economic (micro and macro), societal (safety, public order, mobility, surveillance, civil liberties), and political (international relations, government turf wars, interagency competition) issues at stake in the management of airport security. The constellation of these interests and actors are complex and may generate unexpected tradeoffs. Actors' interests are not always commensurate, even when they cross-cut. Moreover, the tradeoff between direct and indirect costs and benefits may create seemingly irrational calculations. These types of factors may explain why airports invest in expensive metal-detection machinery rather than simply stripsearching every passenger.[26] After all, although airlines are concerned about safety from hijackings and bombings, their prime goal is not to stem hijacking (which they understand are rare events) but to make passengers willing to fly.

Airports are the traffic sites of goods (cargo) and human mobility (citizens, immigrants, tourists, business travelers, foreign students, criminals, and terrorists). More than 1.1 million people enter the United States every day through one of the 326 air, sea, and land ports-of-entry and preclearance stations (in Canada and the Caribbean), which are monitored by Customs and Border Protection (CBP).[27] Of the roughly 417 million people legally entering the United States in fiscal year (FY) 2005 (amounting to more than the entire population of the United States), roughly 81 million entered through airports.[28] Accounting for approximately 25 percent of border crossings, airport space consists of a labyrinthine no-man's land between private actors who fly in the airspace and states who own it.

Nowhere are the economic ramifications and dependence of the airlines on both consumer markets and state authority more obvious and extreme than in the United States in the aftermath of 9/11. Not only did NORAD close all airspace over its territory for almost four days (until September 13, and then a few hours later grounded all civilian airplane traffic again until the morning of September 14). But during that time, all air territory (with the exception of police, military, and humanitarian aid) was effectively closed down throughout Canada in order to receive 255 international flights diverted by the Federal Aviation Administration (FAA). The shutdown of the major U.S. transportation system illustrated the interdependence and vulnerability of foreign states, as well as both the airline industry and the U.S. economy. Share prices of airlines and airplane manufacturers plummeted after the attacks.[29] Thousands of layoffs were announced in the weeks following September 11, 2001. But even when it was reopened, consumer confidence in air transport declined precipitously (illustrated by a 34 percent drop from the previous September) and did not return to pre-9/11 levels until three years later, in June 2004.[30]

These economic effects reverberated much larger on to the macro-scale of the U.S. economy. As some analysts have described, the grounding of commercial air-traffic and intensified border security after the 9/11 attacks "amounted to the U.S. doing to itself what no enemy had done before: an embargo on trade."[31] These calculations were not a one-time affair, coming merely on the precipice of a catastrophic state of emergency. More recently, the Western Hemisphere Travel Initiative—with the new requirement of passports for all those who enter and reenter the United States from Canada, Mexico, Bermuda, the Caribbean, and Panama by 2008—raised the potential for hampering tourism and commercial traffic with the United States' two immediate neighbors.[32] An estimated 60 million Americans (about 20 percent of the national population) have passports, and so the additional price of travel for the consumers of American passports (which currently cost $97) are estimated to be prohibitively costly for commerce and tourism purposes.[33]

These types of issues not only trigger economic concerns but also elicit apprehension about civil liberties, freedoms, and accountability. Since the revolutionary structural changes at the airport after 9/11, several lawsuits have been filed against the FAA, the Department of Justice, and others, arguing that requiring passengers to show identity proof before boarding flights is tantamount to an internal passport and is unconstitutional. Similarly, the infamous case of JetBlue Airways in 2003 politicized the delicate relationship between private and public partnerships; the airline's surrender of (unknowing) passenger information to the Defense Department's contractor, Torch Concepts, a private technology business was seen as breaching consumers' privacy rights and it led to major lawsuits.[34] Private actors have been scrutinized for their skills, accountability, and transparency in managing personal data, so too have government officials. According to a recent GAO report, the State Department and the DHS did not possess enough specialized training in interview procedures, fraud-detection tactics, or native language skills.[35]

These shortcomings not only generate uneven practices, but they have enormous effects on migration and humanitarian flows. A bipartisan federal study by the U.S. Commission on International Religious Freedom of seven ports-of-entry across the United States found extreme variation in the handling of potential asylum cases at different airports.[36] The commission examined the eight-year-old system known as "expedited removal"(introduced by Congress to better secure the nation's borders while still protecting refugees), which allows inspectors to send travelers without valid documents back home immediately, unless they express fear of returning, and to detain the others while evaluating their claims. Beyond extreme variation in implementation practices, the report found that CBP agents frequently failed to follow all the rules intended to make sure that migrants were not returned to persecution.[37] This places an enormous responsibility on border agents to sort out potential terrorists from people fleeing for their lives—an issue that has raised the hackles of civil libertarians and human rights groups.[38]

Finally, the question of who should bear the financial costs for these revolutionary changes looms large. Airport, airline, and port security is much like national defense. That is, creating increased safety through security measures does not only provide concentrated benefits and costs (e.g., to providers and customers) but also creates diffuse costs and benefits (e.g., increased safety for the entire country). In this case, there is a strong justification for federal-government financing. However, the particular use of the industry also provides special benefits to those who use the services, which has led to counterarguments that there should be private provisions of security.[39] The riposte is that user fees may result in the diversion of traffic to ports elsewhere (e.g., Canada, Mexico) and the use of alternative modes of transportation.

The United States has changed course on this question several times in the aftermath of 9/11. On February 1, 2002, the Transportation Security Authority (TSA) levied a surcharge ($5 per passenger) for airline travel as a way to defray the costs of aviation security. However, recognizing the issue of U.S. carrier profitability, Congress later suspended security fees on both domestic and foreign carriers, and the government agreed to finance the shortfall.[40] Thus in Europe, despite, and perhaps because of, the more decentralized structure of European aviation security, security activities have been remunerated by a combination of stakeholders, such as airports, air carriers, passengers, and some state funding. In contrast, in the United States, since the shift to a centralized model of aviation security adopted in November 2001, the remuneration of key security activities has been primarily financed by the TSA out of federal funds.[41] These modifications reflect the impact of corporate culture and particularly the influence of private stakeholders on the U.S. policy agenda.

Given the myriad types of stakes discussed above, what are the constraints and opportunities for aviation stakeholders? To what degree do the emerging partnerships have the specialized interests, skills, and resources of all parties to meet collective public goods?

The Stakeholders

The pursuit of open borders for people and goods is often at odds with the needs to protect airport facilities vulnerable to attack. These competing tasks are complicated by the fact that they involve multiple agencies with different mandates who must engage in interlinking strategies. This section provides a broad portrait of the constellation of actors involved in the U.S. aviation system, with particular emphasis on the changes incurred since security became linked to mobility. It delineates the interest matrix of each set of stakeholders and briefly assesses the implications for U.S. control over its borders.

The Central State and Local Public Actors

Cross-nationally there are vast structural differences with regard to the adoption of centralized or decentralized models in provisions of aviation-related security activities.[42] A predominant feature of centralized models is state control over security activities (via government bodies such as the Ministry of Transportation, or law enforcement),[43] compared to decentralized models, which delegate the main security activities to the jurisdiction of relevant authorities who can manage the airport directly or outsource these functions to a third party.[44] While the United States underwent a dramatic change toward a centralized model of aviation security, the enlargement of governmental involvement was in stark contrast to the direction of its European counterparts, where local law-and-order agencies may compete,[45] and public–private partnerships have dominated the implementation of aviation security standards.[46] The U.S. federal government (through the TSA) thus assumed responsibility for the key security activities at U.S. airports, and moved from the setting and monitoring of security standards to one of setting and implementing the standards. Between FY 2002 and FY 2004, the U.S. government has been estimated to have provided almost $32 billion to the U.S. aviation industry.[47]

The expansive arm of the state to orchestrate neocorporatist types of public–private arrangements and oversee compliance is a testament to the increasing interest and capacity to regulate borders.[48] The attacks on

September 11, 2001, prompted tough, new regulations and implementation strategies. The Aviation and Transportation Security Act obliged federal employees to conduct all passenger screening by that November 2002.[49] Federal responsibility for aviation was divided between the TSA, which was in charge of security, and the FAA, which was responsible for airline safety and operations. As a result, passenger and baggage screening was now provided by the TSA, as part of the DHS.

Although the FAA was concerned by the loss of employees in President Bush's transfer of security duties to a new agency in transportation, their official position was to advocate for an agency that had a single focus of security and to urge formal agreements for communication between the two agencies.[50] Whereas the TSA's security mission was clear—to direct operational control over passenger and baggage screening; it was also designated as the lead agency for overseeing a patchwork quilt of federal, state, and local agencies, as well as private companies that provided security at airports, ports, railroads, highways, and public-transit systems. Interestingly, however, the agency has not assumed much presence in all but security duties of aviation. According to its first Transportation Secretary Norman Mineta, "our responsibility in other areas is not as deep as it is in aviation."[51] To some observers, the rationale was based on the desire to avoid turf wars with state and local governments as well as industry.

Although proposals to merge U.S. border-related agencies numbered in the dozens, dating back nearly one hundred years, 9/11 made it a reality.[52] The need to protect the nation quickly initially produced some policy congestion, with a staggering proliferation of governmental actors and a multiplicity of missions for various agencies of border control. CBP, for example, was given the task of intercepting terrorists, enforcing immigration law, and collecting customs duties at all ports of entry, while also being charged with facilitating lawful trade and travel.

The U.S. government sought more-centralized decision making in an effort to reconcile the competing interests between economic imperatives and border security of the post-9/11 world. In response to the 9/11 Report of the bipartisan commission's appeal for a standardized comprehensive screening system at external borders, airports, and other security checkpoints,[53] the then–DHS Secretary, Tom Ridge, announced the "One Face at the Border" (OFAB) initiative. Designed to eliminate the previous separation of immigration customs and agriculture functions at U.S. air, land, and sea ports-of-entry, the OFAB instituted a unified border inspection process and improved cooperation among the fifteen national intelligence agencies.

The creation of such enormous bureaucracies as the TSA and the DHS represents an attempt to streamline transportation security and mobility, and to raise accountability. However, they have suffered from limitations of staffing, funding, and time, resulting in slippage in schedules and implementation. Opponents have argued that rather than improving security flexibility and mobility, they have in fact hindered them.

Private Actors

Industry stakeholders include airport groups and companies, as well as airline carriers (legacy, charter, regional, budget operators, freight, and express). They also include an extensive business community that contributes in different ways, ranging from implementation and enforcement of security measures to information-gathering and surveillance of suspicious movements of people, cargoes, and companies. Although the majority of critical transportation infrastructure rests in private hands in the United States, even when a facility is in state hands, such as is generally the case in Europe, the business community is usually involved in some way as users, customers, or contractors.[54]

Since the 9/11 attacks, the business community has taken substantial strides in preventive security measures and surveillance back-up systems that can preserve vital records. Though large companies are often the beneficiaries of government bids, for the smaller and medium enterprises, many government initiatives are not cost-effective.[55] On the one hand, private companies are partners in the protection of transport networks and key infrastructure, and they receive government advice and funds to develop new antiterrorism technologies. On the other hand, they are often coerced into government requirements without much leverage. The test is not only whether requirements are being fulfilled but also whether private firms have the ability, not just the willingness, to cover a large share of the costs without serious disruption to economic activity.

The airline industry occupies a unique role in the late twenty-first century, not only because air travel has increased dramatically but also because the industry provides a critical service in the movement of people from one national jurisdiction to another. The nature of its service places the international air transportation industry in a powerful position. Air carriers today represent a resource of personnel, services, and access to migrants and travelers, and if successfully recruited by the state, may significantly ease the burden of border control on national governments.

Clearly, there are many cross-pressures faced by airlines and airports in managing the movement of persons across international borders, especially as such mobility creates new organizational and technological challenges for airline employers and employees with regard to coordination with government officials and others. For airlines, key operational issues include passenger, employee, and baggage screening; operations on the ground and on-board; aircraft protection (including cockpit doors and sky marshal programs); cargo and container screening; documentation processing; and performance (i.e., delays). Carriers have both direct and indirect costs, which have increased dramatically since the increase in security requirements. Costs include staff, cockpit-door reinforcement, security training and insurance, surveillance, and general training.[56]

With minimum out-of-pocket cost, states have incorporated these actors into the governance of international mobility through the use of sanctions and penalties. The implications for the international airline industry have been substantial because airlines are forced to conform to and cooperate with national policy and policy makers in order to continue to operate. In turn, these actors provide the state with the technological and resourceful means to effectively differentiate between the "legal passages for travelers or economic tourists and would-be-overstayers or migrants."[57]

These structural changes have introduced other private actors, as they have spawned a whole new industry of surveillance, personal identity, and remote sensing technologies, with estimates reaching $7 billion by 2007.[58] Given the size of such a market, the production of specialized analysis that can influence policy agenda and lobbying is likely to have substantial impact on policy making.[59] Thus, it is not surprising that some of the most ardent support for DHS policies and the reform of the INS came from a number of private enterprises that had already conducted research on the collection of biometric data but had not found a market for their products.[60] The proliferation of commercial proposals from industries specializing in security services has been dramatic since 9/11.[61] Their role in developing individualized surveillance of national borders underscores the shift in security threats in the post–cold war era.

International Actors and Foreign States

The introduction of innovative technologies, biometric techniques, and new visa and passport procedures has extended the number of regulatory actors beyond national borders. The DHS has made it clear that it considers that the security of American citizens can only be assured by measures taken well outside its frontiers, not simply at border crossings. This reasoning has fueled conflicts between foreign governments and among government agencies. Such battles were reflected in the DHS's challenge to the monopoly over foreign relations exercised by the State Department and Department of Defense.[62]

The U.S. strategy to "push borders out" has largely depended on visa and passport documentation of foreign individuals and the delegation of border inspection and security agenda out to other nations. Transatlantic cooperation with European counterparts became especially important after it emerged that many of the 9/11 hijackers had spent considerable time in Europe. Initiatives—such as the US-VISIT automated entry–exit program, the PNR requirement of airlines to provide European Union (EU)–origin passenger data for flight to the United States (signed in 2004), and the agreement with Europol, the EU police agency (in November 2005), and the Canadian authorities to share data related to terrorism, immigration, and customs matters—have relied on arduous international negotiations. These initiatives have triggered serious disputes among countries with diverse historical experiences with migration control and counterterrorism, as well as divergent political cultures relating to civil liberties and privacy norms. Serious controversies have arisen with regard to airline-passenger information sharing, the need for biometric data on passports, and the use of armed marshals on airline flights.

Legal regimes governing privacy- and personal-data protection vary for public and private agencies. Furthermore, standards of intelligence and information sharing for terrorism are applied differently to migration and asylum issues, and thus involve divergent and multiple agencies (i.e., police forces, ministries, and other law-enforcement bodies, including private security companies). There are also different technical and constitutional constraints with regard to separate databases. The U.S. Secure Flight is intended to allow U.S. government personnel, rather than airline employees, to screen passengers against various watch lists. The Safe Harbor Accord concluded in 2000 established principles designed to ensure the protection of personal data when it is transferred from companies operating in the EU to those operating in the United States. The EU Privacy Directive on commercial data-protection prohibits personal data sharing between governments and private sectors, and is motivated by the fear that U.S. government officials may sell data in the same way that U.S. companies do.[63]

A plethora of cooperative initiatives have developed to negotiate these differences, and some of these disputes have been delegated to international bodies. For example, the U.S. Congress deferred to the International Civil Aviation Organization (ICAO) the establishment of biometric standards for passports issued by Visa Waiver countries (twenty-seven foreign states whose citizens were permitted to enter and stay in the United States without a visa for up to ninety days, but who were later required to enroll in the US-VISIT program).[64] In May 2003 the ICAO announced an agreement, which included a digital photo for facial recognition and optional biometrics of fingers and/or eyes to be stored on contactless integrated chips.[65]

There are a number of other less well-known international and regional organizations associated with aviation-security policy development aside from the ICAO, such as the International Aviation Transport Association (IATA) and the European Civil Aviation Conference (ECAC).[66] The formation of the International Biometric Advisory Council (IBAC), launched by the European Biometrics Forum (established by the European Commission and the Irish government) in November 2003, has also attempted to coordinate expert opinions. Although these organizations have been delegated to create standardized, national programs worldwide, they are limited in ensuring policy implementation.

Public–Private Relations: Four Faces of Airport Politics

Clearly, the airport venue is a critical border site where multiple actors engage in public–private partnerships. This section briefly reviews four contentious aspects of these partnerships.

Passenger Name Records

Though the most notorious U.S. legislation enacted on the heels of 9/11 came in the form of the 2001 USA PATRIOT Act, many policies introduced at the time put in place similar albeit less-politicized control mechanisms. The lesser-known Aviation and Transportation Security Act of 2001 instituted a requirement that foreign carriers "make passenger name record information available to the Customs Service upon request" and provided for this information to be shared with other agencies outside of the TSA. The availability of this information was deemed necessary for purposes of "ensuring aviation safety and protecting national security." As an executive report by Privacy International reminded, this initiative was aimed at foreign carriers only, since U.S. carriers were exempt from such compliance, with the understanding that they would voluntarily disclose data.[67]

Noncompliance or insufficient compliance of airlines entails substantial consequences. Passengers would have to undergo rescreening and additional controls resulting in long lines and waits. Airlines would expose themselves to sanctions that range from high fines to withdrawal of landing permission. It is believed that these types of concerns have greatly influenced European airlines to allow American authorities direct access to the data requested.

Exposing deep political and cultural differences, PNR issues are at the forefront of some of the strongest foreign-policy controversies. Broadly speaking, the tension between comprehensive information and individual privacy involves four issues: (1) timeframe and criteria for deleting information from a data base; (2) procedures for information sharing with third parties; (3) establishing appropriate redress for individuals who wish to challenge information about themselves; and (4) procedures for the appropriate sharing of personal data between national governments and the private sector.

The extensiveness of personal data has been seen to infringe on civil liberties and other privacy issues. That is, PNR data consists not only of all details of reservations, payment, and preferences but all types of social and psychological profiling (e.g., financial data, choice of means, previous passenger itineraries, religious and ethnic information, political affiliations, medical data). Of further contention has been the statute of limitations. Data retention was first proposed to be for 50 years, though in later a agreement made with the European Commission and the TSA the period was reduced to 3.5 years. Finally, the issue of scope concerns whether the data could be used for general law-enforcement purposes or combating terrorism and serious organized crime (which eventually prevailed).

Passenger-profiling systems have come under attack by civil liberties advocates in the United States as well. Data-mining initiatives created an important role for nongovernmental organizations such as the American Civil Liberties Union (ACLU), the Electronic Privacy Information Center, and the Center for Democracy and Technology, who have been relatively influential in policy elaboration.[68] Of particular controversy was the delegation of data mining and profiling to the private sector, where they would fall outside of parliamentary scrutiny or oversight, and away from laws that restrict the processing of personal information by government agencies. That the private sector operates under a different regulatory regime with few restrictions made it appealing to government agencies and obviously to industry, which was willing and able to capitalize on the new market.[69]

To overcome the problems of the PNR system, the Computer Assisted Passenger Pre-Screening (CAPPS) program was introduced and revised in CAPPS II, but then abandoned for the Secure Flight program.[70] This shift reflected the great unease that was felt regarding the extensive amount of information being requested to screen passengers against various watch-lists and the preference to delegate such sensitive information to government personnel, rather than private-entity employees.[71]

Virtual Borders and Airport Infrastructure

The protection of infrastructure and transportation networks includes a range of venues from metropolitan transport systems used by millions of people each day, as in Madrid, to major ports and airports, and the ships and planes that transit through them. Efforts to protect borders and key transportation facilities have been subject to substantial transatlantic debate. Among the most politicized of these issues has been the screening of shipping containers and biometric passports. (Data is kept either on an encrypted chip within the passport or in a central database.)

While issues of biometric passports and screening of shipping containers have met with much resistance from foreign governments, businesses have also had good reason to complain. The replacement of physical borders with virtual borders (e.g., US-VISIT employing networks of computer databases and biometric sensors for identification at sites abroad where people seek visas to the United States) extends borders outward, well into cyberspace, and heavily relies on public–private coordination. The virtual border has been compared to the notion of an air-traffic control center. In this case, the system would allow homeland security officials to monitor travel on a national level, shifting resources and responding as necessary. With a virtual border in place, the actual border guard is meant to become the last point of defense rather than the first, because each visitor will have already been screened using a global web of databases.

Experts agree that no matter how good the technology, the system will rely on timely and accurate information-exchange about the histories and profiles of those entering the country. Such a system depends on a broad interconnection of federal databases ranging from intelligence to law enforcement as well as routine commercial data. It also needs to overcome tremendous variations among airports, which up until now have led to uneven practices, generating the equivalent of commercial advantages to migration and asylum shopping.

Outsourcing

Outsourcing mainly refers to the provision of passenger, hand baggage, and surveillance by a third-party supplier. Although the role of third parties in immigration and border control has grown dramatically in the last twenty years as liberal states have "contracted out,"[72] 9/11 put a notable twist on this momentum and reversed a trend that had been growing over the last century. In what has been described as "privatization in reverse" or the "federalization of a function formerly in private hands," one of the most significant changes of 9/11 was the shift from using private screeners to federal screeners at all but five American commercial airports.[73] The new Transportation Security Administration mandated that only federal employees could screen baggage until November 2004, when airports could petition the TSA to contract screeners. This requirement countered organizational designs of the past forty years, which generally held that new agencies should be largely reliant on the private sector.[74] The diminished role of private companies and the shift to TSA control has been applauded by those who want to reduce the airlines' role and have complained that under the private-run system airlines were often able to negotiate reductions in fines levied by the FAA for security contractors' infractions.[75]

The role of private actors as contractors has not disappeared completely, however. Ironically, as the TSA inherited exclusive duties to conduct passenger and baggage screening at the nations' airports, they have also been required to perform criminal background checks on 750,000 employees with access to secure areas at airports—a job delegated to U.S. Investigations Services, Inc. (USIS), an employee-owned private firm.[76] Furthermore, the Aviation and Transportation Security Act (Section 108) required the TSA to establish the Private Screening Pilot Program by choosing several airports to hire private screening companies (as long as they are owned and controlled by U.S. citizens) to test the operational flexibility that private contractors could provide at the airport level.[77] A GAO review of the pilot program produced mixed results for both private and federal screeners.[78]

A chief impediment to a true comparative assessment of private versus public handling of such tasks comes from the constraints that private companies have to do what they do best.[79] Namely, as the GAO reports, the "TSA provided the screening contractors with little opportunity to demonstrate innovations, achieve efficiencies, and implement initiatives that go beyond the minimum requirements of the Aviation and Transportation Security Act."[80] These findings reveal the emerging relationship between private and public actors in regulating mobility—that is, rather than a collaborative partnership or a delegation to private actors, states are increasingly co-opting and compelling private companies to act.

To be clear, this hierarchical relationship is not applicable to all aspects of border control, as initiatives for new technology make evident. In May 2004 there was a large controversy over the DHS's bid to award a nearly $15 billion contract for a network-database system to track visitors to the United States before they arrive as part of the US-VISIT program. This bid for a virtual border plan raised all sorts of logistical and philosophical questions regarding the three final commercial bidders: Accenture, Computer Sciences, and Lockheed Martin.[81] For example, should a company based outside of the United States in Bermuda get a megacontract? How much will it cost? What about privacy concerns of foreign visitors? Can a virtual-border system really work? The notion of outsourcing DHS business to a Bermudan company, Accenture, for example, led Congressman Lloyd Doggett (D-TX) to push to close a loophole allowing foreign bidders on federal contracts. Opponents pondered whether the federal government should be forced to select an inferior bid because its bidder was incorporated in the United States.

The U.S. government's approach to such outsourcing is revealing. As scholars of information technology have noted, rather than impose a set of requirements for the information systems, the government actively sought ideas from outside. CBP launched a solicitation for the Secure Border Initiative Network (SBI*net*) contract by throwing out an open net.[82] In this way they appeared to delegate the responsibility for developing a strategy to the private sector (mostly military contractors) that may or may not have immigration policy and operational border-security expertise.

Carrier Liabilities

The most punitive component of the private–public relationship regarding the airline industry comes in the form of carrier liability laws, requiring employees such as check-in staff and cabin crew to make decisions on the legality of passengers' travel arrangements. The role of air carriers as private actors in border control is secured through the imposition of governmental sanctions and penalties. The responsibilities placed on airlines by the state are many and represent a large burden in cost and effort to the airline industry. These private actors benefit from business opportunities or face economic constraints, such as the avoidance of fines. That is, since airspace is sovereign, carriers avoid state restrictions on operation. Although often these actors are compelled to partake through negative incentives (i.e., avoiding penalties), more recently, there have been some positive incentives established for compliance. In the United States, for example, the Immigration and Nationality Technical Corrections Act of 1994 mitigated fines for "good performance" of airlines—in other words, a reward for efficacy, if an air carrier can show that it has appropriately screened all passengers in accordance with regulations.[83]

As noted above, the practice of sanctioning carriers does not in itself represent a precedent in legislation governing the rules of entry. Sanctions against ships have been in force since the Passenger Act of 1902 in Ellis Island days. These initiatives were reinforced by the Paris Conference of 1919 (which addressed the issue of international air transportation and established an integral precedent) and reaffirmed by the Chicago Convention in 1944. These international instruments granted states enormous power over such private actors.[84]

At their own expense, carriers have thus long been obliged to transport inadmissible passengers back to their countries, but increasingly countries have introduced laws to raise the responsibilities of carriers to pay fines beyond retransport.[85] As Janet Gilboy notes, though these third-party liability systems in part are decades old, they have become strikingly popular for law-enforcement use.[86]

There has been some resistance, mostly from human rights' advocates and employees groups. Trade unions such as the International Transport Worker's Federation (ITF) have campaigned against the requirement that civil aviation workers should have any involvement in immigration policing. Amnesty International has been concerned that carrier liability laws have been applied in ways that obstruct asylum seekers and refugees fleeing to safety.[87]

Implications: Aviation Security, the State, and the Role of Public Actors as Constituents and Passengers

In gauging the impact of private actors on state sovereignty, we must consider who has been setting the agenda, who is delegating, and who is the agency.[88] It is important to understand that the impetus for the new rules of the game has come from states themselves. Private actors face ever more numerable restrictions, either from central governments or from international agreements, including common legislation and international agreements.

The institutional analysis conducted here identifies the constellation of incentives and constraints that keep new border control practices in motion. Despite the proliferation of public–private partnerships, the case of U.S. aviation security is suggestive of mutual bargaining exchanges that put the state in the ultimate beneficiary and authoritative position. In the cost–benefit equation, which favors the state matrix, one must consider that foreign states, airline carriers, and other private actors have been forced to shoulder the burden of liabilities for border regulation enforcement with little bargaining leverage. States have effectively extended their control of borders to the private sector, in some cases (e.g., airports) even circumventing constraints that may be present at the national or international level by humanitarian, judicial, and civil rights groups.[89]

In this vein, the airlines' cooperation on matters of same-day removals of inadmissible foreigners is critical. Though airlines have some latitude in determining the "carrier's next regularly scheduled departure," cooperation allows the state to avoid the costs of detention, which also include the prevention of access to advocates that one-night's detention may present. Such a costly exclusion process could be avoided by same-day removal, and airlines are key facilitators here.[90] In all of these ways, the political will of states to control border crossing may be compatible with the private actors' economic interests.

Of course, it could be argued that such dispersal of responsibility among actors whose interests do not necessarily coincide may compromise the effectiveness of the entire aviation system (the key overlapping goal of all stakeholders). Ultimately, it could undermine democratic legitimacy. However, if consideration of the common denominator—the passenger, consumer, tourist, voting public constituent, expectant migrant, or terrorist —is any indicator of the effectiveness of aviation security, one can give the United States high marks for maintaining a relatively stable and responsive aviation "system."

Indeed, the dramatic change in the American security environment had the most profound impact on the aviation industry. While this change is reasonable given 9/11 and other terrorist experiences across the Atlantic, what is most surprising is the recovery time. By 2004, passenger traffic resumed its pre-9/11 levels. In fact, while total inspections decreased by 3 percent in FY 2005 compared to FY 2004, and land admissions to the United States decreased by 4 percent, air admissions increased by 4 percent.[91]

Less obvious has been the stability of public opinion.[92] According to longitudinal surveys, consumer perceptions of airline-service quality, risks associated with air travel, and satisfaction with airlines before and after 9/11 did not change that much. Although the number of trips did decline over the course of the research, passengers' overall satisfaction with the airline industry did not change in any statistically significant manner.[93]

In terms of more diffuse public reactions to new regulatory modes, there is no doubt that "big government" receives more support, even over corporate culture, during times of heightened threat—as most Americans perceived during the period following 2001. Although attitudinal data varies depending on question phrasing, there is ample evidence to support that the willingness to compromise civil liberties and curtail freedoms in order to protect safety is great under conditions of heightened threat.[94] According to Amitai Etzioni, the correlation between strong safety measures and democracy is opposite to what civil libertarians may argue—that is, democracy is endangered not when strong measures are taken by government to enhance safety and to protect and reassure the public but when they are not taken.[95] If we extrapolate what we know from crime studies—that public perceptions of threat and actual levels of crime do not necessarily correlate—then it is possible that the visibility component of all the new regulations alone may assuage public anxieties.

Overall, both attitudinal and behavioral evidence of air travel reveal public support in terms of consumer satisfaction and democratic responsiveness. This factor lends enormous legitimacy to the calculated logic of the security–mobility dynamic and serves to reconcile the sometimes-divergent interests of the actors involved. For now, the United States seems to have gradually negotiated an aviation "system" responsive to governmental, commercial, and public pressures.

Notes

I am grateful to Mark Salter, David Lyon, Rey Koslowski, David Budge, and the participants of the "Moving Targets: Politics of/at the Airport" workshop, and the Canadian Aviation Security Conference for promoting a close-up view of one slice of the broader political puzzle.

1. Operation Yellow Ribbon, created by Canada's Department of Transport to handle the diversion of civilian-airline flights following 9/11, re-routed United States–bound passengers to fifteen different airports across Canada.

2. Gallya Lahav, "Immigration and the State: The Devolution and Privatisation of Immigration Control in the EU," *Journal of Ethnic and Migration Studies* 24, no. 4 (1998): 675–94.

3. John Torpey, "Coming and Going: On the State Monopolization of the 'Legitimate Means of Movement,'" *Sociological Theory* 16, no. 3 (1998): 239–59.

4. Virginie Guiraudon and Gallya Lahav, "A Reappraisal of the State Sovereignty Debate: The Case of Migration Control," *Comparative Political Studies* 33, no. 2 (2000): 163–95.

5. See Colin J. Bennett, chapter 3 in this volume.

6. Aristide Zolberg, "Matters of State: Theorizing Immigration Policy," in *The Handbook of International Migration: The American Experience*, ed. Charles Hirschman, Philip Kasinitz, and Josh DeWind (New York: Russell Sage, 1999), 71–93.

7. Guiraudon and Lahav, "A Reappraisal"; Virginie Guiraudon, "European Courts and Foreigners' Rights: A Comparative Study of Norms Diffusion," *International Migration Review* 34, no. 4 (2000): 1088–125.

8. Christina Boswell, "The 'External Dimension' of the EU Immigration and Asylum Policy," *International Affairs* 79, no. 3 (2003): 619–38; Sandra Lavenex and Emek Ucarer, *Migration and the Externalities of European Integrations* (Lanham, Md.: Rowman and Littlefield, 2003).

9. See Lahav "Immigration and the State."

10. Rey Koslowski, *Real Challenges for Virtual Borders: The Implementation of US-VISIT* (Washington, D.C.: Migration Policy Institute, 2005), 19.

11. In 2004 alone, the Department of Homeland Security (DHS) apprehended an estimated 1,241,089 foreign nationals and removed 202,842 foreign nationals (Office of Immigration Statistics, Department of Homeland Security, 2005). The total inadmissible count for September 2005 was 37,535, a 22 percent decrease compared to the total of 48,432 in September 2004. Inadmissible persons include aliens referred to secondary inspection who withdraw, are refused entry, are paroled in, or are referred to an Immigration

Judge for a removal hearing. Also included are expedited cases where an alien can withdraw, receive an expedited removal order, or be referred for a credible fear interview.

12. See Lahav "Immigration and the State"; Antje Ellermann, "Coercive Capacity and the Politics of Implementation: Deportation in Germany and the United States," *Comparative Political Studies* 38, no. 10 (2005): 1219–44.

13. Guiraudon and Lahav, "A Reappraisal."

14. Koslowski, *Real Challenges*, 2. The U.S. Illegal Immigration Reform and Immigrant Responsibility Act of 1996 (Section 110) mandated that the Immigration and Naturalization Service (INS) develop an automated entry–exit control system that would "collect a record of every alien departing the U.S. and match the records of departure with the record of the alien's arrival in the U.S." (U.S. Congressional Record House, "Automated Entry-Exit Control System," *Illegal Immigration Reform and Immigrant Responsibility Act of 1996*, Section 110.a.1 (September 28, 1996), H11787.

15. Jon Haveman and Howard Shatz, "Introduction and Summary," in *Protecting the Nation's Seaports: Balancing Security and Cost*, ed. Haveman and Shatz (San Francisco: Public Policy Institute of California, 2006), 23.

16. Lahav, "The Rise of Non-state Actors in Migration Regulation in the United States and Europe: Changing the Gatekeepers or Bringing Back the State?" in *Immigration Research for a New Century: Multidisciplinary Perspectives*, ed. Nancy Foner, Ruben Rumbaut, and Steven Gold (New York: Russell Sage, 2000), 89–106.

17. Harvey Feigenbaum and Jeff Henig, "The Political Underpinnings of Privatization: A Typology," *World Politics* 46, no. 2 (1994): 185–208.

18. See Mark B. Salter, chapter 1 in this volume.

19. Barry Buzan, Ole Wæver, Jaap de Wilde, *Security: A New Framework for Analysis* (Boulder, Colo.: Lynne Rienner, 1998); Jef Huysmans, "Defining Social Constructivism in Security Studies: The Normative Dilemma of Writing Security," *Alternatives* 27 (2002): 41–62.

20. Alan Cowell, "Rights Group Criticizes U.S. Over 'Outsourcing' in Iraq," *New York Times*, May 24, 2006, p. A16.

21. Lahav, "The Migration, Security and Civil Rights Trilemma in the United States and Europe," discussion paper presented to the Robert Schuman Centre for Advanced Studies, EUI, Florence, Italy, November 15, 2005.

22. See Lahav, *Immigration and Politics in the New Europe: Reinventing Borders* (Cambridge: Cambridge University Press, 2004).

23. Guiraudon and Lahav, "A Reappraisal."

24. Raymond Decker, "Homeland Security: A Risk-management Approach Can Guide Preparedness Efforts," testimony before the U.S. Senate Committee on Governmental Affairs, GAO-02-208T, Washington, D.C., October 31, 2001.

25. See Salter, chapter 1 in this volume.

26. Haveman and Shatz, "Introduction and Summary," 20.

27. Ariside Zolberg, "The Archeology of 'Remote Control,'" in *Migration Control in the North Atlantic World: The Evolution of State Practices in Europe and the United States from the French Revolution to the Inter-war Period*, ed.

Andreas Fahrmeir, Olivier Faron, and Patrick Weil (New York: Berghahn Books, 2003), 195–222.

28. The total number of persons admitted at DHS ports of entry during September 2005 include approximately 13 million U.S. citizens and 19.5 million aliens. These categories of admission include individuals who make multiple entries; for example, citizens who leave and reenter the United States multiple times, permanent residents who make multiple entries, or aliens who hold nonimmigrant visas or border-crossing cards, and commute back and forth each week from Canada or Mexico. Office of Immigration Statistics, U.S. Department of Homeland Security, October 31, 2005, http://www.uscis .gov/graphics/shared/aboutus/statistics/msrnov05/INSP.htm (accessed October 22, 2006).

29. Midway Airlines, already on the brink of bankruptcy, shut down operations almost immediately afterward, and many other airlines were threatened with similar fates.

30. Bureau of Transportation Statistics, "Origin and Destination Survey of Airline Passenger Traffic," U.S. Department of Transportation, http://www.bts.gov/ programs/airline-information/air-carrier-traffic-statistics/airtraffic/annual/ (accessed October 20, 2006).

31. Koslowski, *Real Challenges*, 5; Stephen Flynn, "America the Vulnerable," *Foreign Affairs* 81, no. 1 (2002): 60–74.

32. Canada is not only the United States' largest trading partner, with $1.2 billion worth of goods crossing the border every day, but with nearly 16 million Canadians entering the United States in 2004 alone, this mobility has generated an estimated $7.9 billion in travel-related revenues, according to data provided by the Travel Industry Association (TIA) in Washington, D.C.

33. Associated Press, "U.S. to Tighten Border Controls by 2008," http://www .yahoo.com/news?tmpl=story%cid=542&u=/ap/20050406/ap_on_go_ca_st _pe/u (accessed May 4, 2005).

34. See Bennett, chapter 3 in this volume.

35. Government Accountability Office, "Aviation Security: Private Screening Contractors Have Little Flexibility to Implement Innovative Approaches," April 2004, http://www.gao.gov/cgi-bin/getrpt?GAO-04-505T (accessed October 8, 2006).

36. Based on 1,500 hours of observation and hundreds of cases, the report concluded that the chance of being granted refuge may depend on which airport an asylum seeker used. By all measures, for example, Kennedy Airport stood apart as the toughest for asylum seekers. It was the only airport in the nation where shackles were routinely used, and the only place where intensely personal interviews were typically conducted at public counters. Nearly eleven thousand persons were sent back from Kennedy Airport by federal border agents over a three-year period; this is five times the number of persons sent for in-depth interviews with an asylum officer. In contrast, at Miami International Airport, which handled the most cases overall, nearly thirteen thousand persons were sent for asylum interviews between 2000 and 2003— more than twice the number sent back overseas from that location. Nina

Bernstein, "Kennedy Airport Is Called the Toughest for Asylum Seekers," *New York Times*, February 10, 2005, p. B1.

37. Those sent back under expedited removal are not allowed to return to the United States for five years. The report further suggested that lack of privacy and discomfort of counter interviews could discourage frightened foreigners from providing complete information in their exchanges with officers.

38. See Mark B. Salter, "Governmentalities of an Airport: Heterotopia and Confession," *International Political Sociology* 1, no. 1 (2007): 59.

39. Haveman and Shatz, "Introduction and Summary," 22.

40. By 2004, the Transportation Security Administration (TSA) reimbursed $4.6 billion to carriers for expenses and revenue foregone related to aviation security. Irish Aviation Authority / AviaSolutions, *Study on Civil Aviation Security Financing*, European Commission, Study No. TREN/F3/51-2002 (Brussels: European Commission, 2004), 44–45.

41. The structural differences between centralized and decentralized models of aviation security refer to the degree of exclusive and direct government jurisdiction and responsibility over the security activities (i.e., government bodies versus relevant nonstate actors such as airports or outsourced security companies). Ibid.

42. Ibid., 9; see Salter, chapter 1 in this volume.

43. In some countries (e.g., Canada, Germany, the United Kingdom) military aid to the civil power, or police, to maintain order is permitted. In the United States, however, the Posse Comitatus Act, passed in 1878 prohibits federal military personnel from acting in a law-enforcement capacity within the United States, except where expressly authorized by the Constitution or Congress.

44. Among European countries, Austria, Finland, Germany, Iceland, Italy, Luxembourg, Portugal, Spain, and Sweden have adopted centralized models, whereas France, Belgium, Denmark, Ireland, and the United Kingdom have traditionally followed a decentralized model.

45. Didier Bigo, "Migration and Security," in *Controlling a New Migration World*, ed. Virginie Guiraudon and Christian Joppke (London: Routledge, 2001), 121–49.

46. Irish Aviation Authority / AviaSolutions, *Study on Civil Aviation Security Financing*, 44.

47. Ibid.

48. See Lahav, "Immigration and the State."

49. Prior to the 1970s, American airports had minimal security arrangements to prevent aircraft hijackings. Screening measures were introduced starting in the late 1960s after several high-profile hijackings, but they were generally contracted to private security companies. Sky marshals were introduced in 1970 and were placed on a random basis. Already in late 1972, the Federal Aviation Administration (FAA) required that all airlines begin screening passengers and their carry-on baggage by January 1973.

50. Jason Peckenpaugh, "Aviation Security Agency Gets Off the Ground," *Government Executive*, http://govexec.com (accessed December 21, 2001).

51. Ibid., 3.

52. See Koslowski, *Real Challenges*.

53. Commission on the Terrorist Attacks upon the United States, *The 9/11 Commission Report: Final Report of the National Commission on Terrorist Attacks upon the United States* (New York: W. W. Norton, 2004), 400–408.

54. Roughly 80 percent of critical infrastructure in the United States is estimated to be in private hands, compared to 30 percent in Europe, with the rest owned by the state. David L. Aaron, Ann M. Beauchesne, Frances G. Burwell, C. Richard Nelson, K. Jack Riley, and Brian Zimmer, *The Post-9/11 Partnership Transatlantic Cooperation against Terrorism* (Washington, D.C.: Atlantic Council, 2004), 23.

55. Ibid.

56. Interestingly, in a study of European airlines, more than 50 percent of additional air-carrier security expenditures for 2002 were delegated to insurance premiums, whereas only approximately 2 percent of additional costs went to training (see Irish Aviation Authority / AviaSolutions, *Study on Civil Aviation Security Financing*, 23).

57. Frank Paul Weber, "Participation of Carriers in the Control of Migration: The Case of Germany," paper presented at the International Studies Association, Minneapolis, March 1998; William Walters, "Border/Control," *European Journal of Social Theory* 9, no. 2 (2006): 187–203. See also Lahav, "Immigration and the State," 687; Lahav and Guiraudon, "Comparative Perspectives on Border Control" in *The Wall around the West*, ed. Peter Andreas and Timothy Snyder (New York: Rowman and Littlefield, 2000), 63.

58. Ferruccio Pastore, Jörg Friedrichs, and Alessandro Politi, "The European Union and the Fight against Terrorism: A Brief Assessment of Supra-national and National Responses" in *Is There a European Strategy against Terrorism?*, ed. Ferruccio Pastore, Jörg Friedrichs, and Alessandro Politi (Rome: CentroStudidiPoliticaInternazionale, 2005), 12:10.

59. Ibid., 11; Mark Hubbard, "Fight against Terror Spawns a New Industry: Special Report in Worldwide Security," *Financial Times*, December 2003, p. 1; F. Williams, "Homeland Security Is in the Eye of the Passport Holder," *Financial Times*, October 15, 2004, p. 14.

60. Didier Bigo and Elspeth Guild, "Policing at a Distance: Schengen Visa Policies," *Controlling Frontiers: Free Movement into and within Europe*, ed. Didier Bigo and Elspeth Guild (London: Ashgate, 2005), 221.

61. This program has notably involved companies previously involved in Ronald Reagan's Strategic Defense Initiative program.

62. Ibid.

63. Pastore et al., *The European Union*, 16–17.

64. Koslowski, *Real Challenges*, 18.

65. International Civil Aviation Organization, "Biometric Identification to Provide Enhanced Security and Speedier Border Clearance for Traveling Public," PIO/2003, May 28, 2003.

66. See Salter, chapter 1 in this volume.

67. Gus Hosein, "Threatening the Open Society; Comparing Anti-terror Policies and Strategies in the U.S. and Europe," Privacy International, report to the Open Society Programme, London, December 13, 2005, p. 6.

68. Although their actions were rarely collectively organized, they did lead to the relative demise of the Total Information Awareness program, a computer mining system of all transactions of everyday life. Ibid., 12; see also Bennett, chapter 3 in this volume.

69. A good example of this collusion was the role of the Multistate Anti-Terrorism Information Exchange (MATRIX), established by Seisint, a Florida-based company who proposed to do the data mining for the federal and state governments. The company ultimately shut down in March 2005 because of public opposition to Big Brother conspiracies.

70. See Bennett, chapter 3 in this volume.

71. Pastore et al., *The European Union*, 16.

72. See Lahav, "The Rise of Non-state Actors."

73. Donald Kettl, quoted in Peckenpaugh, "Aviation Security Agency," 2.

74. This mandate put an enormous strain on hiring needs as it called for the training of more than thirty thousand federal employees within a month-and-a-half period of its own creation. Although a daunting task, this move was not without precedent. In August 1981, President Reagan fired roughly 11,600 air-traffic controllers who went on strike, which left the FAA virtually no time to put in place a system to hire and train a new set of controllers. Although training requirements for air-traffic controllers take longer (over one year) than those for baggage screeners (with roughly forty hours of classroom training and sixty hours of on-the-job training), as some observers argue, there was an added burden for the Department of Transportation (DOT) because it was forced to design the screening job while building an agency from scratch. Ibid., 4.

75. Ibid., 6.

76. U.S. Investigations Services, Inc. (USIS), formerly part of the Office of Personnel Management was also charged to conduct background checks on prospective air marshals, who need a higher level of clearance than screeners. Ibid., 4.

77. The five airports chosen for the two-year pilot program in 2002 were San Francisco International, Kansas City International, Greater Rochester International in New York, Jackson Hole Airport in Wyoming, and Tupelo Airport in Mississippi. These facilities were chosen based on several factors, including the airports willingness to participate; a balanced geographic representation of variable costs of living; availability of existing screening company resources; and a mix of business, leisure, and academic passengers. Transportation Security Administration, "TSA Announces Private Security Screening Pilot Program," TSA 26-02, June 18, 2002, http://www.dot.gov/affairs/tsa2602.htm (accessed on October 21, 2006).

78. Government Accountability Office, "Aviation Security: Private Screening Contractors Have Little Flexibility to Implement Innovative Approaches," GAO-04-505T, April 2004, http://www.gao.gov/cgi-bin/getrpt?GAO-04-505T (accessed October 21, 2006).

79. See Subcommittee on Aviation Hearing on the Airport Screener Privatization Pilot Program, April 22, 2004, http://www.house.gov/transportation/aviation/04-22-04/04-22-04memo.html (accessed October 21, 2006).

80. Government Accountability Office, "Aviation Security."

81. Eric Lichtblau and John Harkoff, "U.S. Is Nearing Deal on Way to Track Visiting Foreigners," *New York Times*, May 24, 2004, p. 1.

82. On January 25, 2006, the Customs and Border Protection (CBP) held an SBI*net* "industry day" where over four hundred private-sector participants were told by DHS Deputy Secretary Michael Jackson, "This is an unusual invitation. I want to make sure you have it clearly, that we're asking you to come back and tell us how to do our business. We're asking you. We're inviting you to tell us how to run our organization" (SBI*net* Industry Day transcript cited in Rey Koslowski, "Immigration Reforms and Border Security Technologies," *Border Battles: The U.S. Immigration Debates* (New York: Social Science Research Council, July 31, 2006), 2.

83. Constance O'Keefe, "Immigration Issues and Airlines: An Update," *Journal of Air Law and Commerce* 63, no. 28 (1997): 17–65.

84. Mahlon R. Straszheim, *The International Airline Industry* (Washington, D.C.: Brookings Institution, 1969).

85. The U.S. Immigration and Nationality Act (8 U.S.C.) declares that "It shall be unlawful for any person, including any transportation company . . . to bring to the United States from any place outside thereof . . . any alien who does not have a valid passport and an unexpired visa," with a penalty of $3,000 assessed for each infraction, and the responsibility and cost for the removal of the inadmissible individual (1994), Sections, 1181, 1225–27, 1321, 1323.

86. Janet Gilboy, "Compelled Third-party Participation in the Regulatory Process: Legal Duties, Culture, and Noncompliance," *Law and Policy* 20, no. 2 (1998): 135.

87. Amnesty International, "No Flights to Safety: Carrier Sanctions, Airline Employees and the Rights of Refugees," http://web.amnesty.org/library/Index/ENGACT340211997?open&of=ENG-398 (accessed November 8, 2006).

88. Mark Pollack, "Delegation, Agency and Agenda Setting in the European Union," *International Organization* 51, no.1 (1997): 99–134.

89. Guiraudon and Lahav, "A Reappraisal."

90. Janet Gilboy, "'Third Party' Involvement and Regulatory Enforcement Behavior," American Bar Foundation Working Paper #9408 (1994).

91. Bureau of Transportation Statistics, http://www.bts.gov/xml/air-traffic/src/datadisp.sml (accessed October 23, 2006).

92. Lahav, "The Rise of Non-state Actors."

93. Lawrence Cunningham, Clifford Young, and Moonkyu Lee, "Perceptions of Airline Service Quality: Pre- and Post-9/11," *Public Works Management and Policy* 9, no. 1 (2004): 10–25.

94. Leonie Huddy, Stanley Feldman, Gallya Lahav, and Chuck Taber, "Fear and Terrorism: Psychological Reactions to 9/11," in *Framing Terrorism: The News Media, the Government, and the Public*, ed. Pippa Norris, Montague Kern, and Marion Just (New York: Routledge, 2003), 255–78.

95. Amitai Etzioni, *How Patriotic Is the Patriot Act? Freedom versus Security in the Age of Terrorism* (New York: Routledge, 2004), 21.

5

AIRPORT SURVEILLANCE BETWEEN PUBLIC AND PRIVATE INTERESTS

CCTV at Geneva International Airport

....

Francisco R. Klauser, Jean Ruegg,
and Valérie November

Among the large variety of public and private places affected by recent developments in closed circuit television (CCTV), the application of video surveillance in the context of airport risk management presents several specific issues. Given their privileged, symbolic, and practical position within processes of globalization as departure and arrival points for flows of people and goods, airports are particularly exposed to different types of risks and are thus subject to increased local, national, and international security concern. Within the airport context, security issues in general and the use and design of video surveillance systems in particular provide a symptomatic illustration for three broader tendencies of security politics, which together form the starting point of this chapter.

First, in the case of airport risk management, the challenge of numerous local, regional, national, and international actors is to deal with increasingly globalized social risks (such as organized crime, immigration issues, and terrorism) on the basis of increasingly standardized international security standards. In this light, airport risk management exemplarily illustrates the growing interdependence of local, national, and international security issues within a climate of "globalized surveillance."[1] Second, airports are understood as both national ports-of-entry and areas of commercial interest. Therefore, airport security politics brings together a complex variety of public and private interests, partners, strategies, and instruments—thus highlighting broader trends of public–private partnerships in the framework of neoliberal governance. Third, as burgeoning sociotechnical universes in the state of constant transformation, airports are generally exposed to the challenges of new technologies, economic trends, and sociocultural dynamics. Following Pascoe's analysis of airport representations in literature and arts, "one might claim that throughout the century, airspace, an island of advanced development where familiar standards and definitions begin to seem uncertain, has provided a glimpse of how the world outside the terminal might look in [ten] years or so."[2] For example, airports can be found among the first places to test software-based sorting technologies in order to detect and to prevent at-risk persons, behaviors, or objects.

General Approach

Since the 9/11 terrorist attacks, surveillance technologies used to monitor border-crossing movements by building, sorting, and analyzing data sets of passengers have been widely discussed regarding their implications for both security and privacy issues.[3] At the same time, little research has been completed on surveillance operations aiming to control microscale movements and behaviors of passengers (as well as other airport customers) that occur *within* the airport area itself.[4] We crucially lack knowledge of how the airport space—understood as a differentiated and hierarchically organized national border-crossing zone—is monitored through everyday operations of surveillance.

Police CCTV Operations at Geneva International Airport

This chapter directly addresses this issue, by focusing on the daily surveillance practices of airport police at Geneva International Airport (*Police de Securité Internationale*). CCTV is considered here as a sociotechnical device that involves science and technology, cultural and legal aspects, as well as social representations. This amounts to envisaging CCTV not as a lifeless and inert object but rather as a dynamic sociotechnical system that is constantly "in the making."[5] Furthermore, our approach is based on the hypothesis that the functioning of CCTV—its scope, its impact, and the risks it poses—cannot be understood without referring to the territories concerned with, and created by, the installation of the cameras and their performance.

Anchored within a microgeographical approach, the following analysis engages with sociospatial impacts and dimensions of video surveillance within the context of airport risk management. In fact, much effort has been expended on analyzing CCTV as a tool of social sorting, but there is a current lack of research regarding spatial characteristics of CCTV. The basic line of our argument is that surveillance tends not only to relate to specific categories of persons but also to focus on specific categories of space; we thus not only examine how CCTV focuses on particular social groups and individuals but also how and why CCTV focuses on particular spaces at the airport.[6]

Given this general approach, this chapter deals in particular with the negotiation of CCTV practices between public security politics and private business interests, regarding the publicly accessible airport sections (check-in, arrival, and departure zones of the airport; as well as the airport railway station that functions as a commercial shopping center). Our analysis thus concentrates on CCTV operations by means of the sixteen currently installed cameras within the publicly accessible premises of Geneva International Airport. We do not consider police cameras in access-restricted zones of the airport (such as on the tarmac), nor do we examine the use of private cameras in airport shops, in the freight sections, or within several multistory parking garages nearby the airport.

On a microgeographical level of analysis, referring to daily police CCTV operations, we underline convergences and tensions between private business interests to increase the airport's commercial appeal, on the one hand, and police concerns for the airport area as a national gateway of arriving and departing passengers and goods, on the other hand. On this basis, we point out both the inherent subjectivity of airport security politics (it seems that security does not always trump economy) and the limits of surveillance, which result from daily compromises between numerous actors, interests, and strategies.

Our investigation is empirically based on information gathered within a two-year research project (2004–5), funded by the Swiss National Science Foundation.[7] Regarding the broader conceptual understanding of video surveillance, this project specifically dealt with video surveillance as it is understood, perceived, and practiced by its suppliers (producers, distributors, designers) and its users (owner, technical managers, operators). Facilitated by strong, long-term relations with police forces in Geneva, interviews with numerous types of actors who were involved in the planning, installation, use, and development of the airport CCTV system were conducted. In addition, observational research was done in the police control-room, by closely assisting one week of nightly and daily police operations by means of CCTV. Bringing together two research groups (one group of social scientists and one group of legal specialists[8]), this methodological approach provided deep insights into the complexity of the factors that contribute to the functioning and impact of CCTV systems as well as into the legal rules available to regulate the use of surveillance cameras, and their limits.

An Airport for Travelers and Visitors

Most airport studies focus on famous mega-airports (such as Schiphol in Amsterdam, Charles de Gaulle in Paris, and John F. Kennedy in New York). These airports, situated far away from the city center, are mostly understood as detached universes within their own time-space logics. They are examined as "spaces of flows"[9] and as "zones of perpetual transit"[10] that provide specific services for travelers.[11] However, the study of Geneva International Airport highlights that airports are not always, and not only, detached worlds of transit functioning by their own logic but can also, more banally, become common places for local residents, tourists, and other passers-by.

Geneva International Airport is a relatively small and accessible airport near the city center. It is situated beside an important exhibition center and music venue. Because of its central location, it houses many shops aimed at the general public with convenient business hours. In the most commercially appealing section of the airport, which is mainly (but not exclusively) connected to the airport railway station, regular performances and events (such as flea markets, fashion shows, exhibitions, etc.) take place. Geneva International Airport must thus be considered as a functionally diverse space, providing not only services for passengers but also for people without any intention of traveling.

Regarding the conceptualization of airport space more generally, the Geneva case-study also challenges our basic understanding of the meaning and significance of airports. As we argue, airports cannot be reduced to "nonplaces" of consumption and mobility.[12] They must also, more generally, be understood as complex and diverse, yet particularly commercialized, spaces in various forms of public use, which are not only in many ways treated like shopping malls but also as spaces for social encounters for various actors.

The functional dichotomy of Geneva International Airport—to process arriving and departing flows of passengers and goods, on the one hand, and to attract local customers as a destination in its own right, on the other hand—constitutes the basic structure of this chapter. In fact, as we will show, these two major airport functionalities give rise to different strategies of security politics, which are expressed in different CCTV operations.

First, we concentrate on police CCTV operations in capturing and controlling arriving passengers at fixed *points* between passenger-restricted zones and publicly accessible zones. Standing in for traditional police border-control operations, this type of CCTV operation (to control people and goods entering the national territory) constitutes the first reason for police security operations at the airport.

Second, we examine CCTV operations that help to create a safe, trouble-free, and pleasant airport *area* for arriving and departing passengers. Here our focus lies on the publicly accessible part of the airport in its entirety. However, we assert that CCTV operations do not monitor the whole airport area equally but rather focus on specific "places at risk." Referring to the examples of CCTV operations to combat luggage theft and control "problem" people at the airport, we point out that the higher the density of people and distractions there are at particular places, the more these places are understood to be at risk by the police.

Third, referring to the airport's efforts to further attract local customers for its shops, we explore tensions between business and police interests in the publicly accessible parts of the airport. While the former pushes for the increased commercialization of the airport (aiming to increase the density of people and distractions), the latter aims to create a trouble-free, safe, and presentable airport area for travelers without any "disturbing" people or objects. In this regard, we focus in particular on the "flea market" and Christmas dilemmas.

The Airport as Artificial Border-Control Site: CCTV for National Security Issues

Literally understood as "aerial port," the primary function and *raison d'être* of airports is mobility. Firstly, airports constitute points of arrival and departure from/to international destinations, connecting its local region with the outer world. The airport in its entirety is thus set up to process, organize, regulate, and control constant flows of people and goods. As Gillian Fuller explains,

> An airport processes traffic; it is a machine for capturing and controlling flows at the most literal and abstract levels. The movements of people,

machines, and cargo are kept steady and separate. Moving in relay from point to point, each must connect at certain points and then continue along fixed paths and at fixed speeds. All movement is controlled, from the planes on the apron to the corralling of passengers in retail areas.[13]

For example, 9,411,105 passengers passed through Geneva International Airport in 2005, traveling to the 87 destinations (68 in Europe and 19 on other continents) that are served by direct scheduled flights from Geneva.[14]

This means, in turn, that airports also play an important role for national security issues in controlling and regulating border-crossing flows of persons and objects. Unlike checkpoints at the outer geographical border of each nation-state, security measures for the "virtual borders"[15] within airports do not have to deal with large *borderlines* that need to be monitored and safeguarded but are instead concentrated on specific *check*points, where passengers "naturally" arrive through corridors and moving walkways from their planes. Despite this punctual spatial logic, the airport as a national point of access still stands for the subdivision and differentiation of larger (national) *areas*, which is often carried to the point of segregation between indoor and outdoor space, exemplified by restrictive visa policies.

Since 9/11, depending on the country, border-control measures at airports have been more or less retooled and redesigned as part of a new and expanding "war on terror".[16] Enclosed operations reach from traditional passport checks, registrations of arriving and departing passengers, and luggage controls by customs authorities to the storage and analysis of increasingly detailed passenger data sets. Many of these measures of simulated surveillance aim to anticipate "persons of risk" who would later—once they have reached the larger national territory—be more difficult to monitor.[17] Referring to our empirically based example of Geneva International Airport, three main applications of CCTV can be distinguished within the broader issue of national-access control at airports.

First, not yet used at Geneva International Airport but applied in Switzerland's largest airport in Zurich since 2002, biometrical face recognition through CCTV constitutes one of the purest examples of camera-based access control. While this technology is used in other border zones,[18] airports commonly figure among the privileged places for its use, serving as test beds for further societal applications and developments of preprogrammed control technologies.[19]

At Zurich Airport, the scan of passengers' faces is intended for computer-based identification of asylum seekers without identification papers.[20] In this case, access control is subject to the camera's capacity to confirm a person's identity whose facial characteristics have already been scanned and recorded (perhaps even at places other than at the airport). Knowing that all passengers naturally arrive at the same strategic points of the airport, these high-tech cameras are installed near the immigration desks in order to take high-resolution pictures of the arriving passengers' faces.

Faces consequently become the new territories to monitor. In other cases, at Heathrow Airport in London and Schiphol Airport in Amsterdam, for example, biometrical face recognition is not used to restrict access for unwanted individuals but rather to allow faster border passages for business travelers.[21] In Geneva, a similar system is expected to be installed in the near future, which underlines the broader tendency of airport security devices to become international-standards solutions, which are commonly applied not only in other airports but also in other categories of space.

Second, at Geneva International Airport cameras are used to monitor the microscale behavior of previously identified, arriving "passengers of risk" within the publicly accessible arrival zone of the airport. In our interviews, examples of closely monitored "individuals of risk" ranged from members of the Hell's Angels and religious sects to supposed members of human trafficking rings, criminals, and terrorists. Here, the aim is not only to take high-resolution pictures of arriving passengers of risk, but through active manipulations of the cameras' positions and zoom, to understand his or her behavior within the first parameters of the national territory. Is he/she waiting for someone? Will he/she phone someone? Which type of transport will he/she use?

The spatiality of this second type of CCTV for access control is thus more flexible than the first and refers to a larger geographical *area*.

> For example, the criminal investigation department might know that one specific individual will arrive by airplane. Perhaps, they might even be sure that this . . . individual does indeed carry drugs, but they might not know with whom he will be in contact. We will then be asked to take large-scale photos by surveillance cameras, in order to see how the person is dressed, for example. When he drives out of the airport, we will try to register the number plate of his car and we will also try to see with whom he might speak and if somebody's looking for him, etc.[22]

Regarding this second type of camera operation for access control, the relative advantage of CCTV, compared to on-the-spot police agents, lies in the resulting discretion offered to police operations. Arriving individuals might actually believe that they are neither expected nor monitored by the police at their destination, which makes them behave more naturally and display information that would not have been revealed under the pressure of obvious police presence. Furthermore, cameras make it possible to take pictures in order to document monitored scenes or to reconstruct and further communicate the order of events to other police departments a posteriori.

> Wanted criminals, arriving at the airport, generally are very tense. . . . The cameras make it possible for them to come, because they see no . . . police officers on the spot. . . . Cameras make it possible to be discreet. . . . For example, I personally filmed somebody who was suspected of working for X. For half an hour, this person just stayed on the spot. . . . When he arrived, he was still anxious, looking all around. Then, step by step, he got more confident. You clearly saw that he became calmer because he saw nobody to suspect him. Still, he took another ten minutes to join the person who waited for him.[23]

The third form of access control–related CCTV operations does not specifically deal with persons who might represent particular risks but rather intends to protect arriving individuals who are supposed to be particularly exposed to risks. An example of this would be the arrival of state presidents for political events in Geneva, such as for the 2003 G8 summit in nearby Evian. Special circumstances at that time even led to the installation of additional high-tech cameras.

> We've never before encountered such a high concentration of state and government heads arriving in Geneva. I would say, the installation of CCTV already presents a financial investment. The fact that we had an open budget in order to secure the airport allowed us to obtain these additional four cameras, which we wouldn't have been able to do normally. So, it is true that we did benefit from the circumstances in order to install these cameras, which we were able to keep afterward.[24]

The Airport as a Safe Refuge of Passengers: CCTV for Combined Public and Private Interests

We now move beyond our discussion of police CCTV operations for national security issues through the monitoring of flows of people and goods. From a business point of view, the airport has much more to offer than arrivals and departures. It also constitutes a commercially attractive space with bars, restaurants, car rental desks, newsagents, cash machines, and various shops to accommodate passengers or local clients. In 2005 non-aeronautical income accounted for 52.3 percent of the total turnover of Geneva International Airport.[25] In this light, private attempts to benefit from airport police services in general and from police CCTV operations in particular are not surprising.

Before, the UBS office[26] used to be in the arrival zone. Every morning, we assisted the opening of this office. First, two police agents were present; then, we thought about the cameras. So, we did use them for this as well. We didn't have to lose two agents on the spot, but one person could watch from the control room to scan the place and check if there were any suspect individuals nearby. . . . Finally, the bank's employee opened the office, and we, during all this time, we used the cameras to make sure there were no problems.[27]

The increasingly blurred division between traditional police services and particular services for business interests also finds expression in the financing of the airport police's infrastructure (such as its office space and the CCTV control room), which is placed at the police's disposal by the airport management. Among all of the surveillance cameras within the publicly accessible sections of the airport, none has been paid for by the police. For specific services, the police are even directly remunerated by the airport management.

> The airport management—and I think it is absolutely necessary—does want a permanent police presence at the airport. The infrastructure is therefore placed at the police's disposal. Office space is made available for police use and specific police services are even directly paid for by the airport management. This is a specific service for the police by the building's owner, which is a public building. The airport management does not interfere in the use of funds that are made available. It only pays them. . . . The airport did finance the complete installation of the cameras.[28]

In particular, as regards the planning, financing, and installation of the airport CCTV system, our research emphasizes the myriad microdecisions and micronegotiations within a complex network of relationships between numerous public and private actors that have strongly influenced the processes of both bringing the CCTV system into service and searching for constant improvements. In this, the important role of private actors can be seen on at least two levels. First, the technical competencies required to manage the CCTV system give certain (private) parties more weight. Thus, it appears that there has been a general transfer of competencies from the users of the system (the police) via the owner of the system (the airport administration) to the technical managers of the system (the airport's technical service). Second, the role of independently operating private enterprises, boosting, presenting and selling new technical solutions (to both the police and the airport management) or supplying technical services to improve the system's performance is crucial. Given this heavy involvement of private companies in designing and managing high-tech forms of surveillance, these developments clearly put traditional forms of public governance at stake as they rule out police regulations that were traditionally exclusively put under the responsibility of the nation-state.

Keeping in mind the heavy involvement of private actors in the financing and managing of the airport CCTV system, we now take a more in-depth look at the police's motivations for close public–private security partnerships in this context. In fact, the police's particular interest in the close collaboration with the airport management originates not only from the resulting financial and practical advantages but also from the intrinsic combination of interests in the airport as both a safe and attractive national port-of-entry and a commercially appealing shopping mall. The following discussion of police CCTV operations stresses the strategic combination of interests, simultaneously aiming to clear up and prevent luggage theft on the one hand and to manage and exclude commercially unattractive people from the airport area on the other hand. This illustrates more generally the joint production of airport security between public and private actors. Yet again, our analysis focuses especially on the spatial dimensions of CCTV operations for these matters.

Spatial Logics of Police CCTV Operations against Luggage Theft

Thus far, we have suggested that police CCTV operations to monitor arriving passengers either concentrate on specific access points or on particular airport sections, justifying, for example, the increased density of cameras on the arrival level compared to the departure zone. The spatial logic of CCTV operations to clear up and prevent luggage theft is fundamentally different, because in this case, the security of the airport area and its reputation as a whole are at stake. Nevertheless, police CCTV operations for this purpose follow specific spatial logics, which contributes to the differentiation of the airport area in terms of surveillance. In this respect, the spatiality of CCTV operations can be seen on three levels.

First, in the interviews with police representatives, an explicit link was established between the camera installation points themselves and spatial concentrations of luggage theft at specific "places at risk." For example, no surveillance cameras were installed in the transit zone, which is restricted to passengers, because of the low percentage of luggage theft within the secure area. On the contrary, cameras were exclusively spread over publicly accessible spaces of the airport (with concentrations in the arrival zone, the check-in zone, and the airport railway station), without being put into specific shops (which normally have their own cameras).

Of course, [the specific placement of cameras] had to be decided. We could have put cameras everywhere. However, given the insignificance of offences within the transit area—which nonetheless does not mean that we can neglect them—we also had to think about the cost of installation. . . . The installation was quite expensive. Therefore, we did put the cameras at places where the prevention [of theft] was most necessary.[29]

Hence, as we see by looking at the spatial distribution of police surveillance cameras within the publicly accessible parts of the airport, the cameras' points of installation disproportionately value the surveillance of particular places or zones at the airport, which are presented to be "at risk" in that they constitute locations where luggage theft was predicted to be more likely to occur. This emphasizes that the airport is not homogeneously under surveillance but rather selectively monitored, dividing its surface into hierarchically-organized areas of control.

Second, we cannot only discern the spatial logic of airport CCTV operations through the installation points of the cameras, we must also analyze how cameras are effectively used by the police. Following from our observational research, *real time* CCTV operations to reduce luggage theft are indeed first based on the selection of particularly risky airport sections (where robberies can be committed more easily than elsewhere). Micro-operations with cameras (changing their positions and zooming) rely on each operator's personal experiences, knowledge, and assumptions, which are fundamentally related to space. For example, places with many distractions that attract the victim's attention and thus facilitate luggage theft were described as at risk. Given examples include travel agencies, car rental desks, check-in desks, and so on.

It's [risky at] banks, where clients will change money, which takes all their attention. It's also [risky] at car rental desks because people are asked questions and they have to fill out documents and don't think about what is going on behind their backs. On the upper floor, it is at the check-in desks, because people are anxious to leave by plane. . . . These are the points where we most often have thefts. That's why these places are at risk. It is not that we would have determined these places ourselves, but it is where robberies are most frequently committed.[30]

More generally, highly frequented zones at the airport were also subject to increased risk, which—as we will discuss in the later part of this chapter—strongly divides business and police interests in the airport. A high number of people walking or standing at particular places (e.g., near check-in desks or within the railway station zone) not only facilitates luggage theft but also renders video surveillance more difficult: "What will make us look at specific places? It is the places with a high number of people."[31]

Third, looking at the spatiality of CCTV operations to combat luggage theft, we finally refer to the cameras' positions while not being actively used by police agents. Although it is most gratifying for CCTV operators to catch thieves in the act, cameras often remain unnoticed when in strategic positions. Here again, the operator's knowledge and assumptions regarding places at risk is crucial. In the first stage, places are indeed targeted depending on the operator's mental map of the spatial distribution of risks at the airport.

> We know that there are strategic points where more luggage robberies will occur than elsewhere. In the evening, I will focus the cameras especially on these points. Afterward, if we have to visualize the images, I know that the cameras were already watching these points. We also try to have wide camera angles, in order to see the maximum. Furthermore, even if it is not always possible, we try to arrange the cameras in rows.[32]

Only of secondary importance, on the basis of the preselection of particular places at risk, CCTV operators use representations of specific social groups at risk. Regarding other spatial contexts and applications of CCTV, important research has been completed about the discriminatory social judgments and representations within daily CCTV practices, regarding specific "social groups of risk."[33] As regards the real-time monitoring of suspect individuals at Geneva International Airport, according to the qualitative data of our observational research and interviews, camera operators were hardly ever looking for the "usual suspects," such as marginalized social groups and young men with specific ethnic origins. On the contrary, they were more likely to focus on well-dressed, middle-aged gentlemen (often with female companions) hanging around the airport without any clear intention to leave by airplane.

> One often hears about criminals wearing rapper style clothes with baseball cap. . . . However, given our experiences here at the airport, thieves are not necessarily "badly" dressed. They're mainly normally dressed people, to whom you would not especially pay attention. They're generally well dressed, hardly ever young. Some, you would describe as nice daddies. Their look is "bon chic, bon genre": suit, tie. It's really people who go through without being especially noticed.[34]

CCTV to Exclude Disturbing Individuals from the Airport

Many analysts underline the correspondence between business interests and security politics in general and between the commercialization of city centers and CCTV in particular.[35] For example, it has been argued that CCTV aims to increase the commercial value of monitored areas by helping to exclude "disturbing" individuals. The same tendency can be seen at the airport. Aside from fighting against luggage thieves and other criminals, the police's daily CCTV operations also focus on individuals who might threaten the consumer-oriented airport environment.

As a result, CCTV operations are not only aiming at the reduction of criminal behavior in order to create a safe airport but also at the exclusion of individuals whose behavior is considered to be inappropriate in the finely polished marble landscape of the airport. The *repressive* functionality of CCTV (i.e., to neutralize, control, and avoid specific individuals and behaviors) and the *creative* functionality of CCTV (i.e., to produce a commercially appealing environment) are thus intrinsically related. CCTV is not only of strategic importance to combat different types of risks, it also facilitates the airport's commercial usefulness. CCTV thus serves a clearly defined economic purpose and rationality, understood by Michel Foucault as, "the functional inversion of the disciplines."[36]

Despite the airport's function to receive and accommodate the general public, its publicly accessible parts cannot be understood as "public" in the sense of open, democratically shared, public space.[37] On the contrary, within the picture of a safe, trouble-free, and presentable airport, not every social group has its place. Publicly accessible airport sections are thus restricted to clearly defined social groups, which are only accommodated as long as they are not classified to be "undesirable."

To provide a symptomatic example of this ambivalence, it is worth looking at two examples, including skateboarding youth, on the one hand, and homeless people, on the other hand. In fact, camera operators did not describe these social groups to be of risk, in that they would need to be especially monitored to prevent luggage theft, for example. They were on the contrary exclusively seen as disturbing elements to the airport's reputation as both a prestigious national port-of-entry and as a nice place to go shopping.

> Within the railway station sector, one might easily find juveniles arriving with their music and dancing. In this case we will intervene. Often, it is via telephone [to private security agents], but sometimes, we send our own patrol.[38]
>
> Recently, there was a woman pissing everywhere, smelling badly, and talking to herself. Here as well, we were obliged to gently ask her to leave.[39]

The airport management and the more than sixty shops and services at Geneva International Airport strongly agree with the police's strategy to expel young skateboarders and homeless people from the airport.

The Airport as Shopping Mall: CCTV between Antagonist Public and Private Interests

Unlike the police, however, the busy shops, cafés, and restaurants do not consider arriving or departing passengers as border-crossing individuals but rather as potential customers. They even actively seek to attract additional clients to the airport who do not have any intentions of leaving by plane.

From a Place of Transit to a Destination in its Own Right

These efforts are facilitated by the airport's geographical proximity to the city center of Geneva, its excellent integration in the city network of public transit (accessible by train and three bus lines less than ten minutes from downtown) and by the exceptionally long business hours—7 days a week, 365 days a year "in theory"—of both the specialized, luxury shops and the more general shops for the local population.[40] Furthermore, various kinds of special events are organized by the airport management—whose responsibility for the events is intensely advertised throughout the airport on large information boards—ranging from popular events such as displays of model cars, boats, or helicopters to fashion shows, arts exhibitions, and flea markets. The airport thus becomes a destination in its own right.

> I would say that the wish to organize playful events originates from the airport's intention to animate its commercial spaces. One has to know that shops generate a huge income for the airport. Therefore, the airport needs them. And because shops need to make a profit as well, one has to attract a huge amount of people.[41]

Though some of these entertainments concern all public zones at the airport, the most "chaotic" and "uncontrollable" occurrences (such as the monthly flea markets, most model exhibitions, fashion shows, and Christmas markets) are exclusively held within the airport's railway station. In this light, the organization of well-attended events for business interests at the airport raises important issues about the increasing spatial differentiation of the airport into different levels of more-or-less commercialized zones, which our interviewees often described as public sections. In addition, a central challenge for further empirical research would involve questions about the ways in which the airport in general and these events in particular are perceived by customers, passengers, and visitors, in order to better understand the effect of such events on the perception of the airport as a mixture of shopping mall and commercialized leisure park.

These developments originate from business interests, but they clearly counteract the modernist ideal of the airport, which Le Corbusier expresses when he proclaims, "the beauty of an airport lies in the splendor of its space!"[42] By further reducing purely passenger-destined space, airport events might even lead to increased tension between different types of airport user groups, as the following two posts about Geneva International Airport, found on an internet forum about airport quality, point out:[43]

> Another issue is the lack of seating in an overcrowded . . . airport, which results in people sitting wherever they can, blocking the narrow gangways between high-end shops selling overpriced goods ranging from Rolex watches to caviar—but there are no seats to be had at the cramped self-service restaurant![44]
>
> The main problem is that they have so many shops that there isn't enough space for passengers to sit, and there were over a hundred passengers sitting on the floor. I would have thought providing seats for passengers would be a minimum basic service for an airport. Overall, traveling through GVA was a pretty nasty experience.[45]

Another set of difficulties resulting from the increasing commercialization of Geneva International Airport goes back to the fundamental tension between movement and immobility, or in other words, to the tension between commercial efforts to transform the airport into a space of events in its own right and the police's quest for a safe, ordered, clean, and presentable airport for passenger flows. This tension is further examined in two cases.

The Christmas Dilemma

The police agents we interviewed did not openly disagree with the airport management's efforts to increase the commercial appeal of the airport. However, tension between public interests in the airport as a trouble-free, safe, and easily controllable national entrance gate, on the one hand, and business interests for commercial entertainment, on the other hand, is evident. In this respect, the police's role regarding the authorization of events is exemplary. In fact, to organize events at the airport, in general, no authorization is needed, but particular events could be prohibited by the airport police department if the risks entailed are considered to be excessive. The staging of events thus becomes the norm, while the cancellation remains the exception.

> We are informed of any special event. There is also a police delegate who participates in the competent airport working group. But generally, there is no formal permission to be asked. However, we could prohibit specific

events. There is a general police clause, which would allow us—depending on the circumstances—to prohibit any event if the risk would be too high. . . . Still, there is no 100 percent security. Automatically, we have to assess the situation and decide whether an event could be held or not.[46]

Special events rarely present acute risks, however, they do entail difficulties and complications for police security operations. Regarding CCTV operations in particular, a series of difficulties is linked to commercial events at the airport. These challenges arise because of associated changes of the airport's materiality, such as the specific arrangement of objects, placards, and decorations, which accompanies every event. This problem is particularly obvious at Christmas.

Information placards—toilets, etc.—are found more or less everywhere at the airport. Sometimes, we will ask [the management] to change the locations and positions of placards, because they do limit the view of the cameras. Anyway, we do not have a very good view of the departure level. Recently, the airport workers even put another placard in the middle of the hall, which was not really a good solution for us. We also have to pay attention to Christmas decorations. It's very simple; with all these Christmas decorations, we lose a big part of our vision.[47]

The police's worry about Christmas decorations perfectly illustrates the fundamental need to conceptualize airport-security politics as permanently "in the making."[48] Airport surveillance must indeed be studied as the subject of constant research and development, as a result of convergent and divergent interests and requirements. This is particularly clear during the installation and implementation process, a whole series of microdecisions and of micronegotiations are in play. This exemplary microscale issue strongly underlines that airports cannot simply be described as spaces of complete control, as the omnipresent rhetoric of security politics currently suggests. On the contrary, we have to understand surveillance and security issues at airports to be co-produced compromises between numerous private and public actors. The next case illustrates that security does not always trump economy.

The Flea Market Dilemma

Genuine tensions of airport security become even more evident regarding a second micro-issue of police CCTV operations—the "flea market dilemma." As mentioned earlier, monthly flea markets are organized by the airport management to invite customers who have more time than passengers have to enjoy the airport facilities, to engage differently with the airport space, and—most importantly—to spend money. It is remarkable that, due to advance scheduling, this flea market was even held two weeks after the alleged terrorist strikes on several airplanes between London and the United States in August 2006, which dramatically increased security conditions for passengers. Even in normal circumstances, however, the organization of flea markets at the airport raises some fundamental issues.

First, the increased number of people generally presents an important challenge for airport CCTV operations, regardless of their activities. Huge amounts of people and distractions in particular places are not only more difficult to monitor by surveillance cameras, but they also present ideal conditions for pickpockets and luggage theft within the crowd.

> Every special event—I mean whenever there are many people here, bringing money to the airport—is a moment at risk. Increased departures on public holidays, charter flights on Saturdays. . . . Then, pickpockets will be here.[49]

Second, compared to passengers, flea market visitors are not passing *through* the airport but remain *inside* the building for whole afternoons, which further heightens the challenge they pose for security operations. Unlike normal passengers, they can no longer be subject to clearly prescribed patterns of movement—filtered and controlled through check-in, ticketing, security checks, and so on. On the contrary, flea market visitors follow their own spatial logics, adding complex and opposing micromovements to the general flow of travelers.

Third, flea markets are particularly hard to reconcile with increased security precautions against terrorist threats for airports. Rubbish bins have long ago been removed at Geneva International Airport, as elsewhere. In addition, unattended luggage is routinely detected through CCTV and exploded by specialized police forces. In this regard, CCTV's integrated systems of unattended luggage detection have been tested by the airport police department in Geneva. With all of this in mind, flea markets present the very antithesis of the ideally controllable airport environment. As relatively chaotic events, they lead to fundamentally unforeseeable social relationships and spatial behaviors, which makes it nearly impossible to look for abandoned luggage.

Conclusions

The special magic of airports as symbolic spaces of progress and national pride is often expressed through massive, ostentatious security measures.

We also know about powerful surveillance techniques aiming to closely monitor and profile people and goods passing through airports. In this sense, airports indeed act as powerful filters to international mobility. However, the picture of the airport as a homogeneous world of complete control and surveillance must be differentiated, as our empirically detailed insights in daily police CCTV operations at Geneva International Airport have revealed.

Concerned with the dual functionalities of Geneva International Airport as both a national entrance gate and as a destination in its own right for local clients, the study of CCTV practices by the airport police provided a powerful example of broader surveillance trends in the context of airport-security politics. Our question, in essence, has been: how are everyday practices of CCTV embedded within the complex network of public and private actors, strategies, and interests at Geneva International Airport, and how are CCTV practices actually related to the spaces concerned with the installation of the cameras? Based on interviews with airport police representatives and observational research of daily CCTV operations, our analysis thereby was divided into three parts.

First, the chapter explored both the role of CCTV to "capture" and to "understand" arriving passengers at risk, on the one hand, and to "protect" persons who are particularly exposed to risks, on the other hand. Focused either on specific access points or on the entire airport arrival zone, this type of CCTV operations was compared with traditional border-control measures —that is, monitoring international mobility in order to improve the security of the wider national territory.

Second, our analysis was extended to police CCTV operations, following the general quest for a safe, ordered, clean, and pleasant airport environment without any "disturbing" objects or persons. Exemplified by CCTV operations to combat luggage theft and to reduce damage to the airport's image, we pointed out strategic coalitions of interests to purify the airport space. The study of CCTV, thus, exemplarily expressed the close collaboration between numerous public and private parties (encompassing different types of competencies, strategies, interests, and work philosophies) for the organization and daily carrying out of security operations at the airport. In addition, our concern about the different spatial logics of CCTV operations also helped to point out to what degree airport security politics is actually based on conscious and unconscious prioritizations of certain objects (spaces and persons) and the logics of surveillance.

Despite the combined pursuit of a smart and trouble-free airport, the third part of this paper suggested that police interests and commercial interests in the airport area do not always coincide. Here, the example of CCTV operations at Geneva International Airport suggested that airport-security politics both converges *and* diverges with private business interests. While the resulting challenges and tensions can be small in scale in relation to the overwhelming surveillance machine at the airport, they are not to be ignored. Just consider the example of the "flea market dilemma" which emphasized that airport risk management constantly articulates antagonistic issues and interests. Thus, despite being an important priority, especially after 9/11, security issues do not constitute the sole preoccupation airports. In practice, constant tensions are arising between security issues and commercial interests, which today seem to provide the last obstacles to restrain current trends toward ever-increasing surveillance.

In this, a central issue at stake is to conceptualize the current development of security politics more generally, rather than as pure responses to security threats or as exclusive measures to address heightened fears of vulnerability. The study of security politics in the aviation sector indeed presents highly favorable conditions to provide empirical insight into the complexity of factors that contribute to the implementation, functioning, and impact of surveillance. In particular, understanding the interdependencies between public and private actors, interests, and strategies is of crucial importance in order to consider the potential of legal regulations to restrict and manage the ever-increasing deployment of surveillance measures.

In this, the question at stake is not simply whether to choose between security or privacy. The question, in fact, comes from a different direction. It is deeply embedded in the process of global security politics recalibration, which reveals itself as having put in place a series of mechanisms that reorder security politics toward economic goals: How are security strategies embedded within and coproduced through a complex network of local; national; international; and public and private actors, interests, and domains of expertise? How are these networks developing and circulating across diverse private and public spheres, resulting in the production of security models as expert "exemplars" for more general use, which are increasingly influencing local decisions? In which ways, and to what degree, are trends of commercialization subtly pushed forward beneath these developments, associated with specific discourses and measures of security politics?

Regarding the conceptualization of airports more generally, the study of CCTV operations at Geneva International Airport also contributed to the further discussion of the nature of airports in terms of Marc Augé's conceptualization of "nonplaces," which provides a common point of reference for airport studies. The Geneva case study presented an interesting example to explore the airport environment not only as a transit space but also as a commercially-appealing space, intrinsically connected with its surroundings and presenting a strong wish to draw on the broader urban and regional visitor market. Thus, the airport environment is not only populated by travelers but also by local customers, passers-by, and visitors. In this light, Geneva International Airport not only constitutes a place of transit and movement, resulting in a certain detachment between its users and the spaces they traverse, but also a much richer and more diverse space, which brings together myriad spatial practices, emotional engagements, and social microrelations.

Of course, many particularities from the Geneva case-study might strongly differ in other airports and in other national contexts. Also, our analysis in this chapter was restricted to police CCTV operations, without considering the full extent of security operations, instruments, and techniques at hand in the airport.[50] Therefore, our analysis raises important further questions and issues about airport surveillance. For example, there is scope for much-needed empirical research about the role of other types of private actors interfering on local police strategies of airport security politics, such as airplane companies asking for international security standards, and security companies trying to sell and provide new technical surveillance solutions. Without the exact knowledge of the complex relationships between numerous parties, it is indeed very difficult to know through which procedures, operations, and practices international mobility through airports is managed, filtered, and screened within these sites.[51]

In addition, we crucially lack empirically based knowledge regarding the efficiency of different measures of (airport) surveillance. Based on the assumption that the end justifies the means, the generalization of surveillance technology, not only at airports but in nearly every aspect of social life, remains largely unquestioned in terms of efficiency and proportionality. There is, thus, a desperate need to move beyond generalized and deterministic discourses about the role of surveillance in order to pave the way for a better future and to look, in rich empirical detail, at the complex ways in which different surveillance measures are being used in real ways, in real places, in the real world. Even if the lack of enquiry in the research field is somewhat understandable, given the confidentiality of information about security operations in general and at airports in particular, questioning these issues is long overdue.

Notes

1. See chapters by Salter and Lyon in this volume.
2. David Pascoe, *Airspaces* (London: Reaktion Books, 2001), 34.
3. Gillian Fuller, "Life in Transit: Between Airport and Camp," *borderlands e-journal* 2, no. 1 (2003), http://www.borderlandsejournal.adelaide.edu.au/vol2no1_2003/fuller_transit.html (accessed November 8, 2006); David Lyon,

"Airports as Data Filters: Converging Surveillance Systems after September 11th," *Information, Communication and Ethics in Society* 1, no. 1 (2003): 13–20.

4. Peter Adey, "Surveillance at the Airport: Surveilling Mobility / Mobilizing Surveillance," *Environment and Planning A* 36, no. 8 (2004): 1365–80.

5. Bruno Latour, *Science in Action* (Cambridge, Mass.: Harvard University Press, 1987).

6. See David Lyon, ed., *Surveillance as Social Sorting* (London: Routledge, 2003); Gary T. Marx, *Undercover: Police Surveillance in America* (Berkeley: University of California Press, 1988).

7. Jean Ruegg, Alexandre Flückiger, and Valérie November, *Vidéosurveillance et risques dans l'espace à usage public: Représentations des risques, régulation sociale et liberté de mouvement*, research report, Swiss National Science Foundation, Project No. 101412-101858/1 (Geneva: Universities of Geneva, 2006).

8. This research has been conducted by Jean Ruegg, Valérie November, Francisco Klauser, and Alexandra Felder (social science) and by Alexandre Flückiger, Laurence Greco, and Laurent Pierroz (legal research group).

9. Manuel Castells, *The Rise of Network Society—Volume 1: The Information Age; Economy, Society and Culture* (Oxford: Blackwell, 1996).

10. Fuller, "Life in Transit."

11. Pascoe, *Airspaces*, 11.

12. Marc Augé, *Non-places: Introduction to an Anthropology of Supermodernity*, trans. John Howe (New York: Verso, 1995).

13. Fuller, "The Arrow—Directional Semiotics: Wayfinding in Transit," *Social Semiotics* 12, no. 3 (2002): 133.

14. Geneva International Airport, *Annual Report 2005*, March 1, 2006, http://www.gva.ch/en/PortalData/1/Resources//fichiers/publications/publications_institutionnel/2005_ra.pdf (accessed September 30, 2006).

15. Lyon, "Airports as Data Filters," 13.

16. Peter Andreas, "Redrawing the Line: Borders and Security in the Twenty-first Century," *International Security* 28, no. 2 (2003): 78–111.

17. William Bogard, *The Simulation of Surveillance* (Cambridge: Cambridge University Press, 1996).

18. Irma Van der Ploeg, "The Illegal Body: 'Eurodac' and the Politics of Biometric Identification," *Ethics and Information Technology* 1, no. 4 (1999): 295–302.

19. Lyon, "Airports as Data Filters."

20. Rolf Elsener, "Eine Kontrolle, die unter die Haut geht," *Neue Luzerner Zeitung* (January 10, 2003): 3.

21. Adey, "Surveillance at the Airport," 1370; see also Benjamin J. Muller, chapter 6 in this volume.

22. Police agent and CCTV operator I, Geneva International Airport Police. All quotations are translated from French to English by the authors.

23. Police agent and camera operator II, Geneva International Airport Police.

24. Head, Geneva International Airport Police.

25. Geneva International Airport, *Annual Report 2005*.

26. UBS is a European bank.

27. Police agent and camera operator I, Geneva International Airport Police.

28. Ex-head of the Geneva International Airport Police and initiator of the airport CCTV system.

29. Ex-head of the Geneva International Airport Police and initiator of the airport CCTV system.

30. Police agent and camera operator II, Geneva International Airport Police.

31. Head of CCTV control room Geneva International Airport Police.

32. Police agent and camera operator II, Geneva International Airport Police.

33. Clive Norris, "From Personal to Digital: CCTV, the Panopticon and the Technological Mediation of Suspicion and Social Control," in *Surveillance and Social Sorting: Privacy Risk and Automated Discrimination*, ed. David Lyon (London: Routledge, 2002), 249–81; Heidi Mork Lomell, "Targeting the Unwanted: Video Surveillance and Categorical Exclusion in Oslo, Norway," *Surveillance and Society* 2, no. 2/3 (2004): 346–60.

34. Police agent and camera operator I, Geneva International Airport Police.

35. Mike Davis, *City of Quartz* (New York: Verso, 1990); Alan Reeve, "The Panopticisation of Shopping: CCTV and Leisure Consumption," *Surveillance, CCTV and Social Control*, ed. Clive Norris, Jade Morran, and Gary Armstrong (Aldershot, UK: Ashgate, 1998), 69–88; Roy Coleman and Joe Sim, "You'll Never Walk Alone: CCTV Surveillance, Order and Neo-liberal Rule in Liverpool City Centre," *British Journal of Sociology* 51, no. 4 (2000): 623–39; Coleman, "Reclaiming the Streets: Closed Circuit Television, Neoliberalism and the Mystification of Social Divisions in Liverpool, UK," *Surveillance and Society* 2, no. 2/3 (2004): 145–60.

36. Michel Foucault, *Discipline and Punish: The Birth of the Prison*, trans. A. M. Sheridan (Harmondsworth, UK: Penguin, 1977), 210–11.

37. Stephen Carr, Mark Francis, Leanne Rivlin, and Andrew Stone, *Public Space* (Cambridge: Cambridge University Press, 1992), 50.

38. Head of CCTV control room, Geneva International Airport Police.

39. Police agent and camera operator I, Geneva International Airport Police.

40. Geneva International Airport, *Shopping*, http://www.gva.ch/en/desktop default.aspx/tabid-141/ (accessed July 27, 2007).

41. Head, Geneva International Airport Police.

42. Pascoe, *Airspaces*, 113.

43. Comments on Skytrax, *GVA-Geneva Airport*, http://www.airlinequality.com/Airports/Airport_forum/gva.htm (accessed November 8, 2006).

44. Bulmer, Comments on Skytrax, *GVA-Geneva Airport*, http://www.airlinequality.com/Airports/Airport_forum/gva.htm (accessed June, 10 2006).

45. Smith, Comments on Skytrax, *GVA-Geneva Airport*, http://www.airlinequality.com/Airports/Airport_forum/gva.htm (accessed January 31, 2006).

46. Head, Geneva International Airport Police.

47. Head of CCTV control room, Geneva International Airport Police.

48. Latour, *Science in Action*.

49. Police agent and camera operator I, Geneva International Airport Police.

50. For a wider discussion, see Ruegg et al. *Vidéosurveillance et risques*.

51. Adey, "Surveillance at the Airport," 1365.

6

TRAVELERS, BORDERS, DANGERS

Locating the Political at the Biometric Border

••••••••••••••••••

Benjamin J. Muller

Where's the Biometric Border?

Traveling is risky. From the pages of Richard Preston's novel *The Hot Zone*, one is confronted with the possibility that the person appearing to have motion sickness on the flight seated to your right is in fact the carrier of a deadly strain of the Ebola virus.[1] Your quaint family vacation to the British countryside can quickly turn out to be a confrontation with foot-and-mouth disease; turn the children's eyes from the burning pyres of animal carcasses. Stay on the disinfectant mat when crossing the virtual border at the airport. SARS, AIDS, avian flu—enjoy your holiday. Don't touch anything; don't go anywhere; breathing optional. Oh, and be careful if you're traveling in certain parts of the world and media outlets in the state for which you carry a passport has chosen to print offensive cartoons; you might be the target of violence. Like the great lumpenproletariat of the twenty-first century, tourists and travelers find themselves gawking at the disaster-cum-Disneyland spectacle of suffering and violence, only to find cheap consumer goods and take advantage of the most recent airline seat sale. "Ground zero was so moving. I can't believe how amazing Macy's storefront windows were. Glad we changed plans and avoided post-Katrina Mardi Gras; I heard it was awful. Did I tell you I wore a tie to the airport and they upgraded me to business class!"

Although the celebration of the borderless world might have been put on hold on September 11, 2001, it didn't take long for someone to simply order another round and keep the party going. Mourn the loss; rebuild with imperial magnitude; punish the evil-doers; go shopping. As we well know, the now infamous events of "9/11"[2] were cause for celebration in some quarters, rather than the impetus for the borderless world's suspension that some in the West believed it to be. Those touched more regularly by what Roxanne Doty terms "imperial encounters"[3] might have found the border-less world less liberating than the self-appointed liberators proclaimed. While the end of the Cold War marked the general demise of the so-called second world, the "third world" nonetheless remained a convenient term and practice. As Jean Raspail noted in his apocalyptic novel *The Camp of the Saints*, published in the 1970s, "There's no third world; No, not any-more. That's only a phrase you coined to keep us in our place. There's one world, only one, and it's going to be flooded with life, submerged."[4]

Mark Duffield's analysis of the recent seizure of the development agenda by emerging discourses of security in a supposedly "danger rich" age of terror suggests that this preoccupation with keeping the third world in its place and avoiding the submerging flood maintains a certain resilience.[5] Walter Benjamin's phrase, from his *Theses on the Philosophy of History*, that "there is no document of civilization that is not at the same time a doc-ument of barbarism" seems to ring true, now as much as ever.[6]

In such contexts, the linkages between the biometric border and the North–South border would seem rather obvious. Particularly when the robust territorial connotations of the North–South border are critically reconsidered, the sort of slippage between the territorial border and the bio-metric border, and its productive role for constellations of biopower seem particularly cogent. It would seem the biometric border is a rather subver-sive attempt to cope with the limitations of imagining a "borderless world." In essence, the biometric border is an interface between the corporeal, or materially manifested self, the body, and the data-double, or dossier, it rep-resents.[7] This chapter views the biometric border as an important site for analysis in contemporary politics. Rather than being preoccupied with the role of the travelers/tourists themselves, their constructions of places/spaces, their performances, and so on,[8] this analysis considers the relatively recent classification of the "trusted traveler" and the extent to which this differen-tiation is an integral part of the politics of the biometric border and contem-porary citizenship politics.

In attempting to locate the politics of the biometric border, it is quickly apparent that this is *not* found in the political space of the territorial state vis-à-vis the border; arguably, this is not surprising, since the politics of territorial borders are also regularly found elsewhere. While there are various discriminations made at the territorial borders and boundaries of the state, most often between insiders and outsiders, this chapter suggests the sort of discriminating practices of the biometric border go well beyond such sites of sovereign power. Such discriminations are often made on the basis of social values, North–South constellations, and so-called "biopolitical productions," or what recently Paolo Virno, Michael Hardt, and Antonio Negri have referred to as the "multitude,"[9] which will be discussed later.

Not all travelers are equal. The extent to which the differentiation among travelers is considered something to be preserved, secured, even fortified, and its deviation from the lines of sovereignty or conventional notions of political subjectivity, such as the Marshallian tripartite articulation of citizenship,[10] are worth noting. Travelers have always posed a sort of *risk* to sovereignty, in that, like migrants, they highlight the porous nature of sovereign borders and the tenuous hold Westphalian sovereignty has on little more than the political imagination.[11] Italian philosopher Giorgio Agamben has noted, for example, that such actors expose the "originary fiction of sovereign power."[12] In this sense, the analysis here attempts to consider politics around a particular site—that of the biometric border—as opposed to specific spaces of any territorial border/state.[13] This is to suggest that locating the politics of the biometric border involves looking elsewhere.

Warren Magnusson and Karena Shaw's collection on the political battles over the logging of an environmentally-sensitive coastal rainforest on western Vancouver Island, known as Clayoquot Sound, demonstrates how the *politics* of Clayoquot Sound became more than the politics of the specific place/space, but invoked a wide array of issues and debates that were, in fact, not "there."[14] While the widely contested logging of the fragile environment in Clayoquot Sound caused a "battle in the woods" during the summer of 1994—which resulted in massive arrests and mobilized various communities and interests, including local First Nations—the *politics* of Clayoquot Sound were globally apparent. A world-wide boycott of Scott Towel Products, the company responsible for the logging, and a barrage of protests at Canadian Embassies around the world, particularly in Germany, highlighted the extent to which the politics of this geographically remote space/place was neither domestic nor international, but both global and local.

Similarly, the politics of the biometric border and related "homeland security" strategies, do not sit comfortably within the space/place of the territorial border of the state and the accompanying narrative of sovereignty.

Nor is it obvious where/what the "homeland" is, or "whose security" is its focus. To locate the political of the biometric border is to look elsewhere; one obvious location is the airport. Although the experience of judging particular travelers as "trusted" and others as "risky," often materializes at the border, such practices are increasingly materializing at the biometric border, a site consistently not contiguous with the territorial border.

The politics of these discriminations have much to do with contemporary sovereign power—namely exceptional power. They also have much to do with biopower and what Hardt and Negri have called "biopolitical production," which is constitutive of the "multitude" and its differentiation from a typical "political body."[15] In this sense, the border becomes something of a site (like Clayoquot Sound) that signifies and symbolizes a host of discriminations, (dis)empowerments, and exceptions that are linked with much that lies beyond, above, beside, and at some distance from the border, consistently entangled with assemblages of sovereign (bio)power, corporate power on agenda setting, technological prowess, and the uncritical embrace of particular forms of surveillance society.

The analysis here begins with a rather brief review of the field of Critical Security Studies (CSS), and it appraises the value-added that it offers for the analysis forwarded here.[16] This field of critical scholarship prompts analysts to ask questions, probing "whose security?" and "what security?" In regard to the biometric border, we ask how the subject that comes to be known as the "trusted traveler" is constructed and/or performed. There exists a relatively rich literature on borders, although admittedly much of the most insightful, arguably even the most politically relevant, comes from outside of the discipline of political science.

Anthropological literature, which is at the very least ethnographically sensitive, has much to offer in terms of locating the material and cultural politics of borders. Most notably, much of this literature challenges unsophisticated understandings of borders vis-à-vis sovereignty, as simply limits, and therefore any notion of the border or bordering practices is not simply perceived in discourses of dangers, threats, and risks, beholden to tired geopolitical narratives, but open to borders as "borderlands," and the potential formation of "border identities."[17] Considering the theoretical and methodological innovations of CSS scholarship allows one to raise questions regarding the relationship between security and identity, which are issues integral to understanding the politics of the biometric border.

As the biometric border is a showpiece of "new" homeland security strategies, it is worth considering the extent to which the concept of homeland security itself calls into question the distinction between domestic and international/foreign, a differentiation so integral to specific narratives of world politics given by the field international relations theory. In this regard, not only are links between security and identity relevant to unpacking the puzzle of locating the politics of the biometric border, but specific observations about the relationship between identity and foreign policy are helpful.[18] The biometric border is another site where the deterritorial, extraterritorial, and "virtual" quality of borders in contemporary world politics is exposed.

Looking at issues of security and identity in the context of the biometric border, or more directly, simply asking what contemporary forms of being political look like at the biometric border, leads the analysis toward recent work on the "multitude." Most importantly, considering the subject(ivity) of/at the biometric border with the aid of Virno's brief text *A Grammar of the Multitude*, and Hardt and Negri's *Multitude*, inspiration is taken from the notion that the sort of politics and political being, or ways of being political, that we are concerned with here is the politics that emerges from what can be referred to as "styles of life."[19]

Defining Dangers, Going Shopping, and (Re)imagining "Whose Security?"

Throughout much of what can now presumably be referred to as the field of CSS,[20] scholarly literature considers seriously the extent to which the definition of danger is a subjective and powerful performative exercise. Securitization theory, which finds its origins in the Copenhagen School, has raised such concerns, as have many others whose work considers the relationship between security and identity.[21] Arguably one of the most significant contributions made by CSS is the contention that *security* is itself a contested concept.[22] Considering threats and dangers as subjective constructions and performances rather than objective facts, opens up critical debates about a host of supposedly "security-related" concerns, and most importantly, how issues find themselves within security's frame.

Doctrines of deterrence and mutually assured destruction, for example, are critically uncovered as contributing to insecurity rather than security; in essence, security is regarded as somewhat of an aporia.[23] To invoke discourses of security is to consistently remark on circumstances of insecurity; herein a persistent quest toward some perfected ideal of the former acts as the necessary condition for the ubiquity of the latter. Within such a frame, discourses of risk are particularly appropriate. In essence, it is to take Steve Smith's contention seriously that International Relations (IR) Theory tends to "sing the world into existence."[24]

Risks, dangers, threats, as subjectively constructed and performed, can be defined in terms of the individual rather than the state and its role in directing agendas.[25] The human security agenda, for example, attempts to make the field that is security / to be secured, rather wider than the conventional security frame of strategic studies, shifting the referent object of security away from the state toward the individual. The ways in which this has contributed to deeper complications in terms of an emerging security-development nexus and developments in the field of humanitarian intervention are worth noting, but are not the focus of discussion here. Instead, focusing on the question "whose security?" should prove productive when attempting to locate the politics and subject(ivities) of the biometric border, indeed even moving a step further than human security and considering a shift from a geopolitics of security with a referent object of territory toward a biopolitical one, with life itself becoming the referent object.[26]

Immediately following the events of September 11, 2001, George W. Bush set off, or at the very least contributed to, a politically useful but socially devastating discourse of fear.[27] In response to those catastrophic attacks, President Bush suggested that citizens should "go shopping." However, one should be careful not to underestimate the seemingly innocuous nature of Bush's proposition and realize, as some have, the close connection this has with security, defining dangers, and the rationality for subsequent imperial impositions. Most notably, the suggestion to "go shopping" is symbolic of the close connection between identity and foreign policy in the U.S. case. Given the preoccupation with a discourse of civilizations and barbarians, a liberal free-market and American-style consumptive capabilities/habits might also be perceived as further indications of "civilization."[28]

Foreign interventions, while arguably geopolitically relevant, in fact have much to do with a shift from geopolitical security to biopolitical security. Such contentions are made by David Campbell in his article "The Biopolitics of Security: Oil, Empire, and the Sports Utility Vehicle," which deserves sustained comment here.[29] Campbell's argument, which draws on his earlier work in *Writing Security* and its adept illustration of the relationship between identity and foreign policy through the case of the first Gulf War, has particular relevance for understanding the politics of the biometric border. His analysis helps to reframe questions of risk, insecurity, and most certainly the "unbordered" sense of the world, which appears so integral to dominant dilemmas associated with homeland security border-strategies. Furthermore, in terms of "risk," insecurity, and the contemporary politics of citizenship, Campbell's invocation of Michel Foucault's notions of "disciplinary society" and Gilles Deleuze's "societies of control" is particularly useful in this analysis.

According to Campbell, the "SUV symbolizes the need for the U[nited] S[tates] to maintain a global military reach."[30] Simply put, the consumptive habits of many Americans, specifically their dependence on mobility (primarily the linkage between social mobility and vehicular mobility is of specific interest here, given Virno, Hardt, and Negri's notion of the "multitude") and its role in American society, gives resources such as oil a particular social value, which is *biopolitical* rather than geopolitical.[31] In the spirit of much work in the field of CSS, Campbell considers the way in which threats and dangers are made existential, specifically contesting the way in which resource conflicts emphasize the "outside."[32] Astute to the problems of IR and its articulation of world politics, Campbell takes aim at the way in which the influences of internal factors on state identity are considered, while the external/outside is presumed fixed.

Jeremy Packer's analysis of the "auto-mobility," and/in the "war on terror" plays with this dominant articulation of inside/outside, stressing the extent to which "auto-mobility" is integral to the production of social life in America, but also "making bombs of us all."[33] Both Packer and Campbell's assertions draw on some of the deepest critiques of IR Theory and its dominant narrative of world politics. A critical reading of the caricatured story of sovereignty as the singularly elegant resolution of the universal and the particular, the pursuance of the good life inside (political theory) and the nasty, brutish condition of anarchy outside (IR Theory) is foundational to much of critical IR scholarship. The fundamental way in which this politics of inclusion and exclusion operates is seemingly recast at the politics of the biometric border, in so far as it fails to clearly follow the territorial lines of the sovereign state.

One's "risk factor" is only marginally a result of nationality, but often framed in terms of habits, purchasing patterns, consumptive capabilities, class, ethnicity, or what might be referred to by Virno as the politics that emerges from "styles of life." It also recasts the inside/outside problematique, in that the pursuit of the *good life* is perceived transnationally,[34] as is the barbaric brutality that threatens such pursuits. As contributors to this collection suggest—such as Lyon, Adey, and Fuller—the consumptive habits of the air traveler regularly seem to exceed any preoccupations with security, even informing the airport architecture itself.

The way in which Campbell unpacks identity is to highlight the linkages between identities *inside* with particular definitions of danger *outside*. Certainly the politics of the biometric border involves inclusions and exclusions that are sometimes territorially manifest, but also particular accounts of legitimacy and largely misunderstood articulations of identity. The decisionist exceptional powers of the sovereign, in a Schmittian sense, are relevant, whereas territorial Westphalian articulations of sovereign power seem to have far less purchase. An insightful way of unpacking this is through Campbell's discussion of the shift from geopolitics toward biopolitics, invoking Hardt and Negri's notion of "biopolitical production" and the associated concept of the "multitude."

According to Hardt and Negri: "In the postmodernization of the global economy, the creation of wealth tends ever more towards what we will call biopolitical production, the production of social life itself, in which economic, the political, and the cultural increasingly overlap and invest one another."[35] Herein lays a core portion of Campbell's argument and an important link with discussions of the biopolitical border. When looking at the biometric border and raising the question "whose security?" the extent to which the answer is not simply contiguous with conventional articulations of citizenship would seem obvious. For Campbell, the way in which the genealogy of the SUV, in terms of particular legal rulings and (re)categorizations, the consumptive habits of culture and society, and the integral role of notions of mobility in American culture—social and otherwise—plays into what he terms an "SUV model of citizenship" forwards an understanding of homeland security, specifically in terms of "whose security?" that is far more biopolitical than geopolitical.[36]

He highlights the way in which the danger and the insecurity might be particular biopoltical productions that have produced social life in a particular form. In Campbell's case, that form is the consumptive, automobile—specifically the SUV—obsessed "highway arms race"[37] inside America. In the context of Campbell's "highway arms race," the question of "whose security?" is revealing, to the extent that statistical data questions the safety of SUVs, while illuminating their lethal capacity in motor vehicle accidents.[38] The question of security is flipped on its head in Campbell's example, as the supposedly secure SUV is actually the purveyor and provider of insecurity. Directing attention toward the extent to which the SUV might be the most lethal, or certainly most prevalent, weapon of mass destruction dramatically re-articulates discourses of security/insecurity, us/them, and identity/security.

Moreover, it is the way in which it has come to be "biopolitically produced" as a part of social life itself that is significant. The story of the politics of the biometric border and the construction of the "trusted traveler" is a remarkably similar story of biopolitical production. Not only does Campbell's analysis represent a sound "Critical Security Studies" approach to understanding homeland security and the War on Terror, but it opens some important approaches to locating the politics of the biometric border. Critically engaging the attempt to render existential certain threats through securitizing discourses, Campbell highlights the close relationship between American identity and particular foreign policy objectives, in this case securing access to foreign oil resources. Through his analysis, Campbell exposes the extent to which this marks a shift from geopolitics to biopolitics. In the case of the biometric border, biopolitics are again rather more pertinent than geopolitics. As noted earlier, and will be revisited, the politics of the biometric border are regularly found far from the politics of the contiguous territorial border. Directing attention towards the extent to which the SUV might be the most lethal or certainly most prevalent WMD dramatically rearticulates discourses of security/insecurity, us/them, and identity/security. In terms of the politics of the biometric border, it would appear to be caught up in many more issues to do with biopolitical production, articulations/productions of social life, and the overlap between the social, the political, and the cultural vis-à-vis the accumulation of wealth and/in the global economy, as opposed to some outmoded geopolitical discourse, wherein the border indeed acts as a "limit"—specifically in territorial terms.

Trusted Travelers, Biometric Borders, Biopolitical Production

What or who qualifies to be a "trusted traveler"? Although the criterion for making such discriminations remains muddled, the extent to which the "trusted traveler" is directly produced/constructed by/through the biometric border is worth noting. Bennett's argument in this collection characterizes no-fly lists, and related trusted or registered traveler systems, as policy instruments directed at the identification and prevention/filtration of individuals who pose a potential (or perceived) risk to aviation. Certainly this analysis begs critical questions about the role of the state and private actors in such systems, as well as if and how such measures are deemed legitimate and effective. The analysis here considers such measures in terms of the wider consequences for contemporary citizenship, rearticulated and at times reduced forms of political action and agency, and a general recalibration of access and authorization in and by the state and private actors, reflecting substantively on altered state–society relations.

The performance of the *trusted* traveler is rather different than simply that of the traveler, in so far as the trusted are constituted through the surveillant gaze of technology, where one's inconspicuousness is prized above all else. Along similar lines, the U.S. no-fly list or Canada's euphemistically named "Passenger Protect" is a similarly produced subjectivity that is constituted at/by the borders of the digital state itself. In fact, at least in part, one's ability to access the space of the trusted traveler is governed by whether or not one volunteers to be digitized, to become part of the digital festival that enables privileged and hurried access to various spaces and places; an ever more attractive option as mistaken identities vis-à-vis passenger no-fly lists makes long lines at passenger prescreening checkpoints seem a trivial hindrance of contemporary air travel.

However, this comparatively unfettered access comes at a price: the monetary conditions will be addressed later, but certainly as important is one's submission to this digital reconstitution. As Lon Troyer has noted, when considering the relationship between the individual and the capture of the surveillance apparatus, one's performance is of particular relevance: "To stand out is to be at risk; to become undifferentiated from the mass of other lives translated into the binary language of electronic encoding becomes the goal in the age of Total Information Awareness."[39] There is of course a monetary aspect to such so-called trusted traveler schemes as well, which is relevant. However, a range of far broader and more troubling aspects of the trusted traveler and its performance/constitution at/by the biometric border deserves attention.

While questions of access, the criterion measuring the trustworthiness of the traveler, and so on, remain rather muddled, there are indeed programs or schemes that go by this precise name of "Registered Travelers." Interestingly, such schemes are almost wholly tied to the aviation industry, often piloted by individual private airlines or airports, and then subsumed or regulated by the plethora of regulatory bodies preoccupied with aviation security, such as the Transportation Security Administration (TSA) in the United States, or the Canadian Air Transport Security Authority in Canada.

Unsurprisingly as a part of the Department of Homeland Security (DHS), the TSA is beholden to the sort of preoccupations of the DHS. It has embarked on a pilot program for "Registered Travelers," and numerous airlines themselves have "trusted traveler" programs. In all cases, to enroll one must volunteer to have background checks of various ranges of intrusiveness and be issued a biometric ID, which requires the digitization of some physical and/or physiological characteristics. The background checks, which are necessary for obtaining a trusted traveler distinction, are paid for by the user.[40] In this sense, for those with the means and no fear of having their backgrounds examined, the experience of the biometric border is arguably more of a possibility than a limitation.

As is obvious, and noted by many, according to the TSA, "Registered Traveler" can improve airport security by allowing airport screeners to focus on passengers who have not chosen to enroll or cleared background checks.[41] In other words, it is those of us who have chosen not to become trusted travelers that will find ourselves confronting a more conventional border, in so far as it operates as a limit, while the biometric border is almost solely the space of the trusted traveler. This point is of particular importance in locating the politics of the biometric border, as the dramatic shift from the politics of the border appears ever more obvious.

Unlike the territorial border, where dangers, risks, and insecurities are to be thwarted, stopped, held off, and so on, the biometric border is a space of undifferentiated mass: the trusted traveler and the risky body. The ultimate site of biopolitical production, the biometric border is as much about the trustworthiness of the traveler as it is about the trusted traveler's trust in the state. The voluntary nature of one's participation in the biometric border, the extent to which one chooses (and pays for) a background check and a biometric ID, enables one to participate in the biometric border. In some sense, as the numbers of those at the biometric border increases, the severity of the border experienced by the untrusted travelers steadily rises.

The voluntary nature of trusted traveler programs also fit well within Foucault's notion of "disciplinary society" and Gilles Deleuze's "societies of control." Campbell notes that the extent to which Deleuze's formulation is radically different from Foucault's discussion of "governmentality" and the construction of "societies of security" might be relatively overemphasized, but the ideas contained within are of use here.[42] Campbell goes on to show how Hardt and Negri operationalize the difference between these concepts. It would seem, according to their account, that Deleuze's society of control is particularly cogent in terms of the character of trusted traveler programs. If indeed such societies of control involve, "mechanisms of command [that] become ever more democratic, ever more immanent to the social field, distributed throughout the brains and bodies of the citizens," then trusted traveler programs and the biometric border itself appear to fit the model rather well.[43] Rather than being framed in terms of the "undifferentiated mass" of the trusted travelers at the biometric border, where standing out becomes the risk, it is posed as a site of access, privilege and speed.

Following the sort of logic that homeland security places on the citizens to be terror warriors, voluntary enrollment in trusted traveler schemes makes the biometric border ever more comprehensive, and arguably increasingly robust. Hardt and Negri's point regarding the way in which economic, political, and the cultural overlap and invest in one another to produce social life itself are also worth noting here. In fact, for them, "class" is itself a biopolitical term insofar as it is both economic and political.[44] Along similar lines, Virno notes that "Biopolitics exists wherever that which pertains to the potential dimension of human existence comes into the forefront, into immediate experience; not the spoken word but the capacity of speech. As such, not the labor which has actually been completed but the generic capability of producing."[45] As William Bogard contends, biopolitical production is the "creative energy" of Hardt and Negri's *Multitude*.[46] Here, and for Virno, the extent to which both the consumptive and productive *capacity* of contemporary human existence emerges as vital is of particular relevance to the sort of (political) subjectivity that materializes in the space of the airport and/or the biometric border.

As Henry Giroux has noted: "Biopolitics now touches all aspects of social life and is the primary political and pedagogical force through which the creation and recreation of subjectivities takes place."[47] Drawing on this, he poses a "politics of disposability," which is a specifically contemporary expression of biopower and biopolitics that is "marked by a clean visual and social landscape in which the poor, the elderly, the infirm, and criminalized populations share a common fate of disappearing from public view."[48] The politics of the airport appears a space/place *par excellence* of this contemporary biopolitical form. As this collection attests, the politics of/at the airport, though cloaked in the discourse of the "war on terror" and related risks, dangers and insecurities, tends to take shape along the lines of more stable and long-standing trends associated with market imperatives, capital flows, social sorting, and related aesthetics. Following from Giroux's account of the politics of disposability and the contemporary productive capacity of biopolitics, the trusted traveler is a constitutive aspect of the airport's aesthetic, while all others "disappear."

Multitudes at the Biometric Border?

What forms of politics and political subjectivity emerge from/in the politics of/at the airport? *Politics at the Airport* seeks to address such concerns from a variety of disciplinary, theoretical, and methodological perspectives. However, in spite of this eclecticism, the shared understandings and preoccupations that emerge are remarkable. The intricate interrelationship among market forces, architectural visions, securitizations, and identity formations that emerge from this complex politics of/at the airport are apparent throughout this collection. Preoccupations with technological approaches to social sorting and the deeper (im)possibilities such practices signify for understanding the political and accompanying forms of subjectivity rapidly emerge as integral issues in understanding politics and political subjectivity in the contemporary epoch of biopower, biopolitical production, and even Giroux's politics of disposability.

Akin to Foucault's notion of the *dispositif*, or Deleuze and Guattari's *assemblage*, the analysis here has made attempts to articulate the form(s) of political subjectivity that come to be at the biometric border, or are indeed mutually constitutive of/at this border. The architectural space of the airport, the socioeconomic flows therein, and the exercise of sovereign power through the "virtual border" that is manifest at the biometric border are integral to this story. Traditional understandings of citizenship as the chief form of sovereign subjectivity, articulated as a collection of rights and responsibilities, are at the very least called into question at this site. Hardt and Negri's "multitude" may or may not hold promise here, but in some capacity it enables a richer (re)conceptualization of what sort of political being or being political is possible at the biometric border.

Though the constitution of the "multitude" for Hardt and Negri is based on what is common as opposed to identity or unity, this contemporary reformulation of class consciousness and the subsequent "rule of everyone by everyone"[49] may underestimate the very same capacities among the rather more nefarious promulgators of "empire." Although the requisite passport is a must, reflections on what Virno calls "styles of life" seems sensible in terms of the specific experience of/at the biometric border. Nationality is required—no more, no less, however, than the productive and consumptive capacity of the subject. The emancipatory potential of the multitude raised by Hardt and Negri might indeed be no match for Giroux's politics of disposability. While somewhat less than the death-drive biopolitics of Giorgio Agamben's political vision,[50] the trusted traveler lounge in contemporary airports seems less like Auschwitz and more like classical Athens.

In thinking about the politics of/at the biometric border, this analysis has strained to conceptualize the sort of subjectivity that comes to be in/at this site and the performance/constitution of that subject. It has suggested the discriminatory practices of contemporary sovereign (bio)power are critical. Articulations of insecurity, risk, and danger are recast in ways far more akin to one's proximity to the sort of "biopolitical production" raised by Hardt and Negri that stresses the productive capacity of contemporary biopolitics than the typical territorial tropes of sovereign power.

Risk is reframed as standing out among the homologous mass of digital data; insecurity is the betrayal of one's digital flesh; danger becomes articulated as those outside the biometric border—not outside the border proper, if it even makes sense to refer to such an artifact. This move allows the insecurity/danger to be rendered existential, while simultaneously articulating possible risks as inside the territorial boundaries of the state. It is at once beholden to the existential trick of securitization where danger is always externalized, while accepting the unbordering move of homeland security, as the homeland is defined as both here and there, as is its alternative.

Notes

I wish to thank the participants in the "Governing by Risk in the War on Terror" workshop held at the International Studies Association meeting in San Diego, on March 21, 2006, and especially Louise Amoore and Marieke de Goede for organizing the workshop. Additional thanks for constructive comments go specifically to Wendy Larner, Charlotte Epstein, William Walters, and Jonathan Simon. I also wish to thank Michael Dillon for his insight when this chapter was originally presented as a paper at a panel discussion at the ISA 2006 meeting. Also, special thanks go to Mark Salter for his regular comments and insights into this analysis, as well as his hard work in making this project come to fruition. For funding and intellectual enrichment that helped to bring these scholars together with practitioners as a part of the Canadian Aviation Security Conference, in addition to Mark Salter, thanks go to David Lyon and the Surveillance Project and the Globalization of Personal Data Project, Queen's University, Kingston, Ontario.

1. See Richard Preston, *The Hot Zone: A Terrifying True Story* (New York: Anchor, 1995).
2. On the extent to which "9/11" has gained discursive power well beyond the simple symbolic signification of the date September 11, 2001, see Richard Jackson, *Writing the War on Terrorism: Language, Politics, and Counter-terrorism* (New York: Manchester University Press, 2005).
3. Roxanne Lynn Doty, *Imperial Encounters: The Politics of Representation in North-South Relations* (Minneapolis: University of Minnesota Press, 1996).
4. Jean Raspail, *The Camp of the Saints* (Petoskey, Mich.: Social Contract Press, 1995), 43.
5. Mark Duffield, *Global Governance and the New Wars: The Merging of Development and Security* (London: Zone Books, 2002).
6. Walter Benjamin, "Theses on the Philosophy of History," in *Illuminations*, ed. Hannah Arendt, trans. Harry Zohn (New York: Schocken Books, 1969), 256.
7. For further discussion of "body-identity-file-profile," see Mark B. Salter, "At the Threshold of Security: A Theory of International Borders," in *Global Surveillance and Policing: Borders, Identity, Security*, ed. Elia Zureik and Mark B. Salter (Cullompton, UK: Willan, 2005), 47.
8. For insightful examinations of such issues, see Debbie Lisle, "Gazing at Ground Zero: Tourism, Voyeurism, and Spectacle," *Journal of Cultural Research* 18, no. 1 (January 2004): 3–21; Lisle, "Site Specific Medi(t)ations at the Airport," in *Rituals of Mediation*, ed. Cynthia Weber and Francois Debrix (Minneapolis: University of Minnesota Press, 2003), 3–29.
9. See Michael Hardt and Antonio Negri, *Multitude: War and Democracy in the Age of Empire* (New York: Penguin, 2004); and Paolo Virno, *A Grammar of the Multitude: For an Analysis of Contemporary Forms of Life* (New York: Semiotext[e], 2004).
10. T. H. Marshall, *Citizenship and Social Class and Other Essays* (Cambridge: Cambridge University Press, 1950).

11. On sovereignty and the political imagination, among others, see R. B. J. Walker, *Inside/outside: International Relations as Political Theory* (Cambridge: Cambridge University Press, 1993); Jens Bartelson, *A Genealogy of Sovereignty* (Cambridge: Cambridge University Press, 1995).

12. Giorgio Agamben, *Homo Sacer: Sovereign Power and Bare Life*, trans. Daniel Heller-Raozan (Stanford, Calif.: Stanford University Press, 1998), 131.

13. See Warren Magnusson and Karena Shaw, eds., *A Political Space: Reading the Global in Clayoquot Sound* (Minneapolis: University of Minnesota Press, 2002); also see Simon Dalby, "Political Space: Autonomy, Liberalism, and Empire," *Alternatives: Global, Local, Political* 30, no. 4 (October–December 2005): 429.

14. Walker, "They Seek It Here, They Seek It There: Locating the Political in Clayoquot Sound," in *A Political Space: Reading the Global in Clayoquot Sound*, ed. Warren Magnusson and Karena Shaw (Minneapolis: University of Minnesota Press, 2002), 237–62.

15. Hardt and Negri, *Multitude*.

16. C.A.S.E. Collective, "Critical Approaches to Security in Europe: A Networked Manifesto," *Security Dialogue* 37, no. 4 (2006): 443–87.

17. For insightful accounts of borders from anthropology, see Hastings Donnan and Thomas M. Wilson, *Borders: Frontiers of Identity, Nation, and State* (Oxford: BERG Press, 1999); Wilson and Donnan, eds., *Border Identities: Nation and State at International Frontiers* (Cambridge: Cambridge University Press, 1998). For a reasonably astute analysis of borders in international relations, see Mathias Albert, David Jacobson, and Yosef Lapid, eds., *Identities, Borders, Orders: Rethinking International Relations Theory* (Minneapolis: University of Minnesota Press, 2001). Also see William Walters, "Mapping Schengenland: Denaturalizing the Border," *Environment and Planning D: Society and Space* 20, no. 5 (2002): 561–80; Walters, "The Frontiers of the European Union: A Geostrategic Perspective," *Geopolitics* 9, no. 3 (2004): 674–98.

18. See David Campbell, *Writing Security: United States Foreign Policy and the Politics of Identity* (Minneapolis: University of Minnesota Press, 1992); Campbell, "The Biopolitics of Security: Oil, Empire, and the Sports Utility Vehicle," *American Quarterly* 57, no. 3 (September 2005): 943–72.

19. For a particularly prescient examination of the "multitude," see Stuart J. Murray, "The Rhetorics of Life and Multitude in Michel Foucault and Paolo Virno," *CTheory.net* September 13, 2005, http://www.ctheory.net (accessed September 22, 2005).

20. As the literature in this field is now well into its second decade, replete with textbooks, edited collections, and outlines of the field, it would seem appropriate to refer to it as a subfield within the discipline of international relations. Among many others, see Keith Krause and Michael Williams, eds., *Critical Security Studies* (Minneapolis: University of Minnesota Press, 1997); Ken Booth, ed., *Critical Security Studies and World Politics* (Boulder, Colo.: Lynne Rienner, 2005); Karin Fierke, *Critical Approaches to International Security* (London: Polity, 2007).

21. Campbell, *Writing Security*.

22. See Dalby, "Contesting an Essential Concept: Reading the Dilemmas in Contemporary Security Discourse," in *Critical Security Studies: Concepts and Cases*, ed. Keith Krause and Michael C. Williams (Minneapolis: University of Minnesota Press, 1997), 3–32.

23. Anthony Burke, "Aporias of Security," *Alternatives: Global, Local, Political* 27, no. 1 (January–March 2002): 1–28.

24. Steve Smith, "Singing Our World into Existence: International Relations Theory and September 11," *International Studies Quarterly* 48, no. 3 (2004): 499–515.

25. Salter, "Risk and Imagination in the War on Terror," in *Risk in the War on Terror*, ed. Louise Amoore and Marieke de Goede (London: Routledge, 2008); Salter, "Imagining Numbers: Risk, Quantification, and Aviation Security," *Security Dialogue* 39, no. 2 (2008): 243–66. Also see Claudia Aradau and Rens van Munster, "Governing Terrorism through Risk: Taking Precautions, (Un)knowing the Future," *European Journal of International Relations* 13, no. 1 (2007): 89–115.

26. See Michael Dillon, "Governing Terror: The State of Emergency of Biopolitical Emergence," *International Political Sociology* 1, no. 1 (2007): 7–28. Also see Benjamin J. Muller, "Securing the Political Imagination: Subjectivity, Security, and the Biometric Risk State," *Security Dialogue* 39, no. 2 (June 2008): 199–220.

27. See Benjamin Barber, *Fear's Empire: War, Terrorism, and Democracy* (New York: W. W. Norton, 2004). Also see *Hijacking Catastrophe: 9/11, Fear & the Selling of American Empire*, DVD (The Media Education Foundation, 2004); Jackson, *Writing the War on Terrorism*. On the relationship between economy and security, also see *Why We Fight*, dir. Eugene Jarecki (Sony Classics, 2005).

28. For particular insight on the role of the civilization and barbarian discourse in the politics of the war on terror, see Salter, "Not Waiting for the Barbarians," in *Civilizational Identity: The Production and Reproduction of 'Civilizations' in International Relations*, ed. Patrick T. Jackson and Martin Hall (New York: Palgrave, 2008), 129–46.

29. Campbell, "The Biopolitics of Security."

30. Ibid., 944.

31. Ibid., 966.

32. Ibid., 946. In contrast to and conjunction with Campbell's argument, it is worth considering Jeremy Packer's argument on automobility and securitizations.

33. Jeremy Packer, "Becoming Bombs: Mobilizing Mobility in the War on Terror," *Cultural Studies* 20, no. 4 (2006): 378–99.

34. It is relevant to note that the subtitle to Paolo Virno's *A Grammar of the Multitude* is "An Analysis of Contemporary Forms of Life."

35. Hardt and Negri, *Empire* (Cambridge, Mass.: Harvard University Press, 2002), xiii.

36. Campbell, "The Biopolitics of Security," 951.

37. Ibid., 964.

38. Drawing on statistical information, Campbell points out that when involved in accidents with other automobiles, SUVs often cause large amounts of damage, and rates of death are higher among those who have accidents with SUVs

than those with other vehicles. However, Campbell also notes that in any motor-vehicle accident, the SUVs propensity to flip over due to a high center of gravity leads to higher fatality rates among SUV drivers than drivers of other automobiles.

39. Lon Troyer, "Counterterrorism: Sovereignty, Law, Subjectivity," *Critical Asian Studies* 35, no. 2 (2003): 271.

40. Thomas Frank, "Fees to Fuel 'Trusted Traveler' Program," *USA Today*, October 10, 2005.

41. Ibid. See the Transportation Security Administration Web site, http://www .tsa.gov/public/index.jsp.

42. Campbell, "The Biopolitics of Security," n19.

43. Hardt and Negri, *Empire*, 23.

44. Hardt and Negri, *Multitude*, 105.

45. Virno, *A Grammar of the Multitude*, 84.

46. William Bogard, "Surveillance Assemblages and Lines of Flight," in *Theorizing Surveillance: The Panopticon and Beyond*, ed. David Lyon (Cullompton, UK: Willan, 2006), 117–18.

47. Henry A. Giroux, *Stormy Weather: Katrina and the Politics of Disposability* (Boulder, Colo.: Paradigm, 2006), 16.

48. Ibid., 23.

49. Hardt and Negri, *Multitude*, 100.

50. Agamben, *Homo Sacer*.

7

MOBILITIES AND MODULATIONS

The Airport as a Difference Machine

....

Peter Adey

As opposed to a mere gateway or a doorway, or a warehouse that simply shelters passengers from the elements, we know that airports must do something to movement. Similar to the transformers that convert electricity for transportation over high-voltage power lines, to the step-down transformer that converts it into a more manageable format for your home, the airport transforms or modulates mobility from the ground to the air and vice versa into manageable modes of movement. Essentially the airport is a locus of numerous horizons, thresholds through which we must pass and become changed as we do.[1]

More often than not, this process of modulation is one of disassembly and reassembly. Airports seek to extricate from the passenger all that must be tested and surveilled. As opposed to an atomized individual, passengers are prosthetic subjects, made up of bodies, bags, trinkets, handbags, wallets, keys, and more.[2] These objects are separated out; the prosthetic subject is disassembled into various *vectors* of flow that pass through the airport in different ways.[3] Gillian Fuller and Ross Harley argue that "the airport not only transforms a body on the ground into a body in the air, but it also involves the incorporeal transformation of the travelling body into a series of processing categories, like citizen, passenger, baggage allowance, threat."[4]

Before one arrives at an airport, she/he has most likely submitted information about her/himself: her/his history and her/his travel plans. Although we must be careful not to overemphasize the notion of the "data-double," flows of information *must* be taken from us to permit our travel.[5] This separation allows the processes of preemption and calculation. Airlines will logistically deal with us as passengers and, in some instances, permit various government and security agencies to assess our risk. Without this disassembly we cannot pass.

Once we arrive at the terminal, people traveling to airports by private car, taxi, bus, coach, bike, or by their own two legs (although this is very unlikely) are converted into other configurations. The elements that come with us are separated, channeled away, or refused entry. Passengers are turned into a pedestrian configuration, and once they have checked in, they only have the clothes on their backs, hopefully their passport and tickets, and a few carry on items (perhaps minus a nail file or a pair of scissors). These mobilities are circulated, analyzed, and processed before being spat out to distant or not-so-distant destinations. Upon arrival they are reunited with hand luggage, checked baggage, and remodulated into a form permissible for road, bus, train, or future air travel.

In recent scholarship, airports have been described as incredible identifiers. Symbols of the securitization of public space, airports employ the latest surveillance techniques in order to identify and target terrorists, threats, or risks. In this chapter I suggest that airports do not just identify difference for they are not merely passive identifiers—a supposition commonly leveled at technologies of surveillance. I follow David Lyon's proposition that the critical concern with surveillance since September 11, 2001, is not necessarily the intrusion of government into our private lives or the threat to our privacy in general; Lyon continues, "This is why the common promotional refrain, 'if you have nothing to hide, you have nothing to fear' is so vacuous. Categorical suspicion has consequences for anyone, 'innocent' or 'guilty' caught in its gaze."[6] In continuing the efforts of surveillance theorists to explore the active participation of surveillance in determining people's life chances, I turn these concerns to the airport terminal. I argue that airports actually work to *make* these differences by sorting passengers into different modalities. Moreover, I argue that these differences are not created by accident, but rather they must be attributed to the imperatives of the airport political-economy and security nexus.

This chapter furthers efforts to understand airports as filters. It has been argued that the contemporary surveillance and security machine acts as a mesh or sieve that sorts wanted from unwanted and trusted from distrusted identities.[7] Similarly, David Wood and Stephen Graham posit airports as permeable boundaries that act as open gateways to some people and as barriers to others.[8] Michel Foucault describes the naval hospital in just such a way. He writes, "The naval hospital must therefore treat, but in order to do this it must be a filter, a mechanism that pins down and partitions; it must provide a hold over this whole mobile, swarming mass, by dissipating the confusion of illegality and evil."[9] Categories, records, charts permitted the hospital to make the swarming mass legible. Similarly, Paul Virilio describes the gateways of the city as filtering devices to control the "migrating hordes."[10]

While incredibly useful, such accounts seem to resemble a body of work that treats the airport as merely a node on a transport network.[11] The effect is that the airport is rendered immaterial by the metaphorical abstraction of the filter—constituted by software and informational systems. I will address Mark Salter's charge to engage with the corporeality of the border, a micropolitics of the real physical architecture of the airport within which people spend long hours and make arduous journeys.[12] Furthermore, while considering the very flesh of the airport, we must not forget the corporeal body that inhabits it. In turning our attention toward the physical, the hard, and the visceral airport, we must attend to the sensing and fleshy bodies that move through and feel it. As geographers Alan Latham and Derek McCormack put forward, in attending the material and the corporeal, we must similarly examine the immaterial; the incorporeal dimensions of material experience.[13] The chapter goes on to examine the affective, felt, and emotional modalities of airport passage.

To get within the airport and consider its intimate scale and physicality, however, also requires moving beyond the kinds of political and economic forces that inflect the wider flows in and out of the airport. Recent scholarship has argued that borders and airports are the meeting points of social systems; they "function as spatial mediators of often latent power and governance discourses."[14] I am not trying to argue that the governance of mobility by immigration controls and quotas, visa systems, and more do not have important ramifications for the way in which airports are inhabited. On the contrary, I want to push the notion that these wider imperatives intersect with other and more localized concerns. For example, an airport's operational efficiency or the pervasive issues of consumer spending play important roles in shaping how and why airports are run. In this chapter I explore the interplay between wider, more extensive issues of security and surveillance, and the more localized concerns of airport's consumerist political-economy.

Containment

The airport terminal itself is striated by various impediments designed to shape and control movement. This is reflective of the wider airport functionality of a "machine for capturing and controlling flows in the most literal manner imaginable."[15] Indeed, David Pascoe finds that airports are now marked by the logic of "containment" and "circulation."[16] Today's security climate insists that airports must act as sieves to discern wanted from unwanted flows and high- and low-risk identities, and they work to filter movement further along the logic of controling corporeal passenger flows. Barriers, walls, and bollards create less of a chaotic scenario (depending on the airport you are in!) and more of a permeable space through which passengers are fed. The idea is to change people's movement, to make them move where the authorities want them to go.

One particular way that airports filter movement is for the purposes of consumption. Deregulation, cut-throat competition between airlines, the advent of "low-cost" carriers, airport privatization—all of these factors have increased the importance of nonaeronautical revenues to the airport business.[17] Richard De Neufville describes how by the 1980s airports were using "these revenues to underwrite the cost of runways and related facilities."[18] According to the statistics he presented in 1980, even then, concessionary revenue as a percentage of total airport income ranged from 35 percent for Mexico City to 69 percent for Washington/National. The ubiquitous presence of concessionaries was becoming vitally important to the health of the airport.

The increasing importance of these revenues has had a marked impact on the way passengers are expected to move and inhabit the airport. Aviation expert Rigas Doganis explains the difference between traditional-style airports and more recent developments in design. Doganis states, "In the traditional model the terminal is organized to move passengers through to a boarding gate or lounge with simple and direct flows with little conflict or interruption."[19] Thus, earlier airport designs espoused notions of speed and efficiency in passenger processes. Although pre-1980s airports contained nonaeronautical facilities, at that time airports thrived on being social and local rendezvous for plane spotting and air shows.[20] Often airports had to filter out passengers in order to allow them access to these activities.[21]

Doganis notes, "shops and catering, if any on the landside require a detour and an effort by the passenger to leave the normal flow routes. . . . It is quite possible to walk from the entry doors of some terminals to the aircraft without directly passing by a shop, a service counter or a catering outlet."[22] In the earlier noncommercial airport terminals, shops and retail areas were constructed as afterthoughts to the primary movement of passengers and they were not seen as essential components to the processing of passengers through the building. In this way, the terminals functioned as facilitators of movement; they acted as tunnels or passageways that created clear and free-flowing routes to the aircraft.[23] Balconies, refreshment areas, and restaurants were separated from the main passenger flows. A good terminal was one that distributed passengers to their flights with ease.

However, more recent airport designs have sought to do quite the opposite. Their purpose is less about facilitation than about disruption to the passengers' journeys.[24] Often passengers are directed around shops, cafés, and other concessionaries. Active and passive layouts serve to shape inhabitant's paths of movement. According to Paul Freathy and Frank O'Connell, airport shops must create layouts that are proactive in their influence upon passenger mobility, "In the airport retail environment where time is so important . . . layouts need to manoeuvre or steer the customer to as many merchandise sectors as possible, in particular those with the higher margins."[25]

However, it is important that these new layouts are not *felt* in a disruptive way or become an annoyance. Doganis explains that the changing layout of airports and retail facilities has attempted to make a passenger's movement through the space as natural and as easy as possible, if not as necessary: "The commercially driven airport attempts to direct passengers through the commercial activity areas as a necessary route through the terminal to the aircraft. The principle is to avoid the psychological and physical separation between airport processing time and shopping/refreshment time."[26] Thus, commercial and retail facilities are placed on the primary routes between check-in desk and aircraft.

These kinds of filtering and shaping structures are repeated in the micro-geographies of the airport shop or concessionary. Freathy and O'Connell illustrate the common "snake" and "pinball" layouts. The snake layout works by creating one entryway and an exit. In doing this, the customer "has no choice but to follow the route provided or go back to the entrance."[27] The shop effectively controls passenger movement by forcing the passenger to walk past all the merchandise offered in the shop, increasing the chance of impulse purchases. The passenger is "brought up" to an area and "drawn" though processing' a common word among airport staff is to also "drive" passengers through the terminal. This language of control echoes the way terminal buildings are expected to function. The architecture is intended to literally lead the passengers through the terminal building because of the limitations and capacities forced upon them. Similar to a shopping mall, "the relative permeability of structures" physically limits "the possibility of movement and interaction."[28]

The very same techniques are applied to the security spaces of the airport. Fairly flexible infrastructures line the security areas creating material affordances that shape passenger mobility. The overall layout of the airport creates a pinch point—the physical exultation of the filter that routes most passenger pathways through this site. Within these spaces, lines on the floor, temporary barriers, and other objects work to contain and move passengers along in an orderly way through security. In essence, many airport terminals may resemble exhibition halls, where temporary walls and barriers are placed around the space in order to striate and segment movement. This physical entrainment of movement, however, is supplemented by a social one. Attempting to cross lanes or move the barriers is forbidden. Temporary barriers and airport security staff lead passengers into usually double or single file lines, which are processed by the combination of technologies and personnel.

We might understand this form of airport modulation through Gilles Deleuze and Félix Guattari's description of state power. The aim, of course, is not to necessarily imprison passenger movement but to create "fixed paths in well defined directions, which restrict speed, regulate circulation."[29] Such paths productively regulate passenger mobility so as to smooth the procedures of operational and security processing, or to create exposure to airport consumption.

Incorporeality

The previous section examined the filtering of mobility through its containment and restriction of circulation. But this is not the only process of modulation. For Gillian Fuller, modalities of airport movement are transformed in ways other than constriction. She writes, "this partitioning does occur, but not through traditional modes of confinement (the erecting of barriers and walls). Instead it operates through the patterning of modalities into different streams controlled at various thresholds. . . . We are no longer managed through confinement."[30] In this section, I explore how feelings, sensations, and emotions are sorted out and filtered by the airport. I suggest that particular modes of feeling are limited and curtailed in an attempt to both profit from passengers while also making them be, and feel, more secure.

For Gary T. Marx, borders, like airports, seem not only to construct mobility but also to work to contain, pacify, and amplify the senses: "Many forms of surveillance as border crossing tools and border enhancement tools rely on extending or constricting the senses."[31] For Marx, borders, such as airports, try to channel sensory stimuli; they "often aim at limiting or strengthening sense data" in order to construct specific feelings and emotions.[32] As Debbie Lisle asks us to look beyond the personal experiences that have so often been written about airports, such as "loss, hope, anxiety, joy, adventure, homecoming, and fear," I think we need to understand how these intimate experiences are sometimes intended, engineered, and predicted by the airport authorities.[33] And so we might note that while Marc Augé, Manuel Castells, and others are quick to muse over the airport's feeling of placelessness and transience, they lack a consideration of just *why* these feelings are produced and in whose interests they are produced.[34]

Again, the management of how an airport *feels* is of course not new. Modernist architects of the 1930s, 1940s, and 1950s, influenced by Le Corbusier, wanted to create feelings of drama—an increased connection with the theatricality of flight would see airport buildings disappear into an overexposed space of glass.[35] Architects wanted airports to awaken and not sedate the passenger to the pleasures and sensations of air travel.[36] However, changing structures of financing and regulation have altered the supervision of this register.

For example, some airport designers are using techniques that attempt to engineer specific sensations and emotions in order to motivate particular kinds of behavior, enacting what Nigel Thrift might call a "spatial politics of affect."[37] Airports are obviously noted for the kaleidoscope of emotions that are felt and expressed in them. For Charles Hackelsberger, airports are sites of euphoria as well as relaxation, panic as well as loneliness; one is only ever "a few steps aside from the streams of humanity, the pain of leaving, the joy of arriving, as well as boredom and ill-humour. Airports without people are like an empty stage."[38] Narrowing down this array of emotions and feelings is an increasingly important objective for some airports.

The most obvious to be found are those that attempt to encourage passengers to spend money. In particular, airport designers want to lull passengers into a state of mind so that they might part with their disposable income. One particular way of doing this is by designing atmospheric and architectural triggers that allow "the drama and expressive possibilities of the major public terminal spaces to be exploited."[39] The strategy of theming many terminals with fantastic and imaginative landscapes or reminders to the vernacular has been designed to whip passengers into a spending frenzy, creating what airport retailers have described as "compulsive consumption zones" and "I want" environments.[40] Similarly, according to John Rowley and Francis Slack, the seeming placelessness and timelessness of airports stimulates consumer spending.[41]

As I mentioned earlier, the disassembly of the passenger-prosthetic subject facilitates this process in a way that strips down and opens up the passenger body to the airport's wishes. Airports have discovered that passengers are more likely to spend money in the airport if they are not laden down with luggage. The airport is understood as a differentiated landscape of intensity. The earlier a passenger may relieve him- or herself of such a burden, the sooner their stress levels are seen to lower, and the more willing they will be to enjoy the facilities. Augé comments that this can resemble a form of lib-eration: "As soon as his passport or identity card has been checked, the pas-senger for the next flight, freed from the weight of his luggage and everyday responsibilities, rushes into the 'duty-free' space; not so much, perhaps in order to buy at the best prices as to experience the reality of his momentary availability."[42] Passengers without luggage are more able to negotiate the sometimes narrow shopping outlets and corridors.

Of course, this does not always work. Airports can be extremely stress-ful places, especially if they are difficult to navigate. For other airport oper-ators, the onus has become less one about stimulating excitement and more about triggering particularly calm and soothing emotions within the passen-ger. According to one proponent, the airport shopping environment is able to remodulate passengers from a stressful, anxious, and panicked state into a more relaxed mood susceptible to consumer temptation. "They've been queued, corralled and herded from one process to another, just like their baggage. And then it's highly likely that they'll queue again at the boarding gate. Retailing is not about process, it's about emotion. Our shops are the one place, the one place, where we can make them feel human again where they can have a one-to-one experience, where their individuality is recog-nised and catered for. We can offer retail therapy in the truest possible sense."[43] In this instance, the disassembled passenger can be reunited with consumer products, enabling them to be whole once more.

In other airports, architects have used quite utilitarian and modernistic forms of design in order to communicate power. Such designs are intended to tell passengers that they are being watched and that everything is under control. It could be argued that the purpose of airport security has become as much about making people *feel* safe, as opposed to actually making them safer. Dallas–Fort Worth, for example, has taken this philosophy to task by employing a few hundred helpers to inspire passenger confidence and a more pleasurable security experience.[44]

Such feelings of safety and being under control can also ensure the air-port's wishes of acquiescence and subjection. Starkly designed environments consisting of blank, bland walls and low ceiling heights, without ornament or design, are meant to not only be seen but also felt in a way that will stop passengers from panicking or getting angry and becoming aggressive. Narrowly constructed corridor-like spaces are supposedly articulated through a tapering and constriction of the possibilities of emotional expres-sion. Such emotional states will in-turn affect passengers' *approaches* or ori-entations toward certain kinds of behavior.[45]

Having said that, there are no hard-and-fast rules here. For the modu-lation resonates affectively into an amplification and a magnification of the emotions that the airport may want to contain. John Zukowsky describes the emotional expression of the introduction of security "choke points" in the 1970s.[46] He writes how the security spaces of the "choke point" initiated short tempers and bodily irritability; "moments of departure anxiety were aggravated by the sense of being funneled up another chute like a herd of cattle."[47]

Thus, Salter indicates that some airports are employing design schemes to destress and relax passengers by using natural materials.[48] Seoul's Incheon airport, for example, has installed granite surfaces to enclose three sides of the security area. On the other sides exist, "wood panelling and soothing colors, designed to lower stress levels."[49] It is hoped that the entrainment and constriction of certain moods may be expressed in passenger behavior of an orderly and disciplined manner of compliance. As David Pascoe argues, "individuals need constantly to be pacified, the flow of their progress from check-in to take-off continuously smoothed."[50]

A Politics of Modality

In my final example, I explore how airport mobilities are filtered out from one another by a politics of differential speed and emotion.[51] Let us take the recently introduced opt-in trusted or registered traveler schemes that facilitate the bypassing of security.[52] Within such schemes passengers are encouraged to produce more information about themselves in order to prove that they pose less of a threat and, thus, do not require further and repeated examination.

Similar to the U.S. Immigration Naturalization Service Passenger Accelerated Service System (INSPASS), which has been in place for the last decade, Canada's NEXUS Air works on the premise of prescreening and pre-approving passengers so that they may proceed through airport processing with "little or no delay." Upon entry to the United States or Canada, the passenger may bypass the lanes that ordinary travelers must wait in as NEXUS Air passengers are fed to the automated Kiosks in the Federal Inspection Services area (U.S. preclearance), or the Canadian Inspection Services area.[53] Not only are NEXUS passengers spatially sorted from others through these systems, but they also experience automated questioning. Likewise, the "registered traveler" pilot scheme, which operates in the United States, is designed to prescreen travelers already enrolled in the system so that when they reach the airport of departure they may experience reduced and less-stringent scrutiny and searches.

The point of these systems is a physical and immediate one—that is, they are meant to produce a faster, more comfortable, and speedier service for those who are deemed to be less of a risk than others and can afford it. The filter is not about who leaves the airport and who does not but rather how different people may experience differential passage and treatment throughout the space. The schemes produce narratives, such as the story of Bill Connors, one of the first passengers to be enrolled in the schemes. According to one report, Connors

> lived out a business traveler's fantasy one March morning. When he got to Ronald Reagan Washington National Airport, he marched past fifty people waiting in a security line. Slipping into a special lane, Connors approached a machine resembling a kiosk. He peered into a glass surface the size of a salad plate. Almost instantly, the machine's computer scanned the unique patterns in Connors' left iris and verified his identity. Connors stepped to the front of the security line and through the metal detector.[54]

Discourses surrounding these sorts of schemes emphasise speed. Headlines such as passengers "whip" through security and "shorter waits for passengers" pervade the press and corporate journals. The system is meant to function with the same speed and efficiency of using a credit card. Reports state, "Just as credit cards are accepted once issued at most businesses around the country, if you signed up as a Registered Traveler in Washington, D.C., you ought to be recognized as a Registered Traveler in Minneapolis or any other airport around the country."[55] The system is meant to provide the possibility of a two-tier system of security that reduces the "hassle factor."

But it is important that we understand the filtering mechanism of these systems in terms of how they modulate mobility, emotion, and furthermore, the relationality of these modalities. We can see this figuratively in the kinds of messages the schemes project in order to tempt people to use them. For example, the illustration that I used earlier ended with Bill being watched with envy by other passengers. When asked what it was all about, Connors replied, "I'm a Registered Traveler. They were all like, 'Well, how do you get that?'"[56]

The history of flight has, of course, been a history of difference and class inequality; flight being an activity for the privileged and the elite.[57] Therefore, perhaps we shouldn't be too surprised to learn that these schemes are dependent upon the imaginary construction of difference between registered and nonregistered, as well as a real one. Crispin Thurman and Adam Jaworski's study on the symbolic capital and stylization of frequent-flier schemes states that "there can be no 'special,' 'exclusive,' 'advantaged' or 'privileged' unless one is (made) conscious of the common, the ordinary, the needy, the dispossessed."[58] For them the schemes do not just give greater mobility but also the feeling and the promise of "global citizenship." The systems are marketed in a way that customers aspire to be given "a kind of diplomatic status awarded to 'globals' and marked by ease of passage and freedom of movement."[59] It is in this sense that the registered traveler programs are sold on the separation they give between their members and nonmembers. The schemes reward their customers with a real and an imaginary mobility—a feeling and sensation of difference and privilege. Thus, we might come to the conclusion that such systems work on the principle of what Zygmunt Bauman describes as the "reminder of inequality."[60]

But this relationality is not only figural. The mobility of the registered travelers is connected to their nonregistered counterparts. For example, many civil liberties groups have commented that because of the small numbers expected to actually register, it will make very little difference in terms of speeding up the lines of the nonregistered passengers. Moreover, it may actually work to slow them down: "To date, the TSA has not published any studies demonstrating that either dedicating screening lanes for Registered Traveler participants, or allowing Registered Traveler participants to jump to the front of the line, will not make the lines for the mass of the flying public longer."[61] Concerns abound that the registered passenger programs may well speed up those who are members, while it will slow down the movement of those who are not.

So, there are some obvious issues here regarding the inequity of flying experiences and perhaps worries that the lanes of nonregistered passengers will actually slow down rather than speed up. Registered Traveler is meant to work on a threat-based model, so that the security services can concentrate their resources on those more likely to be a threat. This could perhaps force people into the registered schemes. Or the schemes may permanently exclude those who cannot afford to pay for it, or those with the wrong credit ratings or credentials.

There is obviously a direct link between speed and privacy here. Timothy Sparapani of the ACLU has articulated some of these fears. For instance, Sparapani suggests that "Registered Traveler poses an unacceptable inducement that causes business and other frequent travelers to involuntarily forego their personal privacy for the promise of speed and efficiency in screening."[62] He argues, "No one should be forced to choose between privacy and speed."[63]

But having maintained that registered passenger systems may resemble and point to these more intensive inequalities, we must not lose sight of what Heather Cameron refers to as "quality-of-life" issues evident in registered travel.[64] Perhaps of a more immediate concern is the psychological, emotional, and physical impact of such systems. We must not ignore the very personal experiences of those who simply cannot afford to sign up for the schemes, come from the wrong background, or who refuse to give up the information required of them. Moreover, we must take seriously the sometimes petty, but often real and tangible, feelings and experiences that such schemes may trigger.

Conclusion

In this chapter I have looked at the airport terminal from within rather than from without. As opposed to focusing on the sort of mobility regimes that enter and leave the airport terminal, as if the airport were flattened out and squeezed into a nodal point on a two-dimensional map, I apprehended the terminal as a real and physical environment, which people inhabit, dwell-in, and pass through. While scholars have taken airports in a way that is suggestive of their sorting capabilities through surveillance and security systems, this chapter explored how the metaphor of the filter achieved material form in the shape of the airport terminal itself. The layout of the terminal was seen to create material affordances for movement and navigation. Passenger mobilities are changed, separated, and modulated into controlable forms. These are premeditated by a hydraulic science that shapes and directs them past security pinch-points and compulsive consumption-zones.

In setting out the frame of analysis within the terminal like a magnifying glass, I brought into focus and clearer resolution more complex and localized forms of power and politics. In particular, this involved the conjunction of both security and commercial interests, a trend that reflects the common imperatives of the function of airports. For Mika Aaltola, "The economic function of an airport to distribute global wealth has been blended with the need to defend against 'terror.'"[65] In this chapter I explored how the contemporary airport has twisted this arrangement so that the practices used to defend against "terror" have been combined with those used, not to distribute global wealth, but to absorb and retrieve it. This relationship resonates, of course, with practices such as passenger profiling, techniques, which Adam Arvidson has shown may owe their origin to commercial marketing procedures.[66]

But as well as achieving a form of corporeal filtering, airports act to filter out and sort incorporeal sensations and affects. In resembling an architectural form of what Raymond Williams would describe as a "structure of feeling," airport design was shown to delimit the sensations of its inhabitants in an attempt to control their emotional sensibilities and moods.[67] The intention behind this being that effected passengers would be more susceptible to parting with their cash in the many retail concessionaries, or they would be more submissive and obedient to direction and instructions in the security-check areas.

In the final example, I focused on how passengers are being sorted from one another through opt-in registration schemes that allow those signed-up to avoid lengthy lines and delays. A politics of speed was evident in the ways by which the mobility of the registered seemed to depend upon the reduced swiftness and quality of those who were not. However, this power geometry could also be found at the affective register as a politics of modality—in the relational way that the schemes were intended to and did make people feel.

To conclude, I want to urge future airport scholarship to continue unpacking the black box of the airport terminal and to consider the everyday experiences of their inhabitation and use. I realize that this may not be particularly novel, but if airport scholarship is marked by anything, it is a lacking of understanding of just how these sites are experienced, not just by scholars and academics but by those who do so on an everyday occurrence.[68] We must ask how these sites are designed and run to intervene in quite ordinary and extraordinary inhabitations; we must question how airport politics of control, consumption, and security are articulated in private, personal, insular, felt, and emotional ways.

Notes

1. David Pascoe, *Airspaces* (London: Reaktion, 2001).
2. Robin Law, "Beyond 'Women and Transport': Towards New Geographies of Gender and Daily Mobility," *Progress in Human Geography* 23, no. 4 (1999): 567–88; Celia Lury, *Prosthetic Culture: Photography, Memory and Identity* (London: Routledge, 1993).
3. Peter Adey, "Secured and Sorted Mobilities: Examples from the Airport," *Surveillance and Society* 1, no. 4 (2004): 500–519.
4. Gillian Fuller and Ross Harley, *Aviopolis: A Book about Airports* (London: Blackdog, 2004), 44.
5. Colin J. Bennett, "What Happens When You Book an Airline Ticket (Revisited): The Computer Assisted Passenger Profiling System and the Globalization of Personal Data," in *Global Surveillance and Policing: Borders, Security, Identity*, ed. Elia Zureik and Mark. B. Salter (Cullompton, UK: Willan, 2006), 113–38.
6. David Lyon, *Surveillance after September 11, Themes for the 21st Century* (Malden, Mass.: Polity, 2003), 35.
7. Ibid.
8. David Wood and Steve Graham, "Permeable Boundaries in the Software Sorted Society: Surveillance and Differentiations of Mobility," in *Mobile Technologies of the City*, ed. Mary Sheller and John Urry (London: Routledge, 2006), 177–91.

9. Michel Foucault, *Discipline and Punish: The Birth of the Prison* (London: Allen Lane, 1977), 144.

10. Paul Virilio, *Speed and Politics: An Essay on Dromology* (New York: Columbia University Press, 1986).

11. Adey, "Airports and Air-mindedness: Spacing, Timing and Using Liverpool Airport 1929–1939," *Social and Cultural Geography* 7, no. 3 (2006): 343–63.

12. Mark B. Salter, "The Global Visa Regime and the Political Technologies of the International Self: Borders, Bodies, Biopolitics," *Alternatives* 31, no. 2 (2006): 167–89.

13. Alan Latham and Derek P. McCormack, "Moving Cities: Rethinking the Materialities of Urban Geographies," *Progress in Human Geography* 28, no. 6 (2004): 701–24.

14. Henk van Houtum and Ton van Naerssen, "Bordering, Ordering and Othering," *Tijdschrift Voor Economische En Sociale Geografie* 93, no. 2 (2002): 129.

15. Fuller and Harley, *Aviopolis*, 14.

16. Pascoe, *Airspaces*.

17. See Norman Ashford, H. P. Martin Stanton, and Clifton A. Moore, *Airport Operations*, 2nd ed. (New York: McGraw-Hill, 1997); Marcus Binney, *Airport Builders* (Chichester, UK: Academy Editions, 1999); Christopher J. Blow, *Airport Terminals*, 2nd ed. (Boston: Butterworth Architecture Library of Planning and Design, 1996); Ian Humphreys, "Privatisation and Commercialisation—Changes in UK Airport Ownership Patterns," *Journal of Transport Geography* 7, no. 2 (1999): 121–34; Anne Graham, *Managing Airports: An International Perspective*, 2nd ed. (Oxford: Butterworth-Heinemann, 2003).

18. Richard De Neufville, *Airport Systems Planning: A Critical Look at the Methods and Experience* (London: Macmillan, 1980), 148.

19. Rigas Doganis, *The Airport Business* (New York: Routledge, 1992), 139.

20. Alastair Gordon, *Naked Airport: A Cultural History of the World's Most Revolutionary Structure* (New York: Metropolitan Books, 2004).

21. Hugh Pearman, *Airports: A Century of Architecture* (London: Laurence King, 2004).

22. Doganis, *The Airport Business*, 139.

23. De Neufville, *Airport Systems Planning*; Robert Horonjeff, *Planning and Design of Airports*, 2nd ed. (New York: McGraw-Hill, 1975).

24. Adey, "'May I Have Your Attention': Airport Geographies of Spectatorship, Position and (Im)mobility," *Environment and Planning D-Society and Space* 25, no. 3 (2007): 515–36.

25. Paul Freathy and Frank O'Connell, *European Airport Retailing: Growth Strategies for the New Millennium, Macmillan Business* (Basingstoke, UK: Macmillan, 1998), 80.

26. Doganis, *The Airport Business*, 140.

27. Freathy and O'Connell, *European Airport Retailing*, 81.

28. Jon Goss, "The 'Magic of the Mall'–An Analysis of Form, Function, and Meaning in the Contemporary Retail Built Economy," *Annals of the Association of American Geographers* 83, no. 1 (1993): 31

29. Gilles Deleuze and Félix Guattari, *A Thousand Plateaus: Capitalism and Schizophrenia* (London: Athlone Press, 1988), 386.

30. Fuller, "Perfect Match: Biometrics and Body Patterning in a Networked World," *fibreculture* 1 (2005), http://journal.fibreculture.org/issue1/issue1_fuller.html (accessed April 15, 2008).

31. Gary T. Marx, "Some Conceptual Issues in the Study of Borders and Surveillance," in *Global Surveillance and Policing*, ed. Elia Zureik and Mark B. Salter (Cullompton, UK: Willan, 2005), 20.

32. Ibid.

33. Debbie Lisle, "Site Specific: Medi(t)ations at the Airport," in *Rituals of Mediation: International Politics and Social Meaning*, ed. Francois Debrix and Cynthia Weber (Minneapolis: University of Minnesota Press, 2003), 3.

34. I am referring of course to the classic and groundbreaking work on airports by Marc Augé, *Non-places: Introduction to an Anthropology of Supermodernity*, trans. John Howe (New York: Verso, 1995); Manuel Castells, *The Rise of the Network Society, The Information Age: Economy, Society and Culture, Vol. 1* (Oxford: Blackwell, 1996). For more on the restriction of capacities to feel, see Adey. "Airports, Mobility, and the Calculative Architecture of Affective Control," *Geoforum* 39, no 1 (2008): 438–51.

35. Pascoe, *Airspaces*.

36. Adey, "Architectural Geographies of the Airport Balcony: Mobility, Sensation and the Theatre of Flight," *Geografiska Annaler Series B* 90, no. 1 (2008): 29–47.

37. Nigel Thrift, "Intensities of Feeling: Towards a Spatial Politics of Affect," *Geografiska Annaler Series B* 86, no. 1 (2004): 57–78; see also Sonja Sulzmaier. *Consumer-oriented Business Design: The Case of Airport Management, Contributions to Management Science* (New York: Physica-Verlag, 2001).

38. Charles Hackelsberger, *Munich International Airport Two* (Basel: Birkhauser, 2004), 26.

39. Brian Edwards, *The Modern Airport Terminal: New Approaches to Airport Architecture*, 2nd ed. (New York: Spon Press, 2005), 74.

40. Mark Gottdiener, *Life in the Air: Surviving the New Culture of Air Travel* (Lanham, Md.: Rowman & Littlefield, 2000).

41. John Rowley and Francis Slack, "The Retail Experience in Airport Departure Lounges: Reaching for Timelessness and Placelessness," *International Marketing Review* 16, no. 4/5 (1999): 363–75.

42. Augé, *Non-places*: 105.

43. Mark Riches, "The Great Consumer Obsession," paper presented at the Middle East Duty Free Association Conference, Dubai, 2005.

44. "DFW Airport Survey Reveals Travellers Feeling Safe, Experiencing Short Security Checkpoint Lines," press release (DFW Airport, November 19, 2001), http://www.dfwairport.com/mediasite/pdf/01/Traveler_Survey_Release.pdf (accessed April 15, 2008).

45. See Adey, "Airports, Mobility"; Sulzmaier, *Consumer-Oriented Business Design*.

46. John Zukowsky, *Building for Air Travel: Architecture and Design for Commercial Aviation* (Munich: Prestel, 1996).

47. Gordon, *Naked Airport*.
48. Salter, *Rights of Passage: The Passport in International Relations* (Boulder, Colo.: Lynne Rienner, 2003), 126.
49. Clair Enlow, "New Gates for Asia," *Architecture Week* (June 20, 2001), http://www.architectureweek.com/2001/0606/design_1-1.html (accessed April 15, 2008).
50. Pascoe, *Airspaces*, 215.
51. On speed, see Adey, "'Divided We Move': The Dromologics of Airport Security," in *Surveillance and Security: Technological Politics and Power in Everyday Life*, ed. Torin Monahan (London: Routledge, 2006), 195–208.
52. See Lyon, chapter 2 in this volume; Bennett, chapter 3 in this volume; and Benjamin J. Muller, chapter 6 in this volume.
53. Matthew Sparke, "A Neoliberal Nexus: Economy, Security and the Biopolitics of Citizenship on the Border," *Political Geography* 25, no. 2 (2006): 151–80.
54. Frank Thomas, "Flying through Security," *USA TODAY*, May 30, 2005.
55. Ibid.
56. Ibid.
57. Robert Wohl, *A Passion for Wings: Aviation and the Western Imagination, 1908–1918* (New Haven, Conn.: Yale University Press, 1994); Pascoe, *Aircraft* (London: Reaktion, 2003).
58. Crispin Thurman and Adam Jaworski, "The Alchemy of the Upwardly Mobile: Symbolic Capital and the Stylization of Elites in Frequent-Flyer Programmes," *Discourse and Society* 17, no. 1 (2006): 116.
59. Ibid., 124.
60. Zygmunt Bauman, *Globalization: The Human Consequences* (Cambridge: Polity, 1998).
61. John Harper, "The Promise of Registered Traveler," paper presented at the Subcommittee on Economic Security, Infrastructure Protection, and Cybersecurity Committee on Homeland Security, U.S. House of Representatives, June 9, 2005.
62. Timothy Sparapani, "Testimony of Timothy D. Sparapani, ACLU Legislative Counsel, on Secure Flight and Registered Traveler before the U.S. Senate Committee on Commerce, Science and Transportation," February 9, 2006.
63. Ibid.
64. Heather Cameron, "Sites of Contention in Public Transport," paper presented at the Politics of/at the Airport workshop, First Canadian Aviation Security Conference, Ottawa, 2007.
65. Mikka Aaltola, "The International Airport: The Hub-and-Spoke Pedagogy of the American Empire," *Global Networks* 5, no. 3 (2005): 267.
66. Adam Arvidson, "On the 'Pre-history of the Panoptic Sort': Mobility in Market Research," *Surveillance and Society* 1, no. 4 (2004): 456–74.
67. Raymond Williams, *The Country and the City* (London: Hogarth, 1973). For a delineation of these ideas see Nigel Thrift, "Inhuman Geographies: Landscapes of Speed, Light and Power," in *Spatial Formations*, ed. Thrift (London: Sage, 1996), 256–310.
68. On these arguments, see Mike Crang, "Between Places: Producing Hubs, Flows, and Networks," *Environment and Planning A* 34, no. 4 (2002): 569–74.

8

WELCOME TO WINDOWS 2.1

Motion Aesthetics at the Airport

....

Gillian Fuller

The spectacle is a Weltanshauung that has been transformed into objective force.

—Guy Debord, *Society of the Spectacle*

Sheathed in Glass

The airport is, among many other things, a perceptual machine. Airports do not merely sort and sequence our bodies, they also guide our perceptions. Airports work our feelings, as well as our baggage and identification data. They move us in many ways. We glide on moving walkways in air-conditioned comfort, shielded from the heat of the tarmac and the chill of the rain at the exits and entrances. Cocooned from the smell of avgas and uncontrollable weather, the sound of planes is barely discernible—the threatening roar of jet power dampened by thick layers of clear glass. Within the glassy sheath of the terminal, we can hear the chatter of movement and calm calls of announcement systems. The "trace odors of stress and hustle"[1] intermingle with the vague wafts of brewing coffee and the greasy smells of convenience food. Sensually there is a lot going on, but at the airport the visual dominates. All senses are diverted to a sublime vision of transparency.

As we move through the glass tubes and halls of modern global transit systems, doubled by our digital identities as passengers, divided by glass partitions as impermeable as walls, we see and are seen in multiple modes. This constant and variable movement is a "ravishing balletic spectacle"[2]— a city in miniature, captured through the passing movement of people. Such a panorama is not new, of course. The technological and structural developments of glass and iron, as noted by Walter Benjamin in *The Arcades Project*, reified nineteenth-century mythologies around power, the market, and urban forms in ethereal structures full of movement and light: "These creations undergo this 'illumination' not only in a theoretical manner, by an ideological transposition, but also in the immediacy of their perceptual presence. They are manifest as phantasmagorias. Thus appear the arcades."[3]

How do the phantasmagorias of the nineteenth century relate to the virtualities of the late twentieth century? The experience of the nineteenth-century *flâneur*[4] is one of abandonment to "the phantasmagoria of the marketplace"—a new perceptual realm in which the *flâneur* is disciplined but also consumed. And what is the experience of the twenty-first-century flier, who abandons herself to the total incorporation of the manifold possibilities of a commodified network? An aesthetic realm where vision is no longer just spectacular, no longer just two way (either real or imagined), no longer a fleeting glance or a sustained gaze, but precise, targeted, pattern-matched, and integrated logically and practically into movement systems?

In the world of transit—we are neither inside nor outside but in a zone of exception in which a virtual logic of movement facilitates a new mode of spatiality—in which transparency is a politico-aesthetic method: both a mode of operation and part of the sell. Within the monumental spaces of global transit, the promise of an actual elsewhere has never seemed so present or available. The airport offers a seemingly unmediated spectacle of movement. In this glazed splendor we are both inspired and instructed. A vision of global possibilities is offered to the traveler, but it is a vision that when accessed starts feeling like the protocols of code.

In this chapter I would like to consider just one aspect of airport aesthetics: the use of windows. Great glass caverns and tubes dominate contemporary airport architecture, each designed by a brand name architect—Renzo Piano, Richard Rogers, Norman Forster, Paul Andreu—each with a manifesto about light, glass, space, aviation, and aesthetics.[5] Glass appears to be the perfect match for a cultural fiction that associates commercial international aviation with lightness and airiness, rather than, pollution and war, for example. From Eero Saarinen's jet-age "TWA at New York" to Andreu's latest steel and glass tube in Dubai, the terminal building strives to coalesce the putative qualities of "lightness" with utopian fantasies of flying. This is hardly surprising. As Benjamin points out, glass architecture has been from inception, utopian. By allowing the outside in and the inside out, glass buildings enable cosmos and construction to innocently and transparently converge.

Paul Scheerbart's 1914 technical manifesto *Glass Architecture* instructed that if the coming culture was to evolve to higher levels, then we must, for better or worse, open up our "closed-room" environments by making all walls entirely of glass.[6] We must be open to the world. It is a common refrain. This opening out to, and incorporation of, world as landscape was one of the many innovations in the original Crystal Palace, the large glass structure designed by Sir Joseph Paxton for the Great Exhibition in London in 1851. A reviewer at the time notes, "There is no longer any true interior or exterior, the barrier erected between us and the landscape is almost ethereal. If we imagine that air can be poured like a liquid, then here it has achieved a solid form, after the removal of the mold into which it was poured."[7]

This folding of space (inner and outer) as a form of display recurred elsewhere as new spaces became visible—the space of the product, the space of the consumer, each becoming incorporated into the expanding spectacle. Another contemporary of the Crystal Palace, Thomas Carlyle, remarked on his return from the "glass soap bubble": "Here we are just returned from the wonderful wonder of wonders; which fact was accomplished with every convenience. . . . The edifice and the arrangements are perfect, really a type of English method and dexterity; many of the objects are well worth seeing, and the people—Oh it is the beautifullest, best got up piece of nonsense that was ever seen in the world!"[8]

In the world exhibitions and the birth of the arcade, the crowd and the commodity had converged. The spectacle now incorporated inside and outside, structure and process, product and person. Such techniques continue today in the modern airport, which creates a world of folds and frames, where the binaries of interiority/exteriority, public/private, movement/stasis become architecturally refined and spatially rendered through a series of transparencies. This is made possible by continual development in both steel and glazing technologies, as well as the digital technologies that have evolved with them. Windows, in both the analog and digital worlds, are vision machines. They replace the elements of actual location with a spectacle of virtual movement. Within this space of transformative promise—anything is possible, from escape to far-flung destinations to body and bag searches and biometric data gathering—and each is visible, each is part of the daily spectacle of airports.

The modern airport is made of glass: a technology that materializes transparency, an aesthetic that entwines both "the X-ray gaze of empirical knowledge"[9] and spectacular possibilities of consumption.

"It's a Mall. . . . It's an Airport"[10]

In terms of urban design, airports are a lot like malls; they present little to the streetscape except a series of entry and exits accessed by feeder roads. The enclosed megamall is a controlled environment, its traffic flow is directed, its temperature is constant, and its interiors expand to include exterior elements, such as fountains, theme parks, and tropical atriums. At the mall the outside is no longer necessary: "The window—and any connection to the outside world other than those which admit customers—is finally deemed unnecessary or even hostile to commerce."[11] Only one type of window generally exists in the mall—the one that enables visual access to the goods on sale. Bathed in light, placed on a plinth, the commodity is "enthroned . . . with the glitter of distractions."[12]

Comparisons between airports and malls are now commonplace, and for good reason. The airport terminal does indeed share many of the interiorizing modalities of the mall, with one significant architectural exception. Unlike malls, airport windows face out to the world of flight as well as inward to the franchises. Airports exult in a spectacle of outside. Huge jumbos with exotic livery press against the glass walls of the terminal, people from every place and every time zone move purposefully around us, the planes and the sky are presented in exhilarating panoramas. Windows have pulling power, and the vistas of movement are utterly commodifed at the airport. As Peter Adey notes, tarmac frontage is prime real estate. Citing Rachel Bowlby, he continues, the windows purpose is to "pull him from one space to another, to move him mentally and stop him physically."[13] Windows have the power to arrest a crowd around a commodity, corralling them in chic bars overlooking the runway as they wait for their call, but also guiding them where to go next.

Such guidance is necessary, given the multiplicity of regulatory and commercial zones at the airport. Inside, the terminal is so massive it appears to have many interiors—some visible, some not. Glass partitions organize a sequencing of behaviors and their accompanying spectacles according to where one is located: in customs one is searched; in the café one is served;

in the departure lounge one waits. As you wait and stare outside to the tarmac, you are looking at another country, which you are technically not in. Sometimes inside and outside converge as air bridges seamlessly deliver passengers to planes. Horizons of possibilities are visually and procedurally buffered as we move from one vista—the tarmac, the security line, the concourse—to another. We are pulled in, ineluctably drawn to the next event scene. The momentum of the terminal emulates that of the plane: forward, directed, and controlled. It is hard to stop the forward motion, once you've begun the processes for flight.

Outside of military spaces, penal spaces, and casinos, airports are probably the most controlled spaces in the world. Visible to all, only our thoughts move in private. Our baggage, our bodies, and our movements are all part of an encompassing spectacle. In public lines we see the most intimate of moments: a young man being pulled aside and patted down by security, anxious travelers compulsively fingering their pockets for wallets and passports, an elderly woman repacking her bag to fit the weight allowance, lovers suppressing their tears at the departure gate. The drama of aviation, the intimate and the monumental, the promise and the threat are all visualized and yet also contained in the multiple refractions of light and glass. This transparency enables a spectacle of movement and isolation that is as comforting as it is controlling. As Diller + Scofidio note, "[y]esterday's pathologies have inverted: the fear of being watched has transformed to the fear that no one is watching."[14]

Integrated into a medium of transparency, we witness our own multiple visualizations as we pass through the stages of transit. The process of externalization—of being categorized, isolated, assessed, before being allowed "in" (into the country or onto the plane)—connects to the affectual drives of virtualization as much as it does to disciplinary control. The possibility of always seeing more—more planes, more people, more places—elides traditional subject–object distinctions as vision machines modulate promise and threat into an ineluctable event scene: Visible to everyone, we disappear into the image matrix of the airport.

Seeing Space

The Enlightenment residues are easily discernible in Andreu's linking of transparency to "precision and truthfulness." He writes, "I am interested in attaining a sense of weightlessness and transparency and I strive to tackle all the details of construction with great precision and truthfulness. But to me, what matters most is the space itself, its structure and bound as defined by the material which stands out against the light or dissolves into."[15] Light optically entangled with "weightlessness," forms the antonymic hero to the dead weight of gravity—the thing that keeps us down. From Jean-Jacques Rousseau's belief that transparency was a "fundamental metaphor expressing a utopian state for humans"[16] to current texts by and about Piano, Forster, Andreu, and others, a connotative chain of positivist rationality, openness, and truthfulness unfurls at the mere mention of "transparency."

Its power as political metaphor is evident and has a long and ongoing history. Although cast glass and the glazed display window were pioneered in seventeenth-century Holland, it is Paris—home of Haussmann's geometric urban optics, the grand arcades, and Andreu's tubes at Charles de Gaulle International Airport—that has worked the modernist geographies of body, motion, and visuals so intensely, and inspiring its most insightful critics from Benjamin to Foucault. Of Mitterand's Grand Projets, the latest in a series of Parisian innovations in glass architecture, Annette Fierro notes,

> Located on the urban flanks, [Mitterand's] transparent buildings engage, indeed attempt to become, the life of the city. As the bodies of visitors and general public are displayed and surveyed through the translucent skins of monumental buildings, so are the bodies of buildings themselves, replete in all previously undisclosed and shadowy inner domains. Haussmann's perspectival boulevards add the final context to the unrelenting mechanisms of vision in an enormous and multifaceted display of the potential reach of the rational gaze.[17]

Transparency serves both the rational and irrational, alternating between an illuminating display of the previously unseen to the dark suspicions of "what have you got to hide?" It is a question one often hears today, but it has been heard before. Much like our current "terror," the terror of Revolutionary France also produced a mania for transparency, during which all private activity and association was considered suspect. As Fierro further notes, "If the goal of [Mitterand's] projects was to express accessibility, surely a more benign metaphor was available."[18]

Simultaneous Visions

Transparency may not be benign, but it certainly is apt for rationalist regimes of surveillance and consumption. The complexities of transparency as both trope and aesthetic lie precisely in the power of the visual perspective offered. Transparency offers simultaneous perception, a particular optical quality enabling figures to overlap rather than obliterate each other. In their influential work on transparency in architecture and art, Colin Rowe and Robert Slutsky quote Gyorgy Kepes: "Transparency means a simultaneous perception of different spatial locations. Space not only recedes but fluctuates in a continuous activity. The position of transparent figures has equivocal meaning as one sees each figure now as the closer one, now as the farther one."[19] They continue, "by definition, the transparent ceases to be that which is perfectly clear and instead becomes that which is clearly ambiguous."[20]

This kind of phenomenal transparency generates the opportunity for "continuous fluctuations of interpretation."[21] Transparency enables multiple planes and dimensions to visually coexist, implying a "broader social order"—one beyond the literal sense of transparency through which we see "the product," "the human," "the landscape," but one which re-imagines the surface structures of spatial order, making the world cubist, remixable. The surface tension of transparency seems to be tightening all around, not just in terms of the incorporation of glass and plastics in urban architecture but also in our embodied and disembodied experiences living within modern and supermodern regimes of movement and visuality, or spatiovisuality, as Guiliana Bruno has called it.

The train, the plane, the car, the TV screen, and the moving walkway all present fleeting images of simultaneous spaces at different rhythms, speeds, and angles. The constant shifting of foreground and background, inside and outside shift generates a dynamic space, endlessly renewing and modifying. The new visions enable by mechanized movement skewed spatial perception transferring across all modes of "motion capture" from train to roller coaster to tracking shot. As Bruno notes, "Mobility, a form of cinema—was the essence of these new architectures."[22]

This kinesthetic geography, charted by Benjamin, Wolfgang Schivelbush, Marc Augé, and others, not only "morph[ed] the perceptual world into seductive images and commodified leisure destinations"[23] but also inaugurated a new mobilized subject, circulating in new markets (as a driver, an audience, a tourist, etc.) and circulating almost constantly. Highway, train station, airport—we move in spaces designed to get us elsewhere. These "nonplaces"[24] are mediated spaces, which privilege certain aspects of the relationship of gaze and landscape, of individual and place. In these places of supermodernity, we commodify our own anonymity as the world we move through looks increasingly two-dimensional—a Club Med version of somewhere we once knew. Yet if the world is appearing two-dimensional, the screens through which we increasingly move are gaining yet more perceptual depth.

One no longer just looks at the screen, one operates through it. Screens appear as windows and windows appear as screens. One can see the movie, experience the ride, visit the exact location, and buy the game. In the plane one can witness the landing through the plane's nose camera on in-flight TV and see it from a different perspective by looking out the window. One can experience another form of tubular motion as trains feed directly into the terminal and the terminal tube sorts directly to the plane. All the while, visions and sounds from elsewhere cut across the space in the form of mobile phones, transit TV, advertising billboards, and directional signage. There is so much coextensive vision that the world appears set in a perpetual optical hum and things become a bit blurry and opaque.

Transparent Tech

Things need to be transparent and obvious because the space one is navigating exists on a scale that is beyond big; it is informational. Vision at the megascale of modern, urban structures is no longer panoramic but rather informatic. Windows overlap, looking out to each other—car windows, train windows, terminal windows, screen windows, plane windows—generating a perceptual inside through which one navigates in a space that operates on an informational scale. Transparency, in this context, is a surface for information exchange. Thus transparency acts as a filter for noise as well as providing access to the workings of the machine.

Here transparency manifests the attribute for which it is prized—obviousness—in the field of Human Computer Interaction (HCI). Transparent interfaces are those you do not have to think about. They generate analogous spaces that conceal the complexities of the code but enable access to functions. Windows and other Graphical User Interfaces (GUIs) replaced a text-based line-code interface with a "transparent" visual paradigm based on spatial metaphors, a world of windows, where we soon learn that it is obvious that you grab the mouse and point or that you click on a file and drag. The interfacing of the formal languages of computers and the semantic frames of everyday life, while illuminating is also obscuring, filtering the actual working of the machine from its user. As Kittler notes this all happens in the name of (user) "friendliness": "Consequently, in a perfect gradualism, DOS services would hide the BIOS, WordPerfect the operating system, and so on and so on until, in the very last years, two fundamental changes in computer design (or DoD politics) have brought this secrecy system to its closure."[25]

These two fundamental changes were the established orthodoxy of GUIs and the implementation of "protection" software "in order to prevent 'untrusted programs' or 'untrusted users' from any access to the operating system's kernel and input/output channels."[26] The dominant GUI is the WIMP (windows, icon, menu, point), which presents the user with a series of surfaces, the paradoxically opaque windows. Each new window brings another layer to the foreground of the visual field, partially obscuring the previous layer. Our attention toggles betweens surfaces, unable to get our hands dirty with code, we are presented with another window.

The immersive, mimetic, and above all, interactive space of the computer screen forms a new regime of vision, manifest in neither cinematic gaze nor the televisual glance[27] that we may want to call "glazing," following gaming theorist Chris Chesher.[28] Drawing on the stickiness of the metaphor, Chesher describes how the player is held to the screen through identification with the on-screen character and direct feedback, in terms of the unfolding action and a sense of a mission. For Chesher, the glaze governs a domestic space—the boy's bedroom. And yet, the glazing that Chesher describes both as "a liquid adhesion holding the players eyes to the screen" and a "glazing over" descriptive of the utter absorption of the player in the sensations of their game space, seems pertinent to most contemporary navigators, be they gamer, driver, or frequent flier. Sheathed in a tubular glass terminal, attention toggling from mobile screen to TV to departures information screens, we perform a cybernetic dance, responding to visual cues and commands, initiating sequences, in a machine that we no longer just sit in front of, but traverse through.

The same regimes of vision and involvement now permeate public and private, online and offline space, and even those divisions do not truly hold anymore. Particularly at the airport where a proliferation of domestic, business, retail, and recreational spaces ensure that "no time is wasted time"[29] and where surveillance and security ensure there is no "empty" or unknown space. Transparency makes it obvious what kind of subject one should be to navigate the space—a predictable one.

When things become habitual they become transparent. It now seems obvious to interface with a computer via windows rather than through lines of text. It now seems quite normal that air passengers (and other suspects) should be profiled and probed. In such an interconnected and transversalizing world, the task of power is to flatten the affect of movement, to limit it to the predictable. As Francesco Varela has noted, "when there is no change in affective tone, things are transparent."[30] In order for things to effectively and precisely interface, things must be what they appear. Shampoo must be shampoo. An iPod must be an iPod.[31] And you must be who you say you are and move like you should.

Being a necessarily two-way track, we are as transparent to our architecture, both in the sense of obvious and ambiguous, as it is to us. How do our windows see us? We, too, are fleeting images of anonymous bodies known by their outlines and behaviors on surveillance cameras. But we are also other bodies, "a new body, a multiple body, a body with so many heads that, while they might not be infinite in number, cannot necessarily be counted."[32] The ability to extend our bodies across space and time and connect with other systems has resulted in a strange arrest—one that opens up a body while simultaneously closing it down. These new relations of bodies —to themselves via databanks and biometrics—or to other bodies via travel and teleprescensing, create new dynamics and also new modes of regulatory power, which seem to mark a radical shift in the way we need to think about the technologies of "motion capture." In a world of movement, where variability and instability is constant, flattening the process as well as the visual becomes a pivotal focus of control. Everything has to be able to interface with everything else—flesh to machine, land to air.

What was once clear is now enigmatic. The ambiguity of transparency discussed by Rowe and Slutsky, in terms of expressionist art and architecture, is now utterly banal as we move through the remixed world, which according to Jean Baudrillard accentuates, "the fake transparency of the world to spread a terroristic confusion, to spread the germs or viruses of a radical illusion, that is to say operating a radical disillusion of the real. A viral and deleterious thought, which corrupts meaning, and is the accomplice of an erotic perception of reality's trouble."[33]

On a recent trip through a "SARs scare," I was thermally scanned and appeared through the operator's windows interface as a series of roughly pixellated mauve, green, yellow, and orange blobs. My luggage under X-ray had hypnotic depth as densities appeared as interpenetrating layers of colored translucence. Each of my movements, including the incorporeal ones, where my digital-double was being processed generated another abstraction of me.

Profiled by both marketers offering great deals and paranoid officials demanding explanations, we are given form by a biopolitically informed vision, which sees us statistically as well as individually. Oscillating between an individual as body and an instance in a set matched to patterns of data, we are pulled aside if our data is "scary." Certain patterns, for example, one way tickets, cash payments, and "Islamic itineraries" all flag a passenger before he has even arrived at the airport. Cross-referenced and profiled through information in proscribed data fields, imaged both inside and out— an infinitely variable but consistently coherent subject emerges—the "consumer-suspect." A figure that becomes even more literal, as U.S. authorities demand access to credit card details to all air passengers entering the United States in order to profile potential security threats through spending history.

Airports produce encounters with bodies, architecture, and information in which nothing is inside or outside.

The End of Windows

Walking through an airport like Kansai or Chep Lap Kok, it does feel that the window has mutated, gained extra dimensions and folded itself around us. We are, as David Pascoe notes, intubulated by the architecture that prepares us for the processes, aesthetics, and experiences of jet flight.[34] For him, these tubes induce a narcotic quality, one we may perhaps associate with the glazed integration of an avionic architecture that both seduces and numbs. The layering of vision, the convergence of window and screen to a total aesthetic of transparency, in which everything fluctuates, is the banal condition on every airport, every transit zone and thus almost everywhere. As Scheerbart writes, "When glass architecture comes in, there will be not much more talk of windows either, the word 'windows' will disappear from the dictionaries."[35] Fed by a familiar rhetoric of urgency and fear, further precision, and thus more transparency, is required. In a recent paper on contemporary surveillance, Jordan Crandall states,

> Let's address this question of "precision" on two fronts: one, as a technologically-enabled drive toward efficiency and accuracy—a drive to augment human capabilities by developing new human-machine composites, connecting and joining forces with multiple processing agencies, wherever or whatever they might be; and two, as a technologically-assisted drive to reduce mediation and offer a form of direct connection to our real objects of inquiry. We might call these the effective and the affective. Both aim for the goal of instantaneous vision: a real time perceptual agency in which multiple actors, both human and machinic, are networked and able to act in concert. A real time perceptual agency in which time and space intervals can be eliminated, reducing the gaps between detection, analysis, and engagement, or desire and its attainment. A real time perceptual agency that can somehow touch the real.[36]

The window has become a truly transparent technology in as much as it seeks to erase any sense of mediation between a user and the medium, digital and analog, virtual and actual. Consumptive practice and securities procedure becomes seamless, as each opens out to the other in the name of transparency. Openness gains new connotative dimensions as it now collocates with "data sharing arrangements" as well as a friendly and desirable form of sociality. As obscuring as it is illuminating, it is the ambiguous optical realm of the supermodern world.

Notes

1. Anthony Vidler, quoted in Martha Rossler, *In the Place of the Public: Observations of a Frequent Flyer* (Frankfurt: Cantz Verlag, 1998), 14.
2. Herbert Muschamp, "Architecture Review: Buildings That Hide and Reveal," *New York Times*, September 22, 1995.
3. Walter Benjamin, *The Arcades Project*, trans. H. Eiland and K. McLaughlin (Cambridge, Mass.: Harvard University Press, 2004), 14.
4. Ibid. Benjamin describes the *flâneur* as a wanderer, a man of the crowd, literally "one who strolls."
5. See David Pascoe on le Corbusier, Norman Forster, and Paul Andreu in David Pascoe, *Airspaces* (London: Reaktion Books, 2001).
6. Although Paul Scheerbart did champion the use of colored glass over clear glass, "every wall, which will be made of glass—of coloured glass," in Paul Scheerbart, *Glass Architecture* (New York, Praeger, 1972); B. Taut, *Alpine Architecture*, ed. D. Sharp (New York, Praeger, 1972).
7. Cited in Rem Koolhaas et al., *The Harvard Design School Guide to Shopping: Harvard Project on the City 2* (New York: Taschen, 2001), 240.
8. Thomas Carlyle to John Forster on May 8, 1851, *The Collected Letters of Thomas and Jane Welsh Carlyle* (Durham, N.C.: Duke University Press, 2001), 26, Carlyle Letters Online, http://www.dukepress.edu/carlyle (accessed April 9, 2008).
9. Gerhard Auer in Annette Fierro, *The Glass State: The Technology of the Spectacle, Paris, 1981–1998* (Cambridge, Mass.: MIT Press, 2006), 32.
10. Koolhaas et al., *Guide to Shopping*, 181.
11. S. T. Leong quoted in ibid., 116.
12. Benjamin, *Illuminations* (New York: Harcourt, Brace & World,1968), 18.
13. Rachel Bowlby cited in Peter Adey, "'May I Have Your Attention': Airport Geographies of Spectatorship, Position and Immobility," *Environment and Planning D: Society and Space* 7, no. 3 (2007): 356.
14. Diller and Scofidio, "Post-paranoid Surveillance," *Ctrl [Space]* 2001, http://hosting.zkm.de/ctrlspace/e/texts/16 (accessed April 9, 2008).
15. Quotation featured in Pascoe, "Air Conditioning: The Pressures of the Passenger Terminal," paper presented to Air Time-Spaces: New Methods For Researching Mobilities conference, Centre for Mobilities Research, Lancaster University, September 26–27, 2006.
16. Fierro, *The Glass State*, 37.
17. Ibid., 32.
18. Ibid., 38.
19. Attribution in original text is to Gyorgy Kepes, *Language of Vision* (Chicago: P. Theobold, 1944); Colin Rowe and Robert Slutsky, "Transparency: Literal and Phenomenal-Part I," *Perspecta* 8 (1963): 45.
20. Rowe and Slutsky, "Transparency," 45.
21. Ibid.
22. Guiliana Bruno, *Atlas of Emotion: Journeys in Art, Architecture and Film* (London: Verso, 2002), 17.

23. Ross Harley, "Roller Coaster Planet, Kinetic Experience in the Age of Mechanical Motion," *Convergence: The Journal of Research into New Media Technologies* 6, no. 3 (2000): 77–97.

24. Marc Augé, *Non-places: An Introduction to an Anthropology of Supermodernity*, trans. John Howe (London: Verso, 1995).

25. Friedrich Kittler, "There Is No Software," *Ctheory* (October 18, 1995), http://www.ctheory.net/articles.aspx?id=74 (accessed April 9, 2008).

26. Ibid.

27. John Ellis, *Visible Fictions* (London: Routledge, 1982).

28. Chris Chesher, "Neither Gaze nor Glance, but Glaze: Relating to Console Game Screens," *Scan* 1, no.1 (2004), http://www.scan.net.au/scan/journal/display.php?journal_id=19 (accessed April 9, 2008).

29. In September 2006 Dubai Airport featured a marketing campaign for the many business/relaxation features of the airport. Its slogan: "transit time needn't be wasted time."

30. Francesco Varela, "The Deep Now," in *Machine Times-DEAFOO*, by Joke Brouwer and Arjen Mulder (Rotterdam: NAI Publishers, 2000), 15.

31. A none too subtle reference to the July 2006 critical alert at Heathrow; where a plan was supposedly uncovered to detonate bombs made from such daily items as shampoo, baby formula, and iPods.

32. Michel Foucault, "Seminar of 17 March 1976," *Society Must Be Defended: Lectures at the Collège de France, 1975–1976*, ed. Mauro Bertani and Alessandro Fontana, trans. David Macey (New York: Picador, 1996), 245.

33. Jean Baudrillard, "Radical Thought," *Ctheory* (April 19, 1995), http://www.ctheory.net/articles.aspx?id=67 (accessed April 9, 2008).

34. Pascoe, "Air Conditioning."

35. Scheerbart, *Glass Architecture*, Pt. 47.

36. Jordan Crandall, "Precision + Guided + Seeing," *Ctheory* (January 10, 2006), http://www.ctheory.net/articles.aspx?id=502 (accessed April 9, 2008).

CONTRIBUTORS

Peter Adey is a lecturer at the Institutes of Law, Politics, and Justice and Earth Sciences and Geography at Keele University. His articles have been published in *Environment and Planning A, Environment and Planning D, Progress in Human Geography,* and *Geoforum.*

Colin J. Bennett is a professor of political science at the University of Victoria. His books include *Regulating Privacy: Data Protection and Public Policy in Europe and the United States, Visions of Privacy: Policy Choices for the Digital* (with Rebecca Grant), and *The Governance of Privacy: Policy Instruments in the Digital Age* (with Charles Raab).

Gillian Fuller is a senior lecturer in media in the School of English, Media, and Performing Arts at the University of New South Wales, Australia. She is the author of many essays on airports from a contemporary media perspective and co-author of *Aviopolis: A Book about Airports* (with Ross Harley).

Francisco R. Klauser is a research fellow at the Institute of Hazard and Risk Research at Durham University.

Gallya Lahav is an associate professor of political science at the State University of New York at Stony Brook. She is the author of *Immigration and Politics in the New Europe: Reinventing Borders;* coeditor of *The Migration Reader;* and coeditor of a special issue, *Immigration Policy in Europe,* for the journal *West European Politics.*

David Lyon is Queen's University Research Professor at Queen's University in Kingston, Ontario. His books include *The Information Society: Issues and Illusions, The Electronic Eye: The Rise of Surveillance Society, Surveillance after September 11,* and *Surveillance Studies: An Overview.* He is also a founding editor of the e-journal *Surveillance and Society.*

Benjamin J. Muller teaches international relations theory and critical security studies in the Department of Political Science at Simon Fraser University. He has published in various academic journals, including *Citizenship Studies, Security Dialogue, Refuge: Canada's Periodical on Refugees*.

Valérie November is a professor in the School of Architecture and Civil and Environmental Engineering at Ecole Polytechnique Fédérale in Lausanne, Switzerland.

Jean Ruegg is an associate professor of urban and land-use planning at the University of Lausanne, Switzerland.

Mark B. Salter is an associate professor in the School of Political Studies at the University of Ottawa. He is the author of *Rights of Passage: The Passport in International Relations* and co-author of *Global Surveillance and Policing: Borders, Security, Identity* (with Elia Zureik). He has published in *International Political Sociology, Security Dialogue, Citizenship Studies, Alternatives*, and *International Studies Perspectives*. He is on the editorial board of *International Political Sociology* and is associate editor of the *Journal of Transportation Security*.

INDEX